The Cultures of Computing

Edited by Susan Leigh Star

Blackwell Publishers/The Sociological Review

First published in 1995

Reprinted in 1996

Blackwell Publishers
108 Cowley Road, Oxford OX4 1JF, UK

and
238 Main Street,
Cambridge, MA 02142, USA

British Library Cataloguing in Publication Data

A CIP catalogue record for this book is available from the British Library

Library of Congress Cataloging-in-Publication Data applied for

Printed in Great Britain by Short Run Press Ltd., Exeter
This book is printed on acid-free paper.

for Donna Haraway

ISBN 0 631 19282 4

The Cultures of Computing

Contents

Contents

Introduction

Susan Leigh Star

What is a computer?

Computers have emptied and filled my life for over a decade. I have courted by email,[1] been hired by email, learned of friends' deaths by email. In 1989, when I was living in Southern California, a phone call from my mother in Rhode Island informed me of the Loma Prieta earthquake in northern California. During an anxious night and long into the morning the telephone lines between south and north were clogged with signals, and I could not get through to the Red Cross to find out whether my closest friends in the San Francisco Bay Area were alive. The television showed one single scene over and over, of a car captured on someone's home videotape, backing away from the fractured bridge. Finally, late the next morning, I received two email messages from the East Coast (where the long distance telephone lines from the Bay Area could reach)—Anselm and Fran, Allan and Adele, Linnea and the people on the ranch were all okay. I could breath again.

A few weeks later I visited a state park near San Juan Capistrano. All around were signs, 'Warning: Wild Mountain Lions Loose in Vicinity.' Having never encountered a mountain lion, I pulled up at the entrance gate to ask the ranger what I should do if I met one, and how many there were. 'Well, they're not actually on the loose. What that means is that a mother has had two cubs, and we haven't had time to tag them yet.' All the mountain lions in the park wear electronic collars with encoded sensors, which allows the park rangers to trace their movements and collect ecological data. The two cubs, untagged, represent a kind of wildness about which the public must be informed. 'But what should I *do* if I meet them?,' I persisted. 'Well,' said the ranger, 'I couldn't answer that, because if I told you in my official capacity, and then you did it, and got injured, you could sue me or the park system.' I looked at him. 'Could I tell you in my unofficial capacity, just off the record?' 'Sure,' I said, trying not to laugh, 'That would be fine.' 'Well, my advice there would be just to act really weird. Jump up and down and make funny noises and flap your arms in the air. If the animal can't figure out what you are, she won't chase after you, but just walk away.'

In Champaign Illinois, a man has been arrested for stealing a television. It is his second offence. He broke into the house by a back garden window, took the television, and used the car keys lying on the kitchen counter to use the family's car and remove the television. He was caught trying to sell it to a pawnshop on the other side of town. The jails in Illinois are crowded, and the man is not considered too dangerous. He has a job working for a fast-food chain, and going to jail would make him lose it. The judge decides that he is a good candidate for the town's new electronic jail program. The man will wear an electronic ankle bracelet that is attached to a sensor in his house. He may go to work but must be inside his house from 6pm to 8am. The sensor will record his movements, and if he deviates from them, he will be put in a physical jail instead of a virtual one. The same technology is being used to monitor the whereabouts of frail elders or those with Alzheimer's, allowing them to stay in their own homes longer, and not have to go to nursing homes.

I go to one of several hundred conferences on computing to be held this year. The topic is 'embodiment,' and our business at hand is to discuss the relationship between RW (real world) bodies and VR (virtual reality) bodies, and to think about issues like gesture, presence, and the dimensionality of bodies in communication. I watch a demo tape with little cartoon figures lifting blocks and carrying them across a room, and another with photographs of people's faces pasted over the blocky bodies, sitting around a 'table' and 'conversing' with each other through the VR device across geographical distance. When someone in Sweden moves her hand, the block body on the screen moves; when someone talks from Georgia the words are broadcast to all the participants. I find my thoughts drifting during the discussion to the idea of embodiment and how I have felt in my body around computers. Right now, typing this, my neck aches and I am curled in an uncomfortable position. I try to think about my fingertips and the chips inside this Macintosh as a seamless 'web of computing,' to use Kling and Scacchi's classic phrase (1982). But chips make me think of the eyesight of women in Singapore and Korea, going blind during the process of crafting the fiddly little wires; of 'clean rooms' I have visited in Silicon Valley and the Netherlands, where people dressed like astronauts etch bits of silicon and fabricate complex sandwiches of information and logic. I think of the silence of my European ancestors who wore Chinese embroidery, marveling at its intricate complexity, the near-impossible stitches woven over a lifetime with the eyesight of another generation of Asian women. I think, I want my body to include these experiences. If we are to have ubiquitous, wireless computing in the future, perhaps it is time to have a less boring idea of the body right now—a body politic, not just the substrate for meetings or toys.

I love the idea of being a residual category for a mountain lion, and of the non-computerized lions causing the signs to put fear in the hearts of tourists. I am grateful for the complicated heterogeneous networks bearing news of safety and danger. If I were old and frail, or fearful, I might welcome the reassurance provided by the electronic sensor; if I had to choose between jail and virtual house arrest, I would certainly choose the latter. VR games are fun and so is thinking about new ways to use the games. At the same time, these links crisscrossing the world, these rearrangements of work and play, do shake up my sense of freedom, privacy, and naturalness in ways that scare me. Having destroyed the habitat of the mountain lion, we now track its every move and redefine wildness as that which gives us no information.[2] Having spread ourselves and our intimacies around the world, at great distance, we come to depend on the email message for relief, for connection, for news of life and death. Having filled our jails through the consequences of racism and educational neglect, we place our need to control in a web of electronic signals and police. At every moment, the choices seem like rational choices, and at every moment they seem dangerous and crazy. The Foucaldian consequences of the blurring of boundaries between freedom and jail, surveillance and leisure are everywhere. My brother-in-law is now forced to use his cellular phone while driving to a sales meeting so as not to waste time; I can work anywhere with electricity and a phone line with my portable computer—and so we both work longer and longer hours. As Randi Markussen's complex analysis of 'easiness' reminds us, we may all be moving into a regime of virtual detention simply to manage the information available, with escalating definitions of availability, especially for those traditionally presumed to be available for others, as women have often been.

Feminist scholars have begun to analyse as well the exclusion of women's voices from electronic networks and other technological work (Taylor, Kramarae and Ebben, 1993; Hacker, 1990). This occurs through lack of training and socialization, but also through the reproduction of violence against women in cyberspace. We have known for a long time that home can be a safe haven—or the most dangerous place a woman can be (statistically, it is *the* most likely place for a woman to meet a violent death). Consider the following example of a 'rape in cyberspace.'

Julian Dibbell (1992) describes 'A Rape in Cyberspace,' an event which has caught the attention and imagination of many feminists trying to think through issues of computer-mediated sexual violence. The setting in which the event took place was a multi-user dungeon (MUD), an interactive fantasy/virtual reality game-conversation that is 'played' over the Internet and geographically distributed over space. One of the participants created a fictive character who invented a voodoo doll and used its magical powers to 'rape' and stab a female character (by the rules of the fantasy game, certain characters have powers over other characters given in the initial rules). The event led to a court case in 'RL,' or real life.

Although it is possible to simply say, 'well, it's only a game, why didn't the person just stop and walk away when it became uncomfortable?', Dibbell notes that, just as in physical rape, it is not that simple at all:

'Months later, the woman in Seattle would confide to me that as she wrote those words post traumatic tears were streaming down her face—a real-life fact that should suffice to prove that the words' emotional content was no mere playacting. The precise tenor of that content, however, its mingling of murderous rage and eyeball-rolling annoyance, was a curious amalgam that neither the RL nor the VR facts alone can quite account for. . . . To participate, therefore, in this disembodied enactment of life's most body-centered activity is to risk the realization that when it comes to sex, perhaps the body in question is not the physical one at all, but its psychic double, the bodylike self-representation we carry around in our heads.'

The blurring of boundaries between on-line and off-line is common in computing worlds. Ubiquitous talk which blurs the distinctions between electronic transactions conducted via keyboard, video or other electronic devices, and unmediated interactions. The expanding and nearly ubiquitous presence of networked information technologies of all sorts has raised serious questions about where you live and work. It is possible for some to 'telecommute' from terminals or computers at home, if their work involves data entry, writing, or technical tasks that can be so handled. But it is possible to teach (at least some of the time) via bulletin board, video relays and conferencing systems, and other software and hardware configurations of the sort Margaret Riel describes, thus blurring the traditional classroom boundaries.[3] In high-tech work, the process of production may be spread across continents as specifications are shipped from one site to another, and parts configured according to global economies of scale. Mitter has pointed out how such 'global factories' are especially problematic for women in less-developed nations: 'A growing discrepancy in the wages and working conditions of core and flexible workers characterizes the current restructuring of manufacturing jobs. In a polarized labour market, women predominate in the vulnerable, invisible or marginalized work' (1991: 61). As many have pointed out, the combination of telecommuting with the global factory has proved terrible for women in general—women become isolated in 'the electronic cottage', miss promotion and social aspects of the job, and often are expected to do finicky tasks such as data entry along with full time child care. At first heralded as the liberation of working mothers (sound familiar?), the installation of terminals in homes which allowed for 'home work' via telecommuting over time proved to be disadvantageous for most home workers. It can be an easy way for a corporation to do legal 'union busting' and bypass any particular state's labour regulations.

Other issues of invisibility in the online-offline borderlands concern questions of voice and representation. Markussen notes in her article that 'Giving voice to the traditionally invisible requires a purposeful effort to understand work practices, currently not articulated within the dominant understanding,' and that this is indeed a double-edged sword. In a recent study we did with a group of American nurses who are attempting to classify all the work that nurses do (Timmermans, Bowker and Star, in press), we encountered just such a dilemma. This was very similar to the findings of Wagner in her study of Austrian and French nurses (Wagner, in press). The nurses we studied are making a careful empirically-based and communally-legitimated list of nursing tasks. Their goal is to completely specify the varieties of tasks nurses do, and to provide a classification system that will both allow for comparative research (across countries and hospitals, for example) and will as well demonstrate the scientific nature and extent of nursing work.

Nursing has been one of the quintessential types of work that is taken for granted and made invisible, and it has been deeply bound up in traditional gender roles. By creating a classification system to identify work, these nurses hope to provide simultaneously a greater basis for comparability in nursing research, greater visibility of the taken-for-granted, and a basis for quality control of nursing work. Yet one cannot have maximum value on all three counts due to the pragmatics of work and the dangers of surveillance, especially in the electronic sphere. The more visible and differentiated one makes tasks, the more vulnerable one becomes to Tayloristic intervention, and the more discretionary power may be taken away. The more comparability is provided through standardization, the more risk of rigidity or inappropriateness to local circumstances.

The complexity of naming that which has been part of the background, or legitimating of problems, is always there. Similar arguments have been made about domestic labour, secretarial work, and other types of work traditionally done by women. Electronically, such visibility can also mean becoming a target for surveillance, as with the monitoring of key strokes in data entry (again, largely done by women), to the point of timing breaks to go to the toilet.

Many people in information systems are interested in modeling or 'capturing' forms of invisible labour, such as the articulation work of managing real-time contingencies (Schmidt and Bannon, 1992). Yet the problems with this for those who are disempowered may mean a further reification, and disproportionate burdens, as we have seen in the case of women's work (Star, 1991a, b).

Because computers are simultaneously communication media and product, objects of analysis and infrastructure for analysis, intimate and formal, they form good occasions to study a variety of basic processes: the development of material culture, the formation of practice-based networks, the fallibility of language, the relationship between power and infrastructure. Where they model work processes and facilitate them, they are a mirror of those processes, as in systems and requirements analysis; where they simplify or reify informal and local understandings, they are a house of mirrors for both designers and users.

The purpose of this monograph is to explore a wide range of cultural practices associated with the design and use of computing, both as mirror and house of mirrors. Rather than ask 'what difference are computers making in the world?' or 'is there an information technology revolution?,' this volume examines specific kinds of work that people do together (borrowing Becker's phrase) with and around computers. Adopting Lave and Wenger's (1992) notion of 'community of practice,' each essay examines the ways in which people are brought together in computing practices as computing learners, artists, gatekeepers, and scientists—sometimes as insiders, sometimes as outsiders. As an artistic tool, computers are key parts of new musical, photographic and cinematographic inventions. Writing collaboratively on the computer may change, stretch and challenge definitions of authorship and writing processes themselves. Eevi Beck traces how the work of collaborative writers 'was inseparable from their immediate environment and the culture which it was part of.' To make the whole system work, they had to juggle time zones, spouses' schedules, and sensitivities about parts of work practice such as finishing each other's sentences *as well as* manipulating the technical aspects of the writing software and hardware. They had to build a shared context in which to make sense of the information. Rogers Hall and Reed Stevens present a similar case for both students and professional designers using computerized tools. The building of shared context is equally complex for experts and novices—and thus the traditional distinctions between them are challenged, with the attendant assumptions of cognitive science. Karen Ruhleder's study of classical scholars and the impact of computerization on their work similarly challenges the very notions of textual authority and authorities on a text. All three argue against a long tradition of de-contextualized knowledge where only the technical, or narrowly construed considerations about cognition hold sway.

Although computers are becoming more flexible, they nevertheless embody the limitations of any medium. They simplify, make choices that are often invisible about voice, politics, and knowledge. Computers entail and embody power in many ways, from their capacity to encode certain parts of human life (and exclude others) to their power in the marketplace as commodities. Collectively the essays in this volume embrace both the choices and dangers, reasons and insanity embodied in the relations of computing today. Classrooms using computers at long distance stretch the process of teaching and the boundaries of the classroom, as Margaret Riel analyses in her article. 'Pad pals' (the computerized version of 'pen pals') are becoming common in many classrooms, affording a quick and illuminating bridge across cultural and geographical distances. At the same time, there is no guarantee that interaction over the net will not simply replicate the inequities of gender, race and class we know in other forms of communication. We must argue for the crafting of open and equitable spaces, with the continuing presence of both teachers and activists.

Economist Paul David has used the term 'transition regime' to describe the vast infrastructural shifts occasioned by widespread new technologies, for instance with the introduction of the general purpose engine. Such eras are marked by both possibility and confusion, and often by decreased productivity and efficiency. We are in a transition regime with respect to information technologies: will it make our lives easier or harder? more or less intimate, peaceful, productive, global? We don't yet know, and in some larger sense, may never know, exactly what it is we have gained and lost in the wholesale adoption of information technology and integrated media. Because computers are at once intimate and impersonal, tied up with work, education and entertainment, they may be so woven into the fabric of our lives that 'standing back' is completely an illusion. They are, as I have written elsewhere, not trojan horses but trojan doors—unfolding out into worlds embedded in each other without end (Star, 1992).

From automata to architecture

The monograph has four major themes: computers as a medium for building communities and networks; computers as a way of stretching and redefining specific cultural practices; problems in representing cultural practices for computing; questions of power and cultural conflict in the various worlds of computing.

The study of computing as a social and cultural phenomenon is relatively new and comparatively rare. For the last two decades or so, it has been a mixture of social criticism, workplace studies, and philosophically-informed debate about the nature of mind and cognition, and about the nature of formalism. Most of the essays in this volume draw on a combination of these roots, linked by an ethical concern that computers be a force for creativity and equality, and by scientific concerns which resist rationalist, simplistic or hype-driven descriptions of what computers will do for cultures. During this period, there has been a marked shift in the world of computer design and computer science, and a rising recognition of the importance of information retrieval and navigation through networked information spaces. This shift marks a change from a fascination with what computers can (and can't) do and their possibilities as replicant humanoids—to a focus on computer design as creating affordances, not replacements, for human workers and players.

So in the early days of social and cultural studies of computing, many writers focused on the drive from artificial intelligence to replicate and model human intelligence; they focused as well on the negative social consequences of computer surveillance, rigidity, and job loss through automation (Dunlop and Kling, 1991). Dreyfus and Weizenbaum, for example, argued with those in artificial intelligence about the possibilities and putative benefits of AI. Much of the focus in this work was on the nature of human essence, and what could be separated away from the machine and denoted as truly human. In the wake of these debates grew a series of empirical studies: Suchman (1987) and Forsythe's (1993) ethnographic work on artificial intelligence research, for instance; Kraemer and King's studies of the computerization of local government (Kraemer and King, 1977; Kraemer and King, 1986); and Kling and Iacono's work on computerization in a variety of large organizations (Iacono and Kling, 1987; Kling and Iacono, 1984). Explicit in many of these studies was a sense of the limits of computers, formalization and rationalization, implicit was an alternative model for the conduct of computer design and use. The Scandinavian research on workplaces, conducted jointly by informaticians and workers, gave rise to the tradition of 'participatory design' or co-design.' (Bødker, 1991; Bødker and others, 1991) This approach foregrounded problems of design and brought together many social scientist, computer scientists, and humanists in the service of more human design.

Since the late 1980s, with the widespread adoption of increasingly powerful personal computers and Internet usage, a shift has occurred in the focus of both the scientific computing community and those of us who have studied its social/cultural features.

Human actions and interactions are increasingly centered and mechanized imitation of humans increasingly less central. Metaphors of 'space' and discussions of affordances and tools are replacing discussions of automata and Turing tests. Along with this shift a number of partnerships between social and computing scientists have evolved, where the insights of ethnography, cultural studies, history, and sociology of work are explicitly linked with design (Bowker, et al., 1993).

Possibilities and creativity

Too often, in a time of great publicity and hype, attempts to provide a balanced view of phenomena are dismissed as 'boring,' 'nay-saying' or even 'Luddite.' The mixture of social criticism, grounded ethnography, struggles with the legacy of formalism and rationalism, and a sense of the possibilities of design are all present in the papers in this volume, in balanced measure. As we struggle to make sense of this transition regime, another kind of possibility, not previously clear to any of us, emerges. The as-yet-undefined spaces in networks and computers are still there—even as they are pressed upon by commercialism and militarism, imbued with race, gender and class stratification, and containing frightening possibilities for surveillance. Nevertheless this transition is also a possible occasion for reflection, a chance to quarrel with conservative definitions of human-ness and of cognition, of work and of play. Because computers leak over the boundaries of organizations and the ways we organize our days, and because they are both medium and infrastructure for representation, they can also be fun, opening up and tools for change. Digging into the design choices in large information systems, for instance, we discover questions of voice and silence (Bowker, 1994; Bowker and Star, 1994); analysing email and hypertext, we find new practices emerging, often with great wit and a sense of play. Consider for example the invention of 'geek code', an elaborate set of letters and symbols which self-identified geeks attach to their electronic signatures. Geek is slang for a person who is very deeply involved in the technical aspects of a particular endeavour, somewhat akin to a 'nerd'. A 'computer geek' is someone who spends a great deal of time on computing and is often involved in related activities such as reading science fiction. Robert A. Hayden has collected much of the geek code, here reproduced as of 1993[4] (of course, local variants are endless, and the list has already been much expanded):

THE CODE OF THE GEEKS v1.0.1
JULY 17, 1993

So you think you are a geek, eh? The first step is to admit to yourself your geekiness. No matter what anyone says, geeks are people too; geeks have rights. So take a deep breath and announce to the world that you are a geek. Your courage will give you strength that will last you forever.

How to tell the world you are a geek, you ask? Use the universal Geek code. By joining the geek organization, you have license to use this special code that will allow you to let other un-closeted geeks know who you are in a simple, codified statement.

The single best way to announce your geekhood is to add your geek code to signature file and announce it far and wide. But be careful, you may give other geeks the courage to come out of the closet. You might want to hang on to your copy of the code in order to help them along.

INSTRUCTIONS:

The geek code consists of several categories. Each category is labeled with a letter and some qualifiers. Go through each category and determine which set of qualifiers best describes you in that category. By stringing all of these 'codes' together, you are able to construct your overall geek code. It is this single line of code that will inform other geeks the world over of what a great geek you actually are.

Some of the qualifiers will very probably not match with you exactly. Simply choose that qualifier that MOST CLOSELY matches you. Also, some activities described in a specific qualifier you may not engage in, while you do engage in others. Each description of each qualifier describes the wide range of activities that apply, so as long as you match with one, you can probably use that qualifier.

VARIABLES

Geeks can seldom be quantified. To facilitate the fact that within any one category the geek may not be able determine a specific category, variables have been designed to allow this range to be included.

@   for variable, said trait is not very rigid, may change with time or with individual interaction. For example, Geeks who happen to very much enjoy Star Trek: The Next Generation, but dislike the old 60's series might list themselves as t++@.

( )   for indicating 'cross-overs' or ranges. Geeks who go from c+ to c--- depending on the situation (i.e. mostly 'c+') could use c+(---). Another example might be an m++(*). This would be a person who mostly listens to classical music, but also has an extensive collection of other types of works.

@ is different from ( ) in that ( ) has finite limits within the category, while @ ranges all over.

Type

Geeks come in many flavors. The flavors relate to the vocation of the particular geek. To start a code, a geek must declare himself or herself to be a geek. To do this, we start the code with a 'G' to denote 'GEEK', followed by one or letters to denote the geeks occupation or field of study. Multi-talented geeks with more than one vocation should denote their myriad of talents with a slash between each vocation (example: GCS/MU/T).

GB   Geek of Business
GCS   Geek of Compute Science
GE   Geek of Engineering
GM   Geek of Math
GMU   Geek of Music
GS   Geek of Science (Physics, Chemistry, Biology, etc.)
GSS   Geek of Social Science (Psychology, Sociology, etc.)
GT   Geek of Theater

GO   Geek of Other. Some types of geeks deviate from the normal geek activities. This is encouraged as true geeks come from all walks of life.
GU   Geek of 'Undecided'. This is a popular vocation with new freshmen.

GAT   Geek of All Trades. For those geeks that can do anything and everything. GAT usually precludes the use of other vocational descriptors.

Dress

Geeks come in many different types of dress.

d   I dress a lot like those in Walmart ads
d+   I tend to wear trendy political messages like 'Save the Whales' or 'Free South Africa'.
d++ I tend to wear conservative dress such as a business suit.
d-   I tend to wear trendy political messages like 'Nuke the Humans', 'Question Authority', or 'Big Brother's Watching'.
d--   I wear jeans to work to piss off my boss
d--- At work, I have holes in my jeans and/or obscenities on my shirt.

d?   I have no idea what I am wearing right now, let alone what I wore yesterday.
!d   No clothing. Quite a fashion statement, don't you think?
-d+   I wear the same clothes all the time, no matter the occasion, often forgetting to do laundry between wearings.

Politics

Just as the Geek's sense of fashion is varied, so is his/her political convictions.

p   Politics? I've heard of that somewhere but in all honesty I really don't give a shit.
p+   Let's get the government off big-business's back
p++   All in favor of eliminating free speech, say aye!
p+++ Fuckin' Minorities! Adolf Hitler is my hero!
p-   Bring back the 60's
p--   I'm still living in the 60's
p---   No taxes through no government

-p+   Don't label me you moron! Both sides are equally fucked up!

Computers:

Most geeks identify themselves by their use of computers and computer networks. In order to quantify your geekiness level on computers, consult the following (consider the term 'computers' synonymous with 'computer network'):

c   Computers are a tool, nothing more. I use it when it serves my purpose.
c+   Computers are fun and I enjoy using them. I play a mean game of Wing Commander and can use a word proces-

sor without resorting to the manual too often. I know that a 3.5' disk is not a hard disk. I also know that when it says 'press any key to continue', I don't have to look for a key labelled 'ANY'.

c++   Computers are a large part of my existence. When I get up in the morning, the first thing I do is log myself in. I mud[5] on weekends, but still manage to stay off of academic probation.[6]

c+++   You mean there is life outside of Internet? You're shittin' me! I live for muds. I haven't dragged myself to class in weeks.

c++++   I'll be first in line to get the new cybernetic interface installed into my skull.

c-   Anything more complicated than my calculator and I'm screwed.

c--   Where's the on switch?

c---   If you even mention computers, I will rip your head off!

Linux

Linux is a hacker-written operating system virtually identical to unix. It runs on your standard 386/486 PC computers and offers multitasking support far superior to DOS. Because it is still a young OS, and because it is continually evolving from hacker changes and support, it is important that the geek list his Linux ability.

1   I know what Linux is, but that's about all

1+   I've managed to get Linux installed and even used it a few times. It seems like it is just another OS.

1+++   I use Linux almost exclusively on my system. I monitor comp.os.linux and even answer questions some times. I've aliased Linux FTP sites to make getting new software easier.

1++++   I am a Linux wizard. I munch C code for breakfast and have enough room left over for a kernel debugging. I have so many patches installed that I lost track about ten versions ago. Linux newbies consider me a net.god.

1-   I have no desire to use Linux and frankly don't give a rats ass about it.

1--   Uni sucks. Because Linux = Unix. Linux Sucks. I worship Bill Gates.

!1   I don't even use an 80x86 chip, so linux isn't really a reality for me. (ie, Mac people).

1?   What the hell is Linux? I've never even heard of it.

Unix

Just as geeks sometimes use Linux, a great many geeks also use generic Unix machines to accomplish their geeky ends.

u   I have a unix account to do my stuff in

u+   I not only have a unix account, but I slam VMS any chance I get.

u++ I've get the entire admin ticked off at me because I am always using all of the CPU time and trying to run programs that I don't have access to. I'm going to try cracking/etc/password next week, just don't tell anyone.

u-   I have a VMS account.

u-- I've seen unix and didn't like it. DEC rules!

u--- Unix geeks are actually nerds in disguise.

Education

All geeks have a varying amount of education.

e   K-12, been on a college campus.

e+   Started a B.S./B.A, plan to finish it some day.

e++   Had not learned enough to know better not to go back and try for a master's degree.

e+++ Still pretty stupid, over qualified to work any job, went and got my Ph.D.

e-   Got my bachelors, escaped alive, and am making hoards of money writing unmaintainable (except by me) software.

e--   The company I work for was dumb enough to fund my way through a master's degree, then started paying me even more money.

e---   Achieved a Ph.D, have devoted my life to insignificant research, which my employer pays dearly for.

e*   I learned everything there is to know about life from the 'Hitchhiker's Trilogy'.

Music

Musical interests vary widely, also.

m I occasionally listen to the radio

m+ I own a tape or CD collection (records also count, but you would be admitting how old you really are).

m++ I consider myself refined and enjoy classical and new-age selections.

m+++ I consider myself over-refined and grok that heavy-duty elevator music.

m- Just play it loud

m-- I play air-guitar better than anyone else.

m--- LISTEN! I SAID TO PLAY IT LOUD!

m* I am an expert on so many types of music that I can't even keep them straight

Shape

Geeks come in many shapes and sizes. Shape code is divided into two parts. The first indicates height, while the second indicates roundness. Mix each section to fit yourself. Examples include: s/++, s++/, s++/--.

s I'm an average geek

s+/+ I'm a little taller/rounder than most.

s++/++ I'm a basketball/linebacker candidate.

s+++/+++ I usually have to duck through doors/I take up three movie seats.

s-/- I look up to most people. Everyone tells me to gain a few pounds.

s--/-- I look up to damn near everybody. I tend to have to fight against a strong breeze.

s---/--- I take a phone book with me when I go out so I can see to eat dinner. My bones are poking through my skin.

Nutrition

Geeks usually consume good. Some eat everything they can grab while some others are quite conscious of their food. (Note: 'n' is used for nutrition as 'f' is used elsewhere.)

!n Eh what? never mind the menu, give me something to eat!

n+ I like food—especially when it is healthy.

n++ I like the fibers in food

n- Food? I just grab something from the shelves with meat in it.

n--   I eat only the cheap things—even with artificial meat and vegetables.
n---   I live on snacks and coke.

Housing

h   Friends come over to visit every once in a while to talk about Geek things. There is a place for them to sit.
h+   Living alone, get out once a week to buy food, no more than once a month to do laundry. All surfaces covered.
h++   Living in a cave with 47 computers and an Internet feed, located near a Dominoes pizza. See !d.
h-   Living with one or more registered Geeks.
h--   Living with one or more people who know nothing about being a Geek and refuse to watch 'Star Trek'.
h---   Married, with the potential for children. (persons living with a fiance might as well label themselves h---, you're as good as there already.)
h*   I'm not sure where I live anymore. This lab/workplace seems like home to me.

Friends

Yes, it's true; geeks do have friends. At least, some of them do.

f   Yeah, I have friends. Who told you?
f+   I have quite a few really close friends. We get along great. They are all other geeks, though.
f++   I have so many friends, I make other people jealous.
f-   I have a few friends. They barely seem to speak to me anymore.
f--   I've got about one friend left in the world, who probably wants to shoot me.

f?   I think I have friends.
f*   Everyone is my friend.
!f   I have no friends. Get lost.

Glasses

Geeks have traditionally worn glasses.

!g   I have no glasses
g+   I've got four eyes, what's your point?
g++   I've got four eyes and tape in the middle
g+++   I have coke-bottle glasses that I can use to start leaves on fire in the hot sun.

g-   I have contacts
g--   I have colored contacts
g---   I have those funky contacts that have interesting designs on them such as happy faces or some such.

Weirdness

Geeks have a seemingly natural knack for being 'weird'. Of course, this is a subjective term as one person's weirdness is another person's normalness. As a general rule, the following weird qualifiers allow a geek to rate their weirdness.

w   I am not weird. I'm perfectly normal.
w+   so? what's your problem with weird.
w++   I am so weird, I make Al Yankovic look sane.
w+++ Mainstream?: I heard of that once, I think.
w-   I'm more normal than most people normally are.
w--   Isn't everyone in the p+ group?

Star Trek

Most geeks have an undeniable love for the Star Trek television (in any of its three forms). Because GEEK is often synonymous with TREKKIE, it is important that all geeks list their Trek rating.

t   It's just another TV show
t+   It's a damn fine TV show and is one of the only things good on television any more.
t++   It's the best show around. I have all the episodes and the movies on tape and can quote entire scenes verbatim. I've built a few of the model kits too. But you'll never catch me at one of those conventions. Those people are kooks.
t+++ It's not just a TV show, its a religion. I know all about warp field dynamics and the principles behind the transporter. I have memorized the TECH manual. I speak Klingon. I go to cons with Vulcan ears on. I have no life.
t-   Maybe it is just me, but I have no idea what the big deal with Star Trek is. Perhaps I'm missing something but I just think it is bad drama.
t--   Star Trek is just another Space Opera. William Shatner isn't an actor, he's a poser! And what's with this Jean-Luc Picard? A Frenchman with a British accent? Come on. I'd only watch this show if my remote control broke.

t--- Star Trek SUCKS! It is the worst crap I have ever seen! Hey, all you trekkies out there, GET A LIFE! (William Shatner is a t---)

Role Playing

Role-playing games such as Dungeons & Dragons have long been a part of the traditional geek life. Because geeks often become so involved in their role-playing that they lose touch with reality, include one of the following role-playing codes.

r   Role-Playing? That's just something to do to kill a Saturday afternoon
r+   I've got my weekly sessions set up and a character that I know better than I know myself.
r++   There is no life outside the role of the die. I know all of piddly rules of (chosen game). MY own warped rules scare the rest of the players.
r+++   I worship E. Gary Gygax.
r-   Gosh, what an utter waste of time!
r--   Role-Players worship SATAN!

Sex

Geeks have traditionally had problems with sex (ie, they never have any). Because geeks are so wrapped up in their sexuality (or lack of sexuality for that matter), it is important that the geek be willing to quantify their sexual experiences.

This code also is used to denote the gender of the geek. Females use 'x' in this category, while males use 'y'. For example:
x+   A female who has had sex
y+   A male who has had sex.
For those persons who do not wish to give out any details of their sex life, the use of x? (where x is the gender code) will allow you to so.

!x   Sex? What's that? I've had no sexual experiences.
x+   I've had real, live sex.
x++   I was once referred to as 'easy'. I have no idea where that might have come from though.
x-   I prefer computer sex to real sex.
x--   I was once referred to as a 'cyberslut', but I have no idea where that might have come from.

x*   I'm a pervert.

x**   I've been known to make perverts look like angels.

x?   It's none of your business what my sex life is like (this is used to denote your gender only).'

Understanding this sort of humour and elaborate word-typography play is an important part of understanding the culture of those who spend a lot of time on line, playing with long-distance relationships, and developing identities linked to those activities. To give it a try: a sample geek signature for me would look something like this:

Susan Leigh Star (GSS, @d++, c++, c--, u, g++, w+++, t++). The meanings are as follows. In my case I selected the following codes to indicate myself as a Geek of Social Science, generally conservatively dressed, with computers a reasonably large part of my existence . . . I have a unix account, four eyes (glasses) and tape in the middle, definitely not mainstream, and am quite fond of Star Trek (within limits, of course) . . . and so on.

This elaborate partially tongue-in-cheek encoding is a good example of playing with/around/within one of the cultures of computing, growing out from habits and gestures first associated with 'nerds,' as well as the long tradition in electronic mail of creating funny or thoughtful 'sig files' or signature files, as Nancy Baym discusses. The geek code has hundreds of variants on the net, including sexual codes and other personal indicators. Baym's article discusses such signatures as cultural practices deeply woven into the relations of a community. Sherry Turkle's recent study of a group of MUDders provides a fascinating social-psychological insight into the related phenomenon of developing whole personae on-line, and its links with humor, fantasy, and multiple selves (1994).

Kathryn Henderson's examination of the visual culture of engineers shows similar relational threads. The use of drawings by engineers, and their coupling with computing technologies, encompasses a wide range of practices from looking and seeing, to occasions for involvement and learning, to weighing the value of a contribution. How we see can never be taken apart from our tools or our historical period. Dianne Hagaman's question makes a similar point: what if Mead and Bateson had been able to craft their vision of a hypertext set of linked images of Balinese culture? Their yearning to transmit the sense of complexity and wholeness from their fieldwork to a multi-media vision is palpable in her essay. Indeed, Bob Jones and Rand Spero's investigation of hypertext use in the classroom confirms Hagaman's intuition about Mead and Bateson. By breaking apart and reconfiguring the interpretations of canonical texts, hypertext may support a more cognitively flexible approach to reading—a fuller context by virtue of multivocality.

Cyborgs and monsters: at home in cyberspace?

Much of the cultural criticism of computing has drawn from a mixture of science fiction images, artificial intelligence terms, and earlier work in cybernetics, together with feminist notions of ecology and selfhood. For this reason, terms like 'cyborg' and 'monster' have become commonplace in both the popular literature on computing and in scholarly research. Cyborg, as used for example by Donna Haraway (1991) and Adele Clarke (1993), means the intermingling of people, things (including information technologies), representations and politics in a way that challenges both the romance of essentialism and the hype about what is possible technologically. It acknowledges the interdependence of people and things, and just how blurry the boundaries between them have become. It is at once an exciting, avant-garde notion of the merger of people with technologies, making possible new ways of being, and often a despairing look at the devastation wrought by technophilia as coupled with late capitalism. Paul Edwards balances his essay precisely on the mixture of hope and despair—refusing both a romantic view of the green earth, and an over-inflated view of techno-possibility, he forces us to think in new and sometimes paradoxical ways about these images with which we are playing. Allucquere Rosanne Stone similarly notes that virtual spaces offer powerful, playful and serious possibilities for transforming bodies:

'. . . the troubling and productive impositions of neurology and electronics, musculature and hydraulics, thought and computation, biology and technology that signal the close of the mechanical age and the inception of an age which, for want of a better term. let's call the virtual—happening not in some theoretical space but right there in the next room, not to some research subject but to my own flesh and blood.'

The fact that this transformation is both troubling and productive is a central theme for Mike Hale's account of becoming a change agent in a multinational information technology firm. He is both troubler and troubled by what he sees there: a monster, or producer of monstrous behaviour. But he reminds us, as do all of the authors here, that none of us is purely one or the other in the middle of the transition regime of computing technologies.

For the very privileged, 'navigating the net' is now a viable option, where one can obtain electronic addresses on, for instance, the World Wide Web, and communicate with, obtain papers and images, from millions of others via programs such as Mosaic.[7] It is interesting to note that this convergence of technologies has simultaneously given rise to much hyperbole about global citizenship. For example, a 'Netizen' was defined in a July 6, 1993 post to The Daily News Usenet as follows:

> 'Welcome to the 21st Century. You are a Netizen (Net Citizen), and you exist as a citizen of the world thanks to the global connectivity that the Net gives you. You physically live in one country but you are in contact with much of the world via the global computer network. Virtually you live next door to every other single netizen in the world. Geographical separation is replaced by existence in the same virtual space. . . . We are seeing revitalization of society. The frameworks are being redesigned from the bottom up. A new more democratic world is becoming possible. . . . According to one user the net has "immeasurably increased the quality of my life." The Net seems to open a new lease on life for people. Social connections which never before were possible are now much more accessible . . . Information, and thus people, are coming alive.' (posted by Michael Hauben).

One important lesson of the convergence of feminism and other social justice movements with post structural theory in recent years is the concept that every marked category implies its opposite. So, men 'have gender' too (that is, there are historically specific practices associated with becoming a man in any culture, which differ across times and places)—it is not just women who are gendered. Whites are 'ethnic' and 'have race,' too, not just blacks, Hispanics, and Asians. Furthermore, all designations such as male or female, black or white, rich or poor, can be seen in verb terms, not just as nouns. So in addition to being relational as marked-unmarked (everyone has race, not just minorities), such categories are also achievements—something done, not given. So we can talk about the ways in which boys and girls undergo and produce 'gendering'; Toni Morrison has used the term 're-racing' to describe racial attitudes in the Clarence Thomas-Anita Hill hearing of a couple of years ago.[8] Following this lead, we can problematize the ways in which cyberspace and notions such as home and citizenship are changing. Do we indeed (some of us) 'live on the net'?

Doing much of my work and communication with friends by email, I often find myself feeling lonely and isolated. In a way this is paradoxical—just this month, three old friends with whom I'd lost touch a decade ago found my address on the net and wrote to re-make contact. My sister and I have had more to say on email in the course of a week than we have had time to say over the phone in a year. At the same time, I have moved ten times over this decade, and travel extensively to see old friends, feel a hug, a 'catch up' in a way that the electronic medium does not allow. Cyberspace can foster the illusion that I could live anywhere, and still 'be in touch.' This becomes clear during the weekends, when I have vowed for my sanity not to log on to email—and there is a silence around me, those electronic friends can't come to the movies with me, can't go for hikes in the woods, can't cook together.

Of course, you say. It's only a communication medium. Yet on another level there is a big push, so multi-faceted and overdetermined that the world's largest conspiracy theory couldn't hold it—to make us live our lives on line, to abandon living and working in a particular locale. At times this has made me think of myself with the term 'homeless' or 'nomad.' On reflection, this is both true and the mark of a privileged speaker (perhaps too privileged?).

Two researchers at the University of Illinois, Casey Condon and Dave Schweingruber, have recently done an extended ethnography in a local shelter for homeless men (1994). They define homeless as being unable to obtain permanent shelter and a job—what the shelter calls a PLA: Permanent Living Arrangement. They have made a very interesting case that this sort of being homeless is imbricated with questions of time and morality. The men are treated as if they are incarcerated; they must be inside the shelter from 7pm until 9am; they must be working on their 'problem,' looking for a PLA; they may not stay for more than 30 days if they are not working on their problem. Of course, different residents have different relationships to this Puritan morality and conception of time and progress.

The US, as Britain, presents a country of vast opulence populated with rising numbers of homeless people. The streets of every major city are filled with mini-cities made of cardboard boxes and shopping carts; a walk down the street is filled with encounters with people asking for money. Rich people find this disturbing and unsightly. In 1988, Mayor Ed Koch ordered that people living on the street be examined by mental health workers and if 'found deficient,' forcibly hospitalized (Deutsche, 1990: 111). Rosalyn Deutsche says of these politics that: 'The presence in public places of the homeless—the very group which Koch invokes—represents the most acute symptom of a massive and disputed transformation in the uses of the broader city . . . this reorganization is determined in all its facets by prevailing power relations.' (p. 110) She goes on to specify these power relations as embodied in land development politics and commodification, and in the job losses that have resulted from the internationalization of large corporations.

So, in a very important sense, the homeless are the canaries in the mines for those of us breathing globalized electronic air. I am a *homed person*, by analogy with marking other unmarked categories. That is, I have always had the means to put a roof over my head and bread in my stomach. I do not have to wash up in public toilets, house-sit for others in order to have chance to repair my clothes or cook a meal, as does a heroine in Marge Piercy's remarkable new novel, *Longings of Women* (1994). But that does not get at the feeling of the marked/unmarked, since it is so easy for me to say. Peggy McIntosh's thoughtful article on being white identified white privilege as being 'like an invisible weightless knapsack of special provisions, assurances, tools, maps, guides, codebooks, passports, visas, clothes, compass, emergency gear, and blank checks.' (1992: 71) She lists 46 assumptions associated with being white, including things such as going into a book shop and finding writing of and about one's race represented; being late to a meeting without people thinking that somehow reflects on her race, and so on. Following her lead, I can come up with the following assumptions about home:

• Being homed means that I have an ordered supply of food, clothes and tools, upon which to draw without having to think about it at the moment; in the planning and making the supply, I know that I have a place to put them;

- Being homed means that I can pass through the innumerable interactions that complex state bureaucracy requires, giving my name, address, and social security number, without being ashamed;
- Being homed means that I do not risk arrest in the process of conducting my bodily functions (eating, sleeping, passing waste);
- Being homed means that I can unproblematically link my supplies with my social life and my working life, in a manner more or less chosen by me;
- Being homed means that I may come and go, and during my absences my supplies and address will remain more or less constant, and I may return and leave at will without threat of the law or negotiations with others who live around me.

Yet in this complex freedom, there is too a sense in the words of the song of, 'nothing left to lose.' There is a sense in which the traditional axis of homed-homeless has been torqued by the global electronic network—primarily for we homed, but not exclusively. For example, many of those who work with the homeless have instituted voice mail centers, so that prospective employers may call and not realize that the person does not have a fixed abode. Such passing behaviour is made possible by new electronic technologies—and in ways that are very problematic. We know what passing does to the soul, and we also see that this is a convenient way for the homed to ignore the problems that caused the homelessness in the first place.

The axis along home-homing is also torqued. Do I really 'live on the net'? Do *I* have a fixed abode—or a PLA? Of course, and of course not. I do, however, have a 'Home Page' on Mosaic, which I am constantly building up and playing with. This is a document which holds my picture, a couple of articles and bibliography, and has an address which maybe accessed from a computer anywhere in the world. Any part of that document can be hypertext linked to any other one I know about on the World Wide Web, and after it's set up, I can click on those links and 'travel' to places far away. I think about my Home Page quite frequently (possibly because I just learned how to program one), envisioning future links and additions. It's a new addition to how I think about myself, and my sense of home.

At the same time, I miss going to the movies with my friends whose bodies usually inhabit San Francisco. . . .

To be homed in cyberspace, therefore, has a double-edged meaning: to be both homed and homeless in some sense. Living on top of the earlier sense of physically homed, to be homed in cyberspace means:

- I have enough money to buy the basic setup of a terminal, keyboard, and modem, and I have a traditional home with telephone wires over which to run the device (or I work for an institution which provides them for me).
- I have access to maintenance people who can answer questions for me and help me plug into the larger infrastructure.
- I am literate and can either type, see, and sit up, or have special support (e.g. a Braille terminal or voice recognition) to help me carry out the equivalent of these tasks.
- I have a job which allows me an electronic mail address and does not monitor my communications (such monitoring does occur in the US, especially in large corporations);
- I have time and inclination, and a wide enough social network, to have others to write to and read.

Conclusion: A note on the word 'cultures'

Culture is a word like society, with a number of unfortunate definitional and philosophical problems associated with it. It is an easy concept to reify or make monolithic, easy to freeze or concretize what is in fact always a series of complex motions and improvisations. My intent in using the word *cultures* in the title is to call attention to the multiple, non-monolithic sense in which I am trying to talk about a set of practices with symbolic and communal meaning. Simultaneously, partly because of the legacy of the early years of computing and its associations with rational formalism, the joining of the word cultures with computing is a deliberate attempt to locate computing and information technology in the sphere of these practices, and to link the work of the scholars represented here with that notion.

At the same time, I could think of culture in another meaning altogether, as in cultured milk or yogurt: a small organism that affects change over time. And in that sense, I hope this volume will both leaven and enrich our attempts to understand and survive this regime of transitions.

Acknowledgements

Geof Bowker made many helpful comments on this introduction. Part of the work on the volume was supported by the Institute for Research on Learning, Palo Alto, and a fellowship from the Program on Cultural Values and Ethics, University of Illinois. I am grateful for their help. Thanks also to Cheris Kramarae, Jeanie Taylor and the other women of WITS (Women, Information Technology and Scholarship) at the University of Illinois for insights and support. A portion of this introduction was presented at a conference, 'Between Mother Goddesses, Monsters and Cyborgs: Feminist Perspectives on Science, Technology and Health Care,' Odense University, Denmark, November, 1994. I thank organizers Nina Lykke and Mette Bryld for their support. In addition, I would like to acknowledge the influence of several pioneers brave enough to cross the 'great divide' between the cultures of computer science and social science: John Seely Brown, Diana Forsythe, Les Gasser, Joseph Goguen, Carl Hewitt, John L. King, Rob Kling, Walt Scacchi, Lucy Suchman, Randy Trigg, and Bill Turner.

Notes

1 Electronic mail.
2 Geof Bowker (personal communication) points out that Southern California portrays itself as cities surrounded by 'wilderness'; but it in fact has become one megalopolis dotted with parks. The lion is a marker of this transition.
3 Such blurring has occured since the inception of writing and a postal service in some form, accelerated by television classrooms such as the British Open University. But real time, interactive use of the technology makes a qualitative leap over such asynchronous methods.
4 The Geek Code is copyright 1993 by Robert A. Hayden. All rights reserved. You are free to distribute this code in electronic format provided that the contents are unchanged and this copyright notice remains attached. Reproduced here with permission of Robert A. Hayden.
5 MUDs are multi-user dungeons, interactive fantasy games or discussions played or held over the net. They can go on for days, become extremely elaborate, and be funny or serious. See the discussion in Stone's paper, this volume.
6 As an example here: c- would go in the opposite direction, meaning: 'Where's the on switch?'
7 This software, developed by the National Center for Supercomputing Applications (NCSA) at the University of Illinois, Urbana-Champaign, allows decentralized multi-media access to documents, photographs, sound, and movies. The number of users has well surpassed the six million mark worldwide.

27

8 Thomas, a US Supreme Court judge, is married to a white woman, and during his appointment hearing was accused by Anita Hill, an African-American, of sexual harassment. Morrison contends that the public process took Thomas from his token position as 'white' and 're-raced' him with the stereotyped American black man (1992).

From practice to culture on Usenet

Nancy K. Baym

Abstract

Usenet distributes thousands of topically-oriented discussion groups, reaching millions of readers world-wide. Newsgroup participants often create distinctive sub-cultures, which have been all but ignored in scholarly work on computer networks and computer-mediated communication. I illustrate how Usenet discourse can operate as a culture-creating force, and how practice theory can be used to approach Usenet cultures, with a deep analysis of one message in the group 'rec.arts.tv.soaps.' This group, which discusses television soap operas, is one of the most prolific on Usenet. The use of a single message demonstrates the potential of all Usenet talk as a locus of cultural meaning. The specific claims I make about such meanings in rec.arts.tv.soaps are grounded in my ethnographic research on this group over the last two years.

Introduction

Social involvement in computer-mediated communities is one of the most popular uses of computer-mediated communication. Most work on computer-mediated interaction, however, has focused on its use in organizational contexts. Such work (eg Sproull & Kiesler, 1991) tends to portray computers as stripped of socio-emotional information, hence impersonal and poorly suited for social interaction. Much of the attention that social uses of the computer has been given focused on outstanding incidents of sexual harassment, gender-switching, electronic cads who break women's hearts, flaming and other abuses, rather than the countless rewarding and routine non-problematic interactions. If the impact of computer technology on workplaces or users' lives is to be fully understood, these popular social groups must be granted the scholarly attention they deserve.

The most expansive forum for such social groups is Usenet, a computer network supported primarily by UNIX operating systems on mainframes at universities and colleges, scientific laboratories and computer-related businesses. Usenet distributes topically-oriented discussion groups (newsgroups) through the Internet and other computer networks. In mid-1993, Usenet reached over 2,500,000 estimated readers at more than 97,000 sites world-wide (Reid, 1993).[1] There are thousands of newsgroups, and their participants, all of whom are involved voluntarily, often transform these informal links into distinctive intentional sub-cultures. These cultures are a particularly appealing use of computer technology both on Usenet and on commercial networks, but they have been all but ignored in scholarly work on computer networks and computer-mediated communication.

Introduction to Usenet

There are many means of computer-networked interpersonal communication available. Electronic mail (email) is a point-to-point system, allowing users to send electronic letters to specific users. Chat or talk programs enable two or more users to type conversations in real time despite any geographical distance between them (Reid, 1991). Multi-user domains, or MUDs, involve on-line fantasy play, where users create rich fictional environments. Bulletin boards (BBS) are located on single machines and users, usually local, can dial in for a range of services. Newsgroups share with email the format of letters, but, rather than being sent to individuals, letters (or 'posts') are sent (or 'posted') to specific groups and distributed across Usenet. 'Listserv' groups and DLs (distribution lists), of which there are an unknown number, lie somewhere in-between. The messages are distributed to a whole group; however, they are sent directly to individuals rather than housed on mainframes.

There are currently as many as 5,000 Usenets newsgroups. Although the mainframes are associated with institutions of higher learning and high technology laboratories and companies, most newsgroups are about hobbies or interests rather than professional concerns. The group which distributed the most messages in July of 1993, rec.arts.tv.soaps, is devoted to the discussion of daytime soap operas. The second most prolific, soc.motss, discusses homosexuality ('motss' is an acronym for 'members of the same sex'). Of the fifty groups which distributed more than 2,000 messages in July nine discussed computers and electronics, six discussed ethnic cultures (Indian, Vietnamese, Chinese, Jewish and Hong Kong) and twenty-two were fan-oriented (spanning soap operas to Japanese animation, classical music to rock). Discussions of sex, guns, politics, kids, the trading of insults and jokes, and the electronic equivalents of newspaper personals and classifieds, soc.singles and misc.forsale, rounded out the top fifty (Reid, 1993).

The appeal of these groups is unquestionable. Usenet's growth has been extraordinary. Rick Adams has been tracking Usenet traffic through uunet, one of the larger networks through which Usenet runs, since late 1984. An annual sampling of Usenet traffic in the two weeks in early autumn shows the growth (Table 1).

Table 1 Bi-weekly traffic growth on Usenet 1984–1993

For two-week period ending:	# of Usenet newsgroups through uunet	total number of articles through uunet	total number of bytes through uunet
October 8, 1984	158	4,241	6,248,063
October 8, 1985	187	5,731	9,114,399
October 8, 1986	221	7,828	16,008,177
October 8, 1987	342	17,013	33,544,843
October 11, 1988	453	25,253	43,257,129
October 8, 1989	701	45,084	79,292,363
October 22, 1990	1,231	84,771	160,159,428
October 8, 1991	1,732	137,225	283,010,966
October 9, 1992	4,129	272,941	528,385,604
September 8, 1993	5,464	425,320	810,707,213

Usenet's estimated readership has increased by over 500,000 in the last year and a half alone, bringing it to an estimated 2,641,000 in July 1993 (Reid, 1993). While some of the appeal of newsgroups can be attributed to information distribution, most of its use is clearly entertainment-oriented. People become involved because they want to, not because they have to.

Nancy K. Baym

The practice approach to culture

Because Usenet communities are, of necessity, grounded in linguistic interaction, the practice approach to culture (Ortner, 1984) is particularly appropriate for their study. Though they address a wide range of activities, practice approaches privilege language as an especially rich resource for the creation and recreation of culture. Practice theories view culture as continually reproduced and altered through the behavior of actors making practical choices (Ortner, 1984). Practices are functional; they 'aim to act' on the social world (Bourdieu, 1990). Socially codified representations of situations make particular goals relevant (Ochs, 1991; Bourdieu, 1990). Actors' orientation toward these goals recreates patterns of practice and reinforces the goals' relevance. Situational representations thus emerge through shared engagement in culturally meaningful practices. The coherence of culture results from people's reliance on culturally-consistent representations of situations to formulate appropriate action. O'Keefe (1988: 82) writes that verbal message 'are organized and produced through a rational process of deriving means to serve communicative goals . . . [which are] are conceptualized and analyzed as the central elements in socially codified representations of situations.'

Practice theorists see language use as socially organized and embedded in cultural systems of meaning (Schieffelin and Ochs, 1986; Miller and Hoogstra, 1992; Gaskins, Miller and Corsaro, 1992). Bourdieu (1990: 31) writes that language is used 'just enough for the needs of practice and within the limits allowed by the urgency of practice.' The practical needs served by language go far beyond those addressed in many linguistic theories, which treat language as an abstract system separable from practice and which privilege denotative reference. While language does denote, it also connotes and, perhaps more importantly, invokes. This invocative force makes language a powerful creator of social context (Goodwin and Duranti, 1992). Schieffelin and Ochs (1986: 171), drawing on work in sociolinguistics, claim '. . . that language serves several functions in social life and that consequently spoken and written messages have not only logical (truth-functional) but also social meanings'. These include information about the goals embedded in a situation, its objective structures or conditions, the identities of the interlocutors, the

32

frame or genre of the event, and the affective tone of the inter-action (Bakhtin, 1981, 1986; Schieffelin and Ochs, 1986; O'Keefe, 1988).

Language is able to index such socio-cultural information through the actor's choice of linguistic options (Miller and Hoogstra, 1992: 85). Language choices frame and aid in the inter-pretation of social actions through referential and metacommu-nicative cues to context (Schieffelin and Ochs, 1986). John Gumperz (1992) lists a wide range of such 'contextualization cues', including prosody, paralinguistic signs, code choices, and the choices of lexical forms. The work of Gumperz, as well as that of Hymes (eg 1975, 1986) and Bauman (eg 1975, 1992) has shown some of the many ways actors draw on linguistic resources to invest their behavior with social meaning. In so doing, actors invest those resources with further meaning, thus further codifying socially significant systems. In short, practice theory accords linguistic practice a central role in the creation and recreation of culture.

If language use is an important locus of cultural meaning-mak-ing in traditional cultures, it is only more so for Usenet cultures which are so heavily linguistic in nature. The resources available for Usenet participants to create distinct communities are limited to the Usenet system, shared interest in the topic of discussion, and the approaches the participants take toward one another. There are few if any shared spaces, face-to-face encounters, or physical artifacts to provide cultural foundations. Thus, the dis-course, shaped by the forces of the system and object of interest as well as the idiosyncrasies of the participants, carries inordinate weight in creating a group's distinct environment.

Language use alone, however, is not the sole creator of social meanings, nor should it be the sole source of data for the theorist seeking to explicate the meaning systems underly-ing cultural practices (Gaskins, Miller and Corsaro, 1992). Practice-oriented work is often micro-analytic, focusing on the details of activity, but it seeks to describe holistically the sys-tem in which the activity is embedded. 'The relation between language behavior and cultural ideologies,' write Schieffelin and Ochs (1986: 168), 'is not explicit or obvious but must be constructed from a range of ethnographic data, including inter-views, observations, transcripts.' Practice theorists also strive to make explicit the relationship between researcher and commu-nity (eg Bourdieu, 1977, 1990; Ochs, 1988). Community members are more likely to be treated as collaborators and acquaintances than subjects.

For two years I have been studying the community of rec.arts.tv.soaps (r.a.t.s.), a Usenet newsgroup that discusses daytime soap operas. R.a.t.s. is one of the first Usenet newsgroups and one of the most prolific. It has an estimated 52,000 readers and hundreds of active members who together write over 5,000 messages each month (Reid, 1993). My work examines how participants use communication to create a rich and appealing group culture. I have collected three kinds of data. Responses to a set of open-ended questions I posted to the group reveal demographic information about the users, how and why they use r.a.t.s., what they understand the conventions to be, how they view their relationship to other posters, and how they think reading r.a.t.s. and watching the soap operas influence one another. I also draw on email correspondences with participants. My central data source, however, is a corpus of over 32,000 thousand posts systematically collected over a ten-month period. From these posts I gain structural information about the numbers of participants, the rates of participation, and the sites through which they gained access. Since the language of the posts indexes cultural meanings, they also reveal the dynamics of the group's culture building.

I am recognized by the group as a member. In part this is because I am a soap opera fan and had been participating in the group for almost a year before starting the research. Since then I have continued to participate, both as researcher and fan. My acceptance within the group also stems from the fact that I have sought to involve the members in the work's evolution, and have shared it with those interested. Their responses have been an invaluable source of both data and encouragement.

Example Post

Let me provide an example through which to ground this abstract discussion. The post which follows is from rec.arts.tv.soaps discussion. It is fairly typical in content, tone and length. Except for the names and email addresses, which have been changed at the request of the original posts, this is the complete post as it arrived at the University of Illinois at Urbana-Champaign site:

```
From
news.cso.uiuc.edu!ux1.cso.uiuc.edu!howgard.redkin.ap
s.net!allik!herdfine.university.EDU!nntp.university.E
DU!walter!fargate Sat May 8 20:07:18 CDT 1993
Article: 100045 of rec.arts.tv.soaps
Newsgroups: rec.arts.tv.soaps
Path:
news.cso.uiuc.edu!ux1.cso.uiuc.edu!howgard.redkin.ap
s.net!allik!herdfine.university.EDU!nntp.university.E
DU!walter!fargate
From: fargate@herdfine.university.EDU (Susan Fargate)
Subject: Re: AMC: Tad/Ted
Message-ID: <1993May5.024010.6295@gordon.univer-
sity.EDU>
Sender: news@gordon.university.EDU (Sir Headlines)
Organization: Science Dept, University.
References: <1993May3.231122.28337@IRO.UMontreal.CA>
<13669006@pccupp.cap.pc.com>
Date: Wed, 5 May 93 02:40:10 GMT
Lines: 25
```

In article <136690006@pccupp.cap.pc.com>
Beth@pccupp.cap.pc.com (Beth Hunter) writes:
>Hi Everyone,
>
>I'm still way behind on AMC (getting less as my
>post-work activities schedule is lighter in May),
>but am I missing something here? Are we supposed to
>believe that Ted Orsini looks exactly like Tad
>Martin?????????
>
>The Ted Orsini story was based on the fact that
>Nola's kid disappeared as a child. It would not
>therefore be a requirement that the guy (our
>tadski) who shows up on her doorstep look exactly a
>certain way, similar coloring should be enough/
>
>Obviously, I'm missing something, since the writers
>wouldn't actually expect me to believe anything as
>unlikely as them being identical. Right? :-)
>

```
I agree Beth, but the Erica-turned-30 storyline was
enough to convince me that 'believability' is not a
prerequisite for a storyline. It bugs me because it
is hard to get swept up in any sort of suspense
knowing that your hypotheses (based on logic) are
bound to fall short of the writers' whims, but then
again, I have been watching for 14 years so it must
not bug me too much!

--

Susan Fargate           fargate@herdfine.university.EDU
```

I said earlier that the only resources Usenet newsgroup participants have to create distinctive cultures are the mandatory structures of Usenet, shared engagement with the topics around which groups build discussion, and the types of communal interests of the individuals who participate in the group. This post exemplifies the way all of these function as organizing forces as the group continually negotiates its culture.

Structures of Usenet

Several features of the post are attributes of Usenet. Users access Usenet through 'newsreaders,' programs which allow people both to read and contribute to newsgroups. Newsreaders use a consistent format for posts, identical with that of email. This external structuring provides paths and resources for participants. Three elements of the structure that are common to all Usenet posts are the headers, the quotation system, and the signature file. Here, the top twelve lines are the headers, which provide information about the message's route through the sites, the newsgroup(s) to which it has been sent, its number in this group at this site, the sender of the message, its subject, its unique identification number, the machine and organization of origin, other posts referenced in the message, when the post was sent, and its length. Other lines, such as summary lines, can be added at the time of posting. Headers automatically accompany every post; it is impossible to send a post *without* headers, though some newsreaders allow one to read without seeing all header lines. The lines labelled *article, from, subject* and *organization* stand out as resources for invoking interpretive contexts for practices.

The 'Article' line specifies the number of this post in terms of all posts to the group at this site. This article is the 100,045th message in rec.arts.tv.soaps to arrive at the University of Illinois site. This number indexes several important features. It demonstrates how prolific this group is; few groups boast more than 100,000 messages. The number suggests to newcomers a vast communicative history. This has normative implications for the novice; one would expect that many topics had already been discussed multiple times and that forms of practice have evolved— thus there are more social rules to violate than in a group with only a few thousand messages. If one looks at this number in relation to other statistics, such as previous article numbers on particular dates or the official bi-weekly and monthly Usenet readership statistics posted to the group 'news.lists,' one can assess the changes in posting rates. The growth of r.a.t.s. has been as spectacular as that of Usenet. In May of 1988 it carried only a few hundred messages a month. In May of 1990 it carried over 1,100. In the May of 1992 it carried over 3,500, and by May of 1993 it was carrying close to 5,000 messages monthly.

The 'From' line works as a salient contextualization cue. In identifying the sender, the line helps to set up the situation-relevant identities, or the participant structure of the interaction. Providing the sender's email address helps make the sender accountable for behaviour since it allows others to send email directly to those who violate group standards. In this post, the sender is Susan Fargate. Susan is a 'heavy poster'—she writes over 1.5 per cent of the total discussion of this particular soap opera. Earlier (Baym, 1992), I found that the top 10 per cent of the posters to r.a.t.s., each of whom wrote over 1.5 per cent of the messages, authored half the group's posts. The fact that Susan has written so much means that her name is likely to be familiar to regular readers. Especially prolific posters emerge as personalities in any newsgroup. Thus, their names in the 'from' line invoke implications for those familiar with the contributors. For instance, in the subset of r.a.t.s. which discusses the soap opera *All My Children* (AMC), regular readers know that a post from Anne will surely be friendly, a post from CJ is likely to be funny, and a post from John is guaranteed to offend and stir up unwanted controversy. This familiarity allows regular readers to form expectations about the messages and select which to read. Readers can go straight to the posts from those they like or can skip posts by those they dislike. They can even create 'KILL files' which cause their newsreader automatically to eliminate messages from selected individuals.

The 'Subject' line is also a major organizational resource for Usenet social situations. The subject line is chosen by the sender and intended to make explicit the message's topic. Here the subject line is composed of three hierarchical components separated by colons, reading 'Re: AMC: Tad/Ted.' The 'Re:' indicates that this message is a response to a previous one with the subject line 'AMC: Tad/Ted.' When people reply to messages through the newsreader, the software automatically replicates the subject line, adding 'Re:' to the front. Respondents can modify this if they choose. The continuation of subject lines across posts allows people to organize the messages they read by topic rather than chronological arrival order. New messages with a 'Re:' subject line invoke the existing contexts of previous interaction.

The second component of this subject line is the acronym 'AMC' followed by a colon. This conventionalized system in r.a.t.s. indicates which soap opera the message discusses. Here the post concerns *All My Children*. Because few people watch all soap operas, most readers follow only the discussions of those they watch. KILL files are also used to skip posts about unwanted soap operas; the acronyms for each soap opera allow newsreaders' KILL file mechanisms to recognize posts for deletion. People who omit the acronym often receive both public and private scoldings. One of the group's heavy posters, who has taken on much of the explicit socialization work in the group, writes regular explanations of the acronym system, and other r.a.t.s. conventions.

The third component of the subject line is 'Ted/Tad.' This is notable both for what it includes and what it doesn't. This slot in the subject line is often used on r.a.t.s. to mark genre. In the AMC discussion, for example, there are conventionalized ways to mark *retellings* of the soap opera, *previews* of coming events, *sightings* of soap opera stars in other contexts, *tangential* discussion and more. These genres are marked either because they are unrelated to the soap opera (eg *tangents*) or because they speak authoritatively (eg retellings) (Baym, in press). The unmarked speech, which accounts for more than two-thirds of the discussion, is almost all interpretations. They remain closely linked to the soap, and they make few claims to authority. From the subject line 'Re: AMC: Tad/Ted,' then, the reader infers that the post is an interpretive response to an interpretive message about the characters Ted and Tad on the show *All My Children*.

The specification of topic in terms of characters (rather than issues or events) demonstrates that fans' relationships with the show's characters is central to soap opera involvement. Livingstone (1989,1990) has demonstrated, for instance, that the character with whom the fans identify influences storyline interpretations. Hobson (1982), who studied the viewers and production of the English soap opera *Crossroads*, Ang (1985), who studied 47 Dutch viewers of *Dallas*, and Seiter and her colleagues (1989), who interviewed daytime soap viewers in Oregon, all emphasize that audiences identify with characters. Fans know characters, come to care for them, become involved in their problems, come to feel intimate with them, and use this empathic identification to speculate about what characters think, feel, and may do. It is through vicarious participation in the emotional lives of the characters that the viewer places her/himself in the world of the drama. Jean Rouverol, who has written for the soap operas *Search For Tomorrow*, *As the World Turns*, and *Guiding Light* (as well as acting in the radio serial *One Man's Family*), observes:

> Whatever else a show may offer, it must contain people we *love*, people whose joys and tribulations we can share. It must also provide us with people we love to hate, people who offer a continuous threat to the welfare or happiness of those we are fond of. And though the need for suspense is always a given, there can be no real suspense if we don't care about the people we're watching. Above all, we need to *care*. (1984:36)

That the topic is indicated through character is a linguistic cue to this central dynamic in soap opera fun culture (or 'fandom'). Other aspects of the process of soap opera fandom are also important influences on r.a.t.s. practices.

The 'Organization' line reveals the site of the message's origin. This usually places the sender. The line here reveals that Susan Fargate writes from a social science department at a prestigious university. The person to whom she is responding writes from a high technology company. Though the organizational status of each person is not specified, the grounding of the group in institutions affiliated with higher education is explicit. These lines also suggests how unlikely it is that these interpersonal links would have occurred without this forum. (The organization line is occasionally exploited in the name of humour, as when the poster alters it to read 'Organization: very little.')

A second important structural component of this post, below

the headers, is the quotation system. Susan Fargate is responding to a post written a few days earlier by Beth Hunter. Since the post is a reply, as indicated in the subject line, the newsreader has automatically inserted the line immediately below the headers, which provides the identification number of Beth's post and explicitly attributes authorship to her. Beth's quoted words are marked with '>' in the left margin. This ability to embed previous messages within a new post is an essential resource for establishing the situated identities of the participants.

Bakhtin (1981;1986) and Goffman (1981) each stress the importance of embedding in creating cultural meaning and social organization. Embedding is provocative for Bakhtin because it exemplifies what he calls the dialogic nature of talk. He argues that all verbal utterances presuppose other participants. Indeed, the talk exists *for* their sake and is constructed taking into account their projected reactions. The other side of addressivity is responsivity. Talk is responsive because all speech necessarily draws on previous discourse. We respond directly to others' messages, but, even more pervasively, choose our words from previously heard talk. Utterances thus reflect and create one another. Embedding is the most explicit example of this, but responsivity can be more subtle. Through language's projective and reflective qualities, words take on particular meanings within spheres of activities:

> All words have a 'taste' of a profession, a genre, a tendency, a
> party, a particular work, a particular person, a generation, an
> age group, a day and hour. Each word tastes of the context
> and contexts in which it has lived its socially charged life; all
> words and forms are populated by intentions. Contextual
> overtones (generic, tendentious, individualistic) are inevitable in
> the word (1981: 293).

Embedding is thus one way all utterances are linked in an extensive 'chain of speech communication' rich in cultural significances. Goffman (1981) addresses the structural shifts in social organization implicit in embeddings, seeking to explicate the structural underpinnings of the dynamic alignments between hearers and speakers in conversations. Embedding is notable for the shifts in the relationship of speaker to hearer, and speaker to utterance. There are many kinds of hearers, Goffman argues: those who are ratified and addressed, those who are ratified but not addressed, and those who are unratified bystanders or eaves-

40

droppers. In this post, by using quotation, Susan establishes Beth as her addressed recipient, while granting all readers the right to respond. Beth, by starting with 'Hi Everyone' ratifies and addresses all readers. One feature of Usenet's open structure is that there can be no unratified readers.[2] All messages are broadcast publicly.

Goffman also argues that speakers can have different relationships with their own utterances, owning their words to varying degrees. These shifts in an utterance's 'production format' open different possibilities for and restrictions on future talk. When Susan establishes that Beth is the author of the quote, she establishes that she is not accountable for its contents. The contextualization cue of the '>' indicates this When the '>' disappears, Susan becomes accountable for what is written and can be called upon to apologize, to justify, or to explain inappropriate behaviors. Similarly, she can take credit for particularly good behaviors. While she can't be held accountable for what Beth has said, Susan *can* be held accountable for the accuracy of her quoting. If, for instance, she were to pull something out of context, thus distorting it, or to mis-attribute the authorship, she could be publicly reprimanded. R.a.t.s. is highly concerned with accurate attribution.

Embedding, to summarize, is a structural possibility provided by Usenet's newsreaders. Its use creates cultural cohesion and establishes the situation-specific identities of the posts' writers and readers.

A third structural feature of Usenet newsreaders is the signature file. Here seen in the last line. The double dash just before indicates that the signature file follows. The signature file, usually called a 'sig file' for short, is created by a user and automatically appended to the end of every message. Here, Susan has used her file to give her name and email address—a bare-bones sig file. Most people add an affiliation, possible company disclaimers, and personally identifying components such as quotations or pictures drawn with keyboard strokes. Since the sig file appears at the end of all posts it is an excellent resource for establishing individuality. A distinctive sig file carries far more identifying potential than a name. My own experience of becoming socialized into this group and others is that the sig files are, at least initially, the most salient cues in learning to discriminate individuals.

Nancy K. Baym

Shared engagement in the topic of discussion

This group exists to provide a forum for the discussion of soap operas. The people drawn to this group are fans of the genre. It is because of their engagement with the general topic of soap operas that participants contribute to the group. Soap fandom provides resources of shared practices and shared knowledge on which participants draw to create community. Several aspects of engagement with soap opera impact upon language practices in r.a.t.s., including viewing practices; knowledge of the soap; bringing reality to bear on the interpretation of the soap opera; assessing realism and criticizing; speculation on the drama; and identification with the characters.

Two comments in this post suggest how soap operas are watched and valued in this community. Beth sheds light on the viewing practices of r.a.t.s. participants when she writes that her 'post-work activities schedule' prevented her from keeping up on AMC. The reference to 'post-work' shows that she, like most r.a.t.s. participants, videotapes soaps and watches them after work, not live. This defies the stereotype of soap fans as bored, isolated housewives watching TV all day.

The shift from live-viewing to videotape has practical implications as it brings with it the abilities to fast forward over boring parts (including commercials), to rewatch provocative parts, and to segment and time the episodes at one's convenience. The fact that other activities kept her from AMC shows that increases in external pressures can force even serious fans to miss days or weeks at a time. When 'real life' calls, fans may put the show on hold. When they do this, they are also more likely to put participation on r.a.t.s. on hold.

An interesting dynamic of soap commitment is illuminated by Susan's comment, 'I have been watching for 14 years so it must not bug me too much.' At the same time she states her loyalty, she also shows that being a soap fan is not an all-or-nothing proposition; Susan both criticizes (the soap does bug her at times) and appreciates (she continues to watch), suggesting a relationship with the show that is not always satisfactory. The ability, and tendency, of fans to be critical is usually overlooked. When acknowledged (Ang, 1988; Katz & Liebes, 1989), it is often regarded as a way of distancing one's self from the show. However, here criticism is a mode of close involvement, as I elaborate below; it is often the most committed fans who are the most critical.

The fact that r.a.t.s. participants are viewers of the soap operas they discuss provides them with a base of shared knowledge. In order to make any sense of the post at all, one needs knowledge of the show. Since all language use is shaped in part by structures, all language use is elliptical (eg Bourdieu, 1977). This post makes many elliptical allusions to the soap opera. I summarize the stories below. This retelling is meant both to aid the reader who doesn't follow AMC, and to illustrate the knowledge that cultural membership requires and relies upon.

Two years prior to this post, the character of Tad Martin, played by Michael E. Knight, fell off a bridge, got amnesia and hitched a ride out to California. A year and a half later, Tad, played again by Knight, resurfaced in the fictional Pennsylvania town where the soap opera is set, believing himself to be Ted Orsini, the son of a Napa Valley vintner named Nola Orsini. The real Ted Orsini, it turned out, had been kidnapped when he was eight years old. When Tad Martin appeared on Nola's doorstep with no memories, she 'recognized' him as her long-lost son and took him under her wing. By the time this was posted, Nola had passed away, Tad Martin had regained his memory, and the real Ted Orsini showed up in town, unable to remember anything that happened before he was ten years old (including his identity as Ted Orsini). The characters of Ted and Tad are both played by Michael E. Knight, wearing different styles of clothing and speaking in different registers.

The other story involves one of the five remaining original characters in AMC, Erica Kane, played by Susan Lucci, arguably soap opera's most famous diva. Lucci has been on the show since its inception in 1971, at which time Erica was in her late teens. Twenty-two years later, Erica would presumably be no younger than her late-thirties. In the spring of 1993, however, AMC introduced a new character, Kendall Hart, played by an obviously-teenage actress. Kendall, it was revealed, was Erica's secret daughter, born after Erica's secret rape at age thirteen, prior to the show's beginning. (It didn't take a mathematical genius to realize that either Kendall was about ten years too young or Erica was ten years too old for this scenario to make sense.)

When Beth puts the show on hold because of post-work activities, she loses some of the communal knowledge. The shows are the 'capital' of the fan community (Hobson, 1989). Without seeing the show, one is limited in the ability to speak about it. Beth indicates this constraint on language practice in many ways. She begins with an immediate qualification, 'I'm still way behind on AMC.' She then strategically frames her comments as a series of questions: 'am I missing something here?' 'are we supposed to believe?' 'Obviously, I'm missing something . . . Right?' Her framing of criticism as a question organizes the situation by limiting her accountability for criticisms. If there were a plot development she had missed, eg one which would explain that Tad and Ted were twins separated at birth, other participants could inform her without seeming to be challenging her. Had Beth's criticisms been phrased as assertions, the same information would be read as disagreement.

Participants' knowledge of the 'real world' is brought to bear in this post alongside shared knowledge of the soap opera, as the two stories are evaluated for credibility. There are numerous cues that realism is being assessed in the post. Beth asks explicitly if we are 'supposed to believe' that Ted looks exactly like Tad. She also uses nine question marks after her question. If the first indicates a question, the other eight indicate disbelief. In the second paragraph, in contrast, Beth argues that Nola *could* mistake Tad for Ted even if they were not identical, since Ted was so young when he disappeared. Beth lays out a central fact (Ted's youth) and determines realistic conclusions (Tad and Ted look similar in some way). In the third paragraph she returns to the word 'believe' and again emphasizes her disbelief: 'anything as unlikely' and the sarcastic 'wouldn't actually expect . . .' The smiley face at the end of that line, comprised of a colon, hyphen and left parenthesis, further marks the sarcasm (:-)).[3]

Susan also makes the practice of assessing believability explicit when she says that "believability" is not a prerequisite for a story-line.' Her use of quotation markers around 'believability' suggests its use as a group standard, one which the soap opera may fail to achieve. Beth and Susan's evaluation of the stories rests on their knowledge that in their own worlds people do not meet strangers who look exactly like them and people tend to get older rather than younger. This post points out some of the soap opera's larger logical leaps. Shared knowledge of reality is used in more subtle ways as well, as when participants build arguments about whether or not two characters 'really' love each other, arguments based in cultural understandings of what defines 'real love.'

The assessing of realism exemplified by this post has emerged in recent work in cultural studies as an important practice in fandom. While soap opera fans are the first to admit the absurdity of many tricks of the genre, genuineness is the most valued quality of soap opera fiction, and fans are harsh critics when soaps present things which are too 'unreal' (Hobson, 1982; Ang, 1988). Soap realism is critiqued in terms of internal fictional consistency and in terms of the ideological norms by which the viewers make sense of their own lives (Hobson, 1982). There are several features of soap operas which demand that viewers use social knowledge to make meaning of the show. Allen (1985) argues that soap operas appear to be authorless, in part because there is no narrator. The viewer sees the story from multiple perspectives, thus creating a sense of watching a world that exists even when it is not seen. This sense that the soap opera community is real encourages viewers to infer meaning not by reference to authorial intent, but to their own social knowledge. Media-fan scholar Henry Jenkins (1992), borrowing Michel DeCerteau's notion of 'textual poaching,' claims that the reader of popular culture is drawn not into the world of the fiction, but into a world he or she has created from the textual materials. Geraghty (1991:198) argues this is especially true of soap operas which, 'perhaps more than any other fictional form available to women, stress the relationship between text and reader; their constructions are dependent on the audience to fulfill their possibilities.' Viewers simultaneously rely on the shows' realism to sustain their involvement, and critically assess that realism.

Susan explicates the importance of believability as well as any theorist when she writes 'it's hard to get swept up in any sort of suspense knowing that your hypotheses (based on logic) are bound to fall short.' Her reference to logical hypotheses responds to Beth's defence of the credibility of the first Tad/Ted mix-up, a defence based on 'facts' and 'requirements.' Susan here tell us that an important practice of fandom is building logical hypotheses from the facts presented on the show. Again, soap operas are designed to encourage this speculation. They are 'over-coded' (Allen, 1985), carrying more signifying potential than necessary to move the story forward; they lend themselves to multiple interpretations. The expansive temporal framework and regular commercial breaks of the daily format are exploited to encourage viewers to imagine how the scene will continue. All scenes end at the point of maximum suspense. Geraghty (1991:10) describes each episode as ending with a set of 'unresolved narrative puzzles to carry viewers across the time gap from one episode to another.' The form of the genre takes account both of the audience's temporal relation and mental involvement with it, and uses what is shown to stimulate speculation about what is not. David Buckingham (1987:204) writes that:

> the most effective metaphor for soap opera is to regard it as a form of collective game in which viewers themselves are the major participants. The programme itself provides a basis for the game, but viewers are constantly extending and redefining it.

The game metaphor suggests fan goals. One goal indexed in this post is clearly that of formulating reasonable hypotheses and matching them against the unfolding drama. People on r.a.t.s. are often quick to claim their correct predictions, and often create predictions in hopes of entertaining other readers as well as proving accurate.

The game metaphor also suggests obstacles to the process. This post portrays the writers of the soap opera as a central obstacle. The writers are identified as those who 'actually expect me to believe anything as unlikely as them being identical.' Furthermore, Susan contrasts the 'logical hypotheses' of the fan with the 'whims' of the writers. Beth's sarcasm suggests a lack of faith. Beth questions what she is 'supposed' to believe and what the writers 'expect' her to believe, thus capturing a recognized contrast between real and implied viewers. The implied viewer accepts these leaps of logic. This real viewer does not, nor does she think her peers on r.a.t.s. will. The tension between fans and writers is not unique to soap opera. Jenkins (1992:24) writes:

> Fans recognize that their relationship to the text remains a tentative one. . . . While fans display a particularly strong attachment to popular narratives, act upon them in ways which make them their own property in some senses, they are also acutely and painfully aware that those fictions do not belong to them and that someone else has the power to do things to those characters that are in direct contradiction to the fans' own cultural interests. Sometimes, fans respond to this situation with a worshipful deference to media producers, yet, often they respond with hostility and anger against those who have the power to 'retool' their narratives into something radically different from that which the audience desires.

Buckingham (1987:204) too says that 'although the rules of the game are flexible they are ultimately determined by the programme-makers: while viewers may seek to play by their own rules, they must inevitably acknowledge those which are set for them.'

This post indexes the central practices of soap opera viewing, bringing previous soap opera knowledge and social knowledge to bear on interpreting the stories, assessing realism, criticising and speculating on future storyline developments. It also displays the practice of identification in Beth's explanation of how, from Nola's point of view, Tad could reasonably have been mistaken for Ted.

The world of the soap opera and the real world provide relevant stores of knowledge for reading the soap and interacting in r.a.t.s. Variations in knowledge have organizational implications as they lead to variations in degree of interpretive authority. Soap operas also provide practices for the group. The fans share the activities of taking character perspectives; speculating on the future by building logical arguments from story clues and real world knowledge; and assessing realism, a process which often leads to criticism of writers. Fans also bring shared understandings about the relative importance of soap opera; they sympathize with one another's long-term investments in the show and with the occasional real-world needs which prevent viewing. These shared knowledges and practices provide many of the structural influences on the communicative practices in r.a.t.s.

Communal interests

Usenet's structure and the nature of soap opera involvement are resources for and influences on the language practices in r.a.t.s. Participants also draw on those resources to create a sense of community, both as soap opera fans and as what one poster called 'friendly acquaintances.'

Communality

According to Jenkins (1992:86), '[o]rganized fandom is, perhaps first and foremost, an institution of theory and criticism, a semi-structured space where competing interpretations and evaluations of common texts are proposed, debated, and negotiated and where readers speculate about the nature of the mass media and their own relationship to it.' In fandom, fans' relationship to the show(s) becomes communal. On one level this involves sharing the knowledges and practices discussed above; on another it involves transforming the soap's resources into grounds for group solidarity.

There are a number of linguistic choices in this post which suggest that soap opera fandom is a communal enterprise. Jenkins (1992) shows how participants in the newsgroup alt.tv.twinpeaks make fandom communal. These fans post reactions to the show in part to affirm that others reacted the same way. They are likely to begin posts with comments like 'Is it just me or did anyone else think that . . . ,' much as Beth does. Furthermore, Jenkins argues that fans view their own knowledge of the shows as group property, beginning their comments with phrases like 'I'm sure you all noticed on last week's episode that . . .' Here, we see such a quest for validation in Beth's use of 'Right?' The communality is accomplished when Susan replies 'I agree.'

Fans' solidarity is also formed out of personal relationships to the characters, as Beth suggests when she refers to Tad as 'our tadski.' This group, like most AMC fans, adores the character of Tad and Knight's acting. When he fell off the bridge, the group was dismayed. In the time that he was gone, he remained a popular topic of conversation and the prospects for his return were often discussed. A lottery was even held to guess the exact date and time of his return. The winner placed it within five minutes and, shortly afterwards, started receiving one dollar bills in the mail from all over the country. When Beth adds 'our tadski,' she draws attention to the group's common feelings for Tad. The stances towards characters are one way fans co-position themselves.

Finally, consider Beth's question, 'are we supposed to believe that Ted Orsini looks exactly like Tad Martin?????????' and Susan's claim that 'it is hard to get swept up in any sort of suspense knowing that your hypotheses (based on logic) are bound to fall short of the writers' whims.' The uses of 'we' and 'your' portray r.a.t.s. participants as similar and furthers their solidarity by opposing them to the writers. Even the sarcastic smiley-face icon at the end of Beth's segment implies that we, on r.a.t.s., have a common way of engaging (ie we form logical hypotheses based in part on the show's credibility); we are all the targets for

48

the writers (ie we are all supposed to believe the story developments). This 'us against them' dimension of r.a.t.s. fandom helps fans serve as a resource for one another when the show disappoints. By negotiating consensus on the show's shortcomings, the fans are able both to distance themselves from the show and to stay involved until it picks up again. They can find their pleasures in the community, if not in the show.

Camaraderie

The group's establishment and negotiation of a communal relationship to the soap opera is one reason r.a.t.s is so pleasurable. Much of the pleasure is also due to the group members' active and persistent creation of an environment of camaraderie and affection. This can be seen from the very start of Beth's post when she says 'Hi everyone.' The 'hi' marks and creates the friendliness and casualness. She explicitly addresses all readers, so that none are marginalized. Beth's use of questions to express her criticism also marks the group's efforts at friendliness. By phrasing criticism as a question, she strategically avoids conflict, thus assuring that even if there is disagreement, there need be no opposition within the group.

Susan's response also demonstrates the group's friendliness. Calling Beth by name personalizes the interaction, granting Beth status and helping her to form an identity. Though it is not evident from this post alone, Susan's use of Beth's name is also indicative of Susan's status as a heavy poster. Heavy posters are more likely than lighter posters to refer to others by name, one of the many ways they take on a disproportionate share of creating group solidarity. Camaraderie is also created and sustained on r.a.t.s. through other means, eg personalized chit-chat. In some of the soap opera discussions, the acronym 'TAN' emerged as a subject line marker indicating tangential discussions, establishing a legitimized space for social interaction that is off topic.

Such friendly cheer is unusual on Usenet, where many discussions are highly and personally oppositional. The emergence of the network-wide term 'flame' to describe insulting disagreements indicates the practice's cultural significance. The high traffic to the newsgroup alt.flames, a forum for people to insult one another, is one indicant of antagonism. R.a.t.s. participants, on the other hand, strategically avoid antagonism, instead creating a social context of accepting affection. The friendliness of the group is one of the main things that draws new members and keeps people watching their soap operas.

Conclusion

Language use in this one post results from, indicates, and invokes a multitude of significances. Through Usenet, soap opera fandom, and the group itself, r.a.t.s. participants create a rich and well organized community. They have conventionalized meaningful and functional ways of marking messages, as seen in the subject lines, greetings and exaggerated uses of punctuation. They create situation-relevant identities, taking advantage of the headers and sig files, and using quotation, qualification, forms of address, and so on. The fans on r.a.t.s. collectivize solitary practices: taking the perspectives of soap opera characters through identification; bringing real life to bear on interpreting the soap; speculating on the meaning of soap opera events; and criticising the show. They create and sustain an affective tone toward one another of friendliness and solidarity. They also take affective stances on characters and the show's writers.

All of these processes on r.a.t.s. are functional. Collaboration on the four modes of involvement in soap opera enhances enjoyment of the soap. Indeed, the opportunity to join in the pooling of interpretations can be an incentive to take up soap opera viewing. The desire to engage in social interaction has emerged in many studies of soap opera fans as a critical motivation for watching (Rubin, 1985; Rubin and Perse, 1987; Babrow, 1990; Hobson, 1989; Brown, 1990; Geraghty, 1991). Talking about soap operas with other viewers is the fifth practice of soap opera enjoyment. The creation of a forum in which everyone can share their talks on the soap opera provides fans with a way to extend and enhance the pleasure of viewing outside of the watching experience, and create new pleasures of collaborative discussion. R.a.t.s. enables fans to remain involved with the show while they are not able to watch it or when they are not enjoying it. The fan solidarity supports the fan's involvement with the show and makes it harder to stop viewing. Since r.a.t.s. is oriented toward enhancing fun, social practices are shaped to ensure fun. Humour is prized. Insults are taboo, confrontation strategically minimized. People call one another by name, and praise one another's contributions.

The atmosphere is also important because of the topics involved. Since soap operas dwell on private emotionality, when people bring their real experiences to bear on interpreting them, they often draw on intimate and occasionally unpleasant experiences. Storylines about rape, or other forms of violence toward women, draw out personal stories of victimization and survival. This is also true with soap opera custody cases, divorces, racism and so on. The environment of r.a.t.s.' good cheer and aversion to conflict creates a safe space in which to discuss these rarely publicly-disclosed domains. Such disclosures allow others greater insight into both the soap opera and their own world.

R.a.t.s. is only one electronic community on one computer network. There are thousands more Usenet groups, many with richly developed cultures, and countless groups on other burgeoning networks. Computer-mediated communities show users transforming a new medium into something unforeseen by its creators. This essay has suggested a number of routes scholars might take into this phenomenon. Interviews with users illuminate features of the groups they recognize as compelling, as well as those they see as problematic and also allow insight into individual uses of the group. Summary statistics, such as traffic figures, growth figures and comparative ratings of groups show what kinds of groups generate the most participation. Analysis of the possibilities and limits of the computer network and its accompanying software lends understanding of each group's possibilities. Analysis of the topics of discussion, in this case soap operas, in terms of thought and discourse practices rather than abstract issues, also leads to insight into the community. Finally, the nuances of language in each group provide a window into the interests which motivate and sustain participation in each group. It is my hope that a body of work will emerge that allows for comparative analysis of different groups within and across systems and topics, and which begins to account for the dramatic emergence, popularity and growth of these provocative new cultures.

Notes

1 No one really knows accurate figures for Usenet use. These figures come from monthly arbitron-like ratings using a sample of users.
2 In this group, lurkers (i.e. those who read but don't post) are embraced as legitimized participants. The only people ostracized are those who attack the

legitimacy of soap opera fandom. These invaders, but not the lurkers, might be considered unratified. Other groups, however, are less fond of lurkers and treat them as eavesdroppers. The nature of the network, however, is such that eavesdroppers are granted the same access to messages that full-fledged members are, and posters know this when they write. The relational possibilities between posters and lurkers have yet to be systematically examined.

3 The smiley-face is one instance of a vast repertoire of socio-emotional markers known as 'emoticons.' For more on this, see Sanderson (1993).

Changing documents/documenting changes: using computers for collaborative writing over distance

Eevi E. Beck

Abstract

This chapter presents data from a case study of two academic authors writing together across great geographic distance, using telephones and computers connected over an international network. Not only the document being written but also the process itself was continuously changing, with the authors making creative use of the technology available to them. The information they offered each other concerned not only changes in the document, but also the authors' individual context of work. Rules and agreements were open to reinterpretation. The context sensitive interpretation of agreements facilitated a highly flexible process. The observations have implications of how collaboration is conceptualized in Computer Supported Cooperative Work (CSCW), and for what kinds of computer systems would be best suited to support this kind of distributed work.

Respondent's comment introducing new section in manuscript draft: This section is an experiment. Bits of it may get broken up, reworded and put somewhere else. I'm making some strong claims here that we've not really discussed, and you might disagree violently!

Articulation work amounts to the following: First, the meshing of the often numerous tasks, clusters of tasks, and segments of the total arc. Second, the meshing of efforts of various unit-workers (individuals, departments, etc.). Third, the meshing of actors with their various types of work and implicated tasks. (Strauss, 1985)

1 Introduction

Collaborative writing (and its coordination) brings together a number of complex tasks with few explicit guidelines and no structured training. In academic publication, as in many other fields, feedback on the success of the writing is ultimately given only once it is over, and then highly indirectly (the authors receive feedback on whether the product of the process, the article, is acceptable or not, but rarely on the process itself).

In the field of Computer Supported Cooperative Work (CSCW), research aims to develop computer systems which support people working together. What this means in practical terms is the subject of considerable debate in the field, the main tension arguably being between approaches focusing on the development of new technology and those focusing on understanding how people collaborate. Schmidt and Bannon (1992) address this debate, proposing a conception of 'CSCW . . . as a research area devoted to exploring and meeting the support requirements of cooperative work arrangements' (p. 11), central to which is the question of 'how to support the "articulation work" that people must engage in to make the cooperative mechanisms developed to support different aspects of work in complex environments fit together and fit to local circumstances' (p. 22). Writing as an activity may be particularly subject to articulation work, because not only must the cooperation mechanisms of the task be developed and articulated, but the task of writing is itself subject to development and creative change. Having a particular set of people write manuscripts together is a non-routine task, in that it takes place over a relatively long time (weeks, months, or years, for academic co-authors), and is rarely repeated. Academic writing is articulation work which requires the juggling of political as well as content and syntax constraints (Law and Williams, 1982). Furthermore, 'supporting' a process is itself not unproblematic; if something is being supported, certain aspects are being made more easy, which may influence the process itself.

It is therefore particularly important to understand some of the fundamentals of what co-authors do to achieve the coordination required to produce a single document together. This chapter considers some of the circumstances around how two authors, who were in different places, wrote an academic publication together making use of computers, and how the work they were doing and the way in which they did it was inseparable from their immediate environment and the culture which it was part of.

In the following sections, I will first examine alternative conceptualizations of collaboration which may influence system design. I then draw on a case study of two co-authors in different places to show how technology, managed by social agreements, can make collaboration over distance possible. An important point is the constant evolution of the process and the integral part played by social agreements in managing it. Some conclusions are drawn, including general implications for CSCW. (For the Method, see appendix.)

2 Conceptions of collaboration

Systems of ideas about how the world works, are important because they influence decisions we make. The designer of a CSCW system will be influenced by how she sees collaboration, just as designers of robots in Artificial Intelligence have been influenced by notions of plan execution (Agre, 1988, and Suchman, 1987).

One way of conceptualizing collaboration, is seeing collaboration as processing of agreement. This would go something like: 'a proposal/suggestion/problem is brought to the attention of group members; they discuss the issue, and when they reach agreement on a solution (and probably a timetable/deadline, or perhaps postponement), execution of the plan follows, or should follow, as agreed.' Such a view of collaboration seems to correspond with many people's (idealized) picture of what collaboration should be like, making it tempting to use as the basis for a computer system. It translates neatly into a host of ideas for how a computer system may make the process more 'efficient' by providing functions which would 'help' the participants collaborate according to the ideal (eg the system might remind participants of deadlines). Suchman, 1993, analyses the impact of one such line of thought in CSCW, the Language/Action Perspective, criticising its Coordinator system for not taking account of the situatedness of action, and considers some of the vested interests that lead to an admiration for controlling interactions.

What are the practical consequences of seeing collaboration as the process of identifying the next issue(s), reaching a decision on what to do about it, and doing it, repeatedly, until finished? A system which aims to support collaboration by structuring the work according to this model, would, for example, probably ask for the names of the project members in order to register them as having permission to make changes to the document. Non-members might be allowed to read the document, but would perhaps not be allowed to make changes. The plan—that these are the members of the group, and that only they should be allowed to access the document—is executed and, according to his model, that is that. Any changes would have to be explicitly registered as such.

Some immediate problems with this approach are: what if some of the group members' names are not known at the outset? What if the number of members changes during the project? What if someone who was not initially part of the group, and perhaps is not supposed to be one, needs to make changes after all (a reviewer may want to correct spelling mistakes, or another person help out by typing in amendments made on a paper copy)?

An alternative would be to allow for the continuously changing nature of the process, focusing instead on the situated nature of activity (Suchman, 1987) and the articulation work required by collaborators (Schmidt and Bannon, 1992). An integral part of the process is adjusting to, initiating, and keeping up with the continuous change. Part of the work of collaboration, therefore, is exchanging information about changes. Support for the process must therefore be flexible enough to allow not only changes about the state of the process and potential influences to take place, but also information contributing to the coordination of the work. Because the whole environment of the work is highly relevant to individual decisions, the process is too complex to be completely described in models. Instead, technological support could be provided for parts of the process in a way which allows its users to define and develop their own methods of coordination and control. A central part of the work being done is making a range of information available to the others at times and on subjects which would not be predictable to even the most complex computer system. Such a view of collaboration allows a great deal of variability. Instead of seeing it as a technical modelling problem, the approach poses *variation as central* to collaborative work.

The following sections examine evidence for this latter perspective on collaboration, drawing on a case study of two co-authors who were writing a paper together as part of their ordinary work.

3 Technology allows collaboration across distance

Two people, who worked in the same multinational organization but in different countries, had done some work together and wanted to write about it in an academic paper. Their work environment was one where using computers was considered natural. To the two authors and their colleagues (except administrative staff), computer systems were both the objects of their work (research on computer systems), and the tools for reporting the results. The authors also had access to, and were regular users of, electronic mail (e-mail).

The two authors had previously worked together in the same place for a few months, and they had subsequently met a few times and exchanged e-mail messages. The idea to write the paper was conceived at one of the meetings. However, while writing the paper, over a period of three to four weeks, the two co-authors did not meet face-to-face and all their communication was mediated by technology. They both had access to a sophisticated word processor, and used their international computer network to send electronic copies of manuscript drafts between the two sites. They also used the network for sending e-mail messages to each other, a technology they were both familiar with. Finally, they had access to free telephone use for work, which would occasionally include international calls.

Thus, it was highly natural for these two collaborators to use technology to communicate with each other across distance—in this case, they were eight time zones apart. In writing the document, one co-author at a time would make changes to the document for a while (usually a day or some hours), and then make an electronic copy and send this to the person at the other site. Telephone conversations were less frequent and usually planned well ahead.

The computers and network used by this pair of co-authors, were in many ways highly sophisticated as tools for an individual user. However, they had not been designed for collaborative work practices, and had no elements intended to structure the collaborative writing process. (Of course, the fact that this particular technology was being used did affect the way the work was done; for example, exchanging pieces of text separately from other text or comment, was relatively well supported, in a variety of forms, while there was little support for making connections between spoken dialogue and text, or between different pieces of text.)

The word processors used by the two co-authors, although they were of the same kind, were not linked together. There was no 'knowledge' in the word processors that the manuscript had been passed, or was going to be passed, along the network to another computer with its own, albeit similar, word processor. It was up to the co-authors, and their understanding of the way these word processors and the computer network worked, to find (or create, or evolve) ways of achieving the communication between sites which they wanted.

In coordinating their work, the two co-authors made creative use of the technology available to them. For example, there was no technical reason why one co-author could not make changes to their last saved version of the document while the other was making changes to theirs. Doing this would, however, have resulted in the problem of how to merge the two parallel versions that would have been created. Instead, the co-authors mostly avoided this parallelism by treating the electronic file as if only one of them was able to access it at a time. I saw no evidence that they had explicitly agreed to do this, but both had a clear understanding that this was how they were doing it: the transfers were often talked about in terms of which one of them now 'had' the document, and under normal circumstances they did not make changes out of turn. One author, when finished changing the document using the word processor, would save a copy of the document in a file, and use a different program to pass the document file to the site of the other author. This meant that when one co-author had sent off the latest version for the other to work on, he retained a copy of the version he had sent, and his word processor (or indeed any other part of his computer) had no record of the agreement between him and his co-author that 'it is her time to make changes now.'

In this case, then, the co-authors chose to treat an electronic document as if it was a single physical object, not unlike paper, which can only be 'had' by one person at the time, unless they are in the same location. While one could regard this as a failure of the technology to cater for a need to deny someone access to the manuscript, the lack of technological 'support' actually turned out to be useful. At one point, the co-authors temporarily lost the facility to send files or messages to each other because of technical problems with the network. They discussed their electronic communication problem over the phone and agreed explicitly to work in parallel and deal with the merger problem later. This unplanned change of working style was only possible because there was no technical enforcement of their previous arrangement. Through an alternative technology, the telephone, they were able to develop a new mutual understanding of what was appropriate to do, without having to rely on the computer system to support the change of strategy (a situation which, even if foreseen by a designer, would have· been difficult to resolve, given that the computer communication between sites was not functioning).

Another case of the technology letting them down was at the beginning, when one fairly long and important e-mail message from 'Fiona' got lost and never reached 'Mark' (identities have been disguised). This was only realized several days later. The message was immediately re-sent, and this time Mark received it. However, it had by then lost much of its importance. Why the message got lost was never fully established.

The non-arrival of the e-mail message had been discovered when Fiona referred to its contents in a telephone conversation. It was a common practice for these two to duplicate communication channels: e-mail messages would summarize comments contained in the manuscript, and e-mail messages and manuscript contents would be referred to in phone calls. Repeating issues was a way of keeping them salient, with apparently problematic issues remaining current by being referred to time and again. Given that the technology could not be fully trusted to deliver messages, an amount of double checking may have ensured that important points really did get communicated. There was also, however, some indications that the different channels of communication—telephone, e-mail and manuscript transfer with embedded comments—each had their different strengths, which the co-authors were making use of. In telephone calls, much subtle feedback (positive and negative) was given. Embedding comments in the manuscript provided a textual context and a point of reference for the comment, as evidenced in the following excerpt from an e-mail message from Mark: '[The new draft I've sent you] has the changes I've made today, as well as more comments on what needs to be done. I'll also put that stuff here—the bits in the paper are more to grab your attention while you're looking at it.' This is followed by a summary of changes, including: 'Mainly I added comments. The main themes of the comments are: [list of comments]'. E-mail messages frequently contained such summaries of comments.

4 Social protocols and technology

Social protocols are conventions for interaction, whether explicit or implicit, in contrast to formal agreements or rules enforced technically. 'Protocol' is here intended in the computer science sense as meaning the rules, or syntax, of interaction. The above is one example of how social protocols were used to structure the collaboration. Explicit agreements and implicit understandings served to inform each co-author's individual decisions on what to do when, and did so with a flexibility rarely achieved in current computer support systems.

In part, social protocols were explicitly discussed and agreed, in part they evolved organically. For example, having started making comments on the manuscript in the manuscript text itself, a practice of making a visual distinction between text and comments on the text evolved. Comments were successively enclosed in square brackets; then enclosed in square brackets and put into a special font, italics; then a preceding initial was added to indicate which of the two co-authors had written the comment. The practice of making comments more readily noticeable when scanning the page took on the dimension, for one of the co-authors, of a shorthand check-list of have-we-dealt-with-everything-on-this-page-yet. This example also, therefore, illustrates how an aspect of the technology intended for other purposes (characters being shown on the screen in their real fonts in order to help visualize what the text will look like in print) can be developed by the users of the technology to take on other meanings which are socially determined (in this case, that text in a particular font was not to be read as part of the final text, and, furthermore, the significance, in that particular situation, of the presence of 'non-final' text in some part of the manuscript).

Although the initial discussions included the purpose and contents of the paper, these issues remained a topic for discussion and amendment throughout the writing process. The following is part of a telephone conversation between the co-authors:

Fiona: '[. . .] what is the bottom line of this paper, what is it
that we want people to walk away with?'

Mark: 'I'm . . . to be honest, I'm not sure on that . . . right
now.'

Fiona: 'So we may want to . . . I mean it's fine with me if we
wait a few days and talk about that.'

Mark: 'Yeah, I think I'd like to see it all together . . . and . . .
and see . . .'

Fiona: 'Right.'

Mark: '. . . what seem to be the main themes. Because there's
all sorts of things we could say.'

In fact, despite this being a successful writing project (the submitted paper was accepted by the reviewers, and neither of the
co-authors reported major misgivings about it), it is not clear
that an agreement was ever reached on exactly what the purpose
of the paper was. Thus, the process of writing these co-authors
were engaged in, required and provided a significant degree of
flexibility on differences in perspective between the individual
co-authors. In this sense, the emerging manuscript may have
served as a boundary object (Star, 1993) between the co-authors,
ie an object which enables successful cooperative work without
consensus.

The organizers of the conference to which the paper was to be
submitted, had issued a set of format instructions which specified
not only the overall length of papers, but also went into detail on
the required shapes (fonts) and sizes of characters in the main
text and in various headings and layout, including exact margin
widths. Among most western academics it is common to have
access to the sophisticated word processors and printers with
typesetting capabilities required to do this, and it is quite common to expect papers to be submitted in print quality. In the
organizational culture of the two co-authors considered here, it
was natural that such computer systems were used, and the
researchers already had considerable practice in manipulating
their documents to meet such demands.

For some of their tasks, such as writing on a particular topic,
the co-authors had fairly clear notions of which of them was
more expert, and therefore was considered to have the main
responsibility (at least initially). This was not the case with formatting. The required formatting changes were done gradually
and right from the start of the writing, not just at the end. This

task was shared. However, a focus of the formatting discussions was not who should do what, but how exactly to interpret the written instructions. They eventually agreed that one part of the instructions—leaving a blank space for the publisher's notice—was not important for their submission, because even if accepted, they would get another chance to revise the paper before publication. Thus, they made a conscious choice to ignore one of the stated requirements in order to free up more space—a scarce resource—for text. So even the apparently straightforward task of following formatting instructions, a task which on the face of it would be easy to automate, called for (human) assessment of what was in the best interest of those particular people in that particular situation.

We see how social protocols played pivotal part in the complex coordination that was part of the writing work, and that they were subject to change as the writing project evolved and the nature of the work changed. The next section deals with the issue of change, and how the co-authors were keeping each other informed of changes.

5   Changing documents and documenting changes

The co-authors informed each other of what they were doing in a number of ways. They offered each other information which kept the other in touch with their context of work. This often enabled them to make informed assessments on the likely course of action of their co-author. For example, in a telephone conversation where the two co-authors were arranging the time for the next call, one co-author, 'Fiona', displayed awareness of the work habits of the other, by anticipating 'Mark's' habitual evening break:

> Fiona: 'Is there any chance you could do earlier, like around
> um . . . 9.15; 9.15 is 5.15?'
> Mark: 'Yes, that's fine too.'
> Fiona: 'Before you go for a pint?'
> Mark: 'Yep.'
> (Simplified from transcript of telephone conversation.)

Another example, from an e-mail message from Fiona, displays her awareness of Mark's habit of working at the week-end. Interestingly, we also see how she assumes Mark is interested in her whereabouts on the Friday, although there was no obvious reason why he should need to know just then—an example of pre-emptive provision of information: 'Do you plan to work any this weekend? If not, then [. . .] If you will be in this weekend, let me know when (if you know) and perhaps we can overlap[. . .] I have appointments and meetings on Friday morning at 7am (running), 9am, 10am, 12noon (thus should be available around 11am/7pm but I don't encourage you to be at [your office] at that hour :-)' (The symbol ':-)' is widely used in e-mail to denote a smiling face (on its side).)

Another example of sensitivity to the individual's context for the joint work, arose as part of a telephone conversation where Fiona and Mark were fixing a time to call each other next time. Fiona said Mark could ring her at home early in the morning on the proposed day, adding that her husband usually goes to work early. The information about her husband was not, strictly speaking, necessary to make their arrangement, but it contributed to Mark's understanding of Fiona's constraints. One of the effects of Mark knowing this was that he was in effect given license to generalize to other mornings: if Fiona's husband was up early every day, and she usually got up with him and/or didn't mind getting up with him that day, it was likely to be the case on other mornings too. This is an example of off-task talk which task-oriented models of collaboration do not capture and which some CSCW system developers aim to eliminate on grounds of 'efficiency' of communication. It is, however, part of a practice of offering background information that may become useful in the future, and contributes to the work of coordinating the efforts of the two co-authors.

Similarly, Fiona shared some of her troubles with Mark one day. In this case she not only provided an explanation for why she had not worked as much as she had expected, but also conveyed her own dissatisfaction with it: 'Somehow it does not seem like I've gotten much done (though I have worked on it!). I've had several yucky system problems today—some [computer system] error loading my cpu up to 100%, out of memory stuff, inability to print [e-mail messages], . . . The usual occurrences when you care about getting something done!' (From an e-mail message.)

We see that the co-authors sought to keep each other up-to-date on a range of developments. However, not all changes were, or could have been, documented. Changes in thinking may take place only gradually, and articulation requires effort. One can imagine reasons for a co-author not to draw attention to changes, for example if they did not want the other to notice a change, or thought the problem had been resolved and the other would spend their time better focusing on something else. The question of when and how changes were documented is therefore of interest.

Most commonly, changes were documented around the time of transfer, when the current draft was passed from one co-author to the other. The handover consisted of one co-author saving a copy of the manuscript in a file which they could both reach via the international computer network. He or she would tell the other that there was a file ready for her or him to pick up, and give the precise name and location of the file. This was usually done by sending an e-mail message. Occasionally, the message would contain little more than the actual name/location, but more commonly, further content was also added. These regular announcements—another task which in itself could be auto-mated—generated a lot of spur-of-the-moment remarks as well as discussion of more general and long-term issues.

Some changes simply appeared as minor corrections to the text itself. Others were explicitly documented in communication about the document or about the process of writing; some both appeared in text and were explicitly discussed, as shown above. Another example of the latter was when, in electronic mail mes-sages, attention would be drawn to changes in the document. For example, in the following e-mail message from Mark: '[Fiona], as we said on the phone, there's a new copy of the paper at [the electronic file address] with some new words about [a topic].'

Drawing attention to changes could happen even when the change was quite striking, like when the document had been reformatted from one text column per page to two columns. Therefore, it was not only done to provide information that changes had been made. Rather, documenting changes could be an opportunity to justify one's actions, open up for comments, gain credit for work done, or displaying willingness to take responsibility.

In the following comment in another e-mail message from Fiona, she clearly displays wanting to be in touch: 'Yeah, this doesn't say much 'cept that I'm around and listening'.

These co-authors seemed, from time to time, to think 'for' the other: they would think of something which according to their agreement 'belonged' to the other (whether because of the content or the timing of the idea). For example, one co-author made changes to the document when the other was explicitly supposed to be the one making changes, and subsequently informed the other of this. The separation of responsibilities was therefore not interpreted absolutely. On the other hand, there were frequent incidents evidencing sensitivity: a breach of agreement would typically be raised in a way which asked for approval. For example, early on, even though the one who 'had' the document could make any changes they wanted, one co-author preferred to make comments on, rather than change, a section written by the other and seen as within the other's area of expertise. In this case he was being *more* careful than their agreement required. Closer to the deadline, and after the two had been writing together for a while, there was less evidence of sensitivity to or awareness of different areas of expertise.

Documenting changes to the manuscript was therefore a way of drawing attention to some of the changes above others, a way of making one's rationale for changes available to the other co-author, and a reason to keep in touch and an opportunity to 'piggyback' other comments.

6 Related work

The work reported on in this chapter is part of a general, increasing interest in broadening the scope of issues addressed in the design of computer systems. It owes much to the inspiration of the work of sociologists and anthropologists, mainly from Suchman, 1987 onwards, who have ventured into the branch of computer science known as Computer Supported Co-operative Work. Suchman (1987, 1993) questions assumptions evident in much system design that action can sensibly be isolated from the particular situation the person is in. Rather, rational accounts of action in the form of plans are regularly constructed before and after the event as stories of what happened, but do not actually describe what happens in situated action, which is better characterized by contingencies and expectations to how interaction works (Suchman, 1987). Agre (1988) demonstrates how taking seriously the perspective of situated action—or action in context—can fundamentally affect the technical design of a computer system (in this case, in the domain of Artificial Intelligence rather than CSCW). Heath and Luff (1991) show, in detail, finely tuned collaboration in a workplace, including a practice of making information available to others in a way which allows them to choose whether or not to act on it.

In computer support for collaborative writing, a sub-field of CSCW, much research effort has gone into developing new (computer based) technologies for writing. Apart from some studies of use of those technologies, however, less attention has been given to what work people do when they write collaboratively. Some exceptions are Newman and Newman (1993), who conducted two case studies of collaborative writing for decision making, and identified social practices, organizational micropolitics, the purposes of writing, and the patterning of time as important elements of computer-mediated collaborative writing. Kraut, Galegher, Fish, and Chalfonte (1992) conducted a suite of experimental studies of co-authors' choice of communication media for different types of tasks. Plowman (1993) analysed how five co-authors wrote an essay together in a two-hour session, tracing how talk was changed from discussion through notes and drafts into the final text. Both Posner (1991) and Rimmershaw (1992) interviewed co-authors, examining the number of writing groups they had taken part in, as well as what tasks they had taken on when writing with others.

Outside CSCW, the more established interest in collaborative writing in the classroom is being complemented by studies of collaborative writing in other settings, eg Lunsford and Ede, 1990, and Forman, 1992. Cases are being collected, and an understanding of what the process entails is gradually built. However, with word processors as a common writing tool, the linking up of computers in nationwide and international networks has for some people opened new possibilities for remote collaboration (though note that collaborative writing over distance does not depend on computers; early remote collaborators have used postal exchange of letters (Lunsford and Ede, 1990)). At present, little is known about how these fast-exchange distance collaborations work.

7 Conclusions

Broadening the scope of work practice studies for computer systems development to include the environment in which computers are used and the culture which they are part of, can provide important insights into how work gets done. This can contribute to an improved sensitivity to where, and in what ways, it may be appropriate to provide computer support for the work, and thus has the potential to improve substantially the design of computer systems to support such work.

The co-authors observed used computers all day, had done so for many years, and apparently found it natural to do so. For the joint writing reported on here, they relied extensively on the power of their computers and the network which connected the computers. Indeed, it is hard to see how they could have done the work in the time they did without computers. Close observation of their joint work revealed that they regularly discussed the conduct of the work, which changed and evolved as the writing progressed. Rules and agreements were constantly open to renegotiation, and were routinely overruled.

Coordination, at times quite complex, was part of the writing work, with the establishment and evolution of social protocols playing a pivotal part. The social protocols were subject to change as the writing project evolved and the nature of the work changed. The modularity and relative simplicity of the technology used by these co-authors (ie different parts were not integrated and could be mixed and matched as the co-authors pleased), was in many ways advantageous, as it allowed certain ways in which the technology was being used to evolve with the evolving process.

Thus, the computing technology was the tool which enabled the joint work reported on here to take place, but only in the context of social protocols for its use and adaptation to the particular circumstances these co-authors at any point found themselves in.

The trend towards more technically integrated and functionally specialized computer systems is a double-edged sword, and is not necessarily what is of most benefit to collaborating authors. In CSCW, more effort should instead be directed to supporting the flexible organization of work identified here and elsewhere. The question of precisely what functions would be most useful for distributed, collaborating authors, needs further consideration.

Eevi E. Beck

Acknowledgements

Leigh Star has contributed large amounts of patience, encouragement, and support through a difficult period, as well as constructive comments on this paper as the ideas have been developing.
Ronald Lemmen and Yvonne Rogers provided useful comments
on early versions. I thank the participants in the case study for
allowing me to follow (and inevitably disturb) their work, for their
patience with me, and for helping me record their communication.

Appendix: method

To address the question of what beneficial role, if any, a computer system can play to support the work of collaborative writing over distance, I studied how academics do this work at the
moment. Academics were chosen partly because many, like the
two studied here, collaborate and co-author remotely as part of
their work.

I got access to almost all communication between the co-
authors, either as it took place or through delayed, but literal,
copies of the exchanges, with great help from the participants. I
got audio recordings of their telephone conversations, and copies
of their e-mail messages and electronically exchanged manuscript
drafts. One of the participants collected manuscript drafts for me
by saving a copy each time he sent or received a draft from his
co-author. This built up to a chronological record of the paper at
different points in its development, which I was later able to
print out on paper and also manipulate electronically. I was able
to compare versions of the draft both quantitatively (lengths of
drafts) and qualitatively (what parts of the text and layout had
been changed or moved and how) (for more details, see Beck and
Bellotti, 1993). All electronically stored material (e-mail messages
and drafts of papers) had dates attached which identified the
point of exchange.

I conducted semi-structured interviews with the participants separately at several points during their writing: soon after the start
of their writing project, during the writing, and after they had sent
the finished manuscript to reviewers. Briefer and more informal
interviews followed up on specific developments. All interviews
were audio recorded or extensive notes were taken (or both).

Cyberpunks in cyberspace: the politics of subjectivity in the computer age

Paul N. Edwards

Abstract

In the Cold War, Americans constructed the political world as a closed system of ideological conflict. Computers were developed to support a closed-world discourse with centralized, computerized military command and control, embodied in Vietnam-era systems and Reagan's Strategic Defense Initiative. Simultaneously, at the level of individual minds, a cyborg discourse about intelligent machines linked the microworlds constituted by computer programs to human thought processes. Popular science fiction of the 1980s, such as the *Star Wars* film trilogy, *Neuromancer*, and *The Terminator* merged closed-world political themes, such as military computing and global conflict, with cyborg discourse about machine subjectivity and virtual space. This political history provides a critical counterpoint to cyberpunks' over-enthusiastic embrace of cyberspace.

Introduction

Digital computers transform complex, sophisticated techniques into everyday tools. As marketing campaigns so tirelessly proclaim, they thus confer a kind of power. But the significance of computers in modern life extends far beyond this practical capacity.

For half a century, along with television, space flight, nuclear weapons, and automobiles, computers have formed a technological backdrop for the American mental landscape. Revered as the consummate representatives of an ever more technological civilization, they are tools for work and toys for play, assistants to science, fixtures of daily life. They are icons of efficiency, social status, and a high-tech future. Reverberating across the intricate webworks of language and community, images of computers weave a dense and energetic fabric of signifying forms. Computers have been absorbed into the collective American imagination.

By 'imagination' and 'culture' I mean to include not only the fantastic high-tech futures of science fiction, but also the visions that guide public policy and science in a world of very-large-scale integrated circuits (Haraway, 1985). Computers were the enigmatic object of profound hopes and hatreds even before their invention during the Second World War. They have always been as much symbols as practical devices: 'giant brains,' standards of precision, signs of scientific values, evidence of omnipotence. Ideas about artificial intelligence, a networked society where computers instantaneously handle calculation, communication and control, and the view of the human brain as a biological computer are now commonplaces. We can make sense of the material roles of computers as tools only when we simultaneously grasp their roles as cultural metaphors.

Igloo White

In 1968 the largest building in Southeast Asia was the Infiltration Surveillance Center at Nakhom Phanom in Thailand, the command centre of US Air Force Operation Igloo White. Inside the ISC technicians pored over banks of video displays, controlled by gigantic IBM computers and connected to thousands of sensors strewn across the Ho Chi Minh Trail in southern Laos.

The sensors—shaped like twigs, jungle plants, and animal droppings—were designed to detect any human activity: the noises of truck engines, body heat, even the scent of human urine. When they picked up a signal, it appeared on the remote display terminals of the ISC as a moving white 'worm' superimposed on a map grid. As soon as the ISC computers could calculate the 'worm's' direction and rate of motion, coordinates were radioed to Phantom F-4 jets patrolling the night sky. The planes' navigation systems and computers automatically guided them to the 'box,' or map grid square, to be attacked. The ISC central computers were also capable of controlling the release of bombs automatically. The pilot might do no more than sit and watch as the invisible jungle below exploded into flames. In most cases no American ever saw the targets at all.

This entire process normally took no more than five minutes.

Operation Igloo White ran from 1967 to 1972 at a cost near $1 billion a year. Visiting reporters were dazzled by the high-tech scene inside the windowless ISC. Young soldiers sat at their displays in air-conditioned comfort, faces lit weirdly by the dim electric glow, directing the destruction of people and equipment as if playing a video game. One technician is reported to have said, 'We wired the Ho Chi Minh Trail like a drugstore pinball machine, and we plug it in every night.'

Air Force officials made extraordinary claims for Igloo White. They said it destroyed over 35,000 trucks, each carrying about 10,000 pounds of supplies destined for the communist insurgency in South Vietnam. But the official estimates, like so many other official versions of the Vietnam War, existed mainly in the never-never land of public relations. In 1971 a Senate report pointed out that the figure for '. . . truck kills claimed by the Air Force . . . last year greatly exceeds the number of trucks believed by the Embassy to be in all of North Vietnam.' Daytime reconnaissance flights rarely located the supposedly destroyed vehicles. Traffic over the Ho Chi Minh Trail continued as the guerrillas adopted countermeasures such as sensor-confusing decoys and anti-air-craft weapons. The antiseptic efficiency of the ISC control room was belied by the 13,000 civilian refugees created by its operations—and the loss of three to four hundred American aircraft.

Finally, despite more than four years of intensive computer-controlled bombardment of their heavy-equipment supply lines, the communists were able to field a major tank and artillery offensive *inside* South Vietnam in 1972. (See Dickson, 1976: 83–97, Gibson, 1986:396–399).

Operation Igloo White's centralized, computerized, automated, power-at-a-distance method of 'interdiction' resembled a micro-cosmic version of the whole US approach to Vietnam. Van Creveld has noted, in his masterful study of command in war, that once President Johnson ordered US bombing of North Vietnam in 1965, 'the air war . . . was run by McNamara and his assistants from Washington. . . . Directives emanating from the Office of the Secretary of Defense specified the targets to be struck, the weather conditions, and even the minimal level of training that individual pilots had to possess.' Johnson himself sometimes took part in targeting decisions. It was 'the revolution-ary explosion of electronic communication and automatic data processing equipment . . . [that] made effective worldwide command and control from Washington a practical technological proposition' (Van Creveld 1985:244).

Because of the length and complexity of these chains of command, this drive to centralize command and control created serious impediments to accurate understanding of what was going on in the field. The elements of Operation Igloo White exemplify both the 'information pathologies' of Vietnam (Van Creveld 1985) and its problems at the regional level: centralized, remote-controlled operations based on super-sophisticated computing and communications gear, an abstract representation of events (sensors, maps, grids, 'worms') justified in terms of statistics, and a wide gap between an official discourse of overwhelming success and the pessimistic assessments of independent observers.

I begin with Igloo White because it shows how the story of the computer is nested inside another, larger narrative about the grand politics of globalist American foreign policy. There are strong, concrete connections between what I call the 'closed world' of post-WWII American global political hegemony and the 'microworlds' of computer simulations and artificial intelligence.

In the post-WWII era, especially during the Cold War, the Vietnam War, and the Reagan administration, military priorities played a major role in the general direction of American computer research (Flamm, 1987; 1988). In turn, the development of computers—for real-time control of automated forces, for modeling of military situations and world dynamics, and eventually for 'smart' weapons—helped create new military capabilities, new forms and locations of authority, and new techniques of analysis that reinforced closed-world political thought (Gray, 1991; Edwards, forthcoming).

The notion of a 'closed world' is intended to signify a bounded psychological and conceptual space. Sherman Hawkins used this term to define one of the major dramatic spaces in Shakespearean theatre (1968). Closed-world plays are marked by a unity of place, such as a walled city or the interior of a castle or house. Action centres around attempts to invade and/or escape its boundaries; its archetypal form is the siege. The central problematic of the closed world is psychological, an inward confrontation of characters with the power of rationality and social convention which, in tragedy, leads to self-destruction (eg Hamlet) and in comedy to exorcism of these forces (eg Jaques' punishment).

The alternative is not an open world, but what Northrop Frye called the 'green world,' an unbounded natural setting such as a forest, meadow, or glade. Action moves in an uninhibited flow between natural, urban, and other locations, frequently affected by magic and mysterious natural events (think of *A Midsummer Night's Dream* or *The Tempest*). The green world is indeed an 'open' space where the limits of law and rationality are transcended, but this does not mean that anything goes. Rather, the opposition is between a human-centered, inner, psychological logic and a magical, natural, transcendent one.

The 'closed world' discussed here is political and ideological, rather than literary. Post-WWII American politics were dominated by a closed-world unity of place. The stage was the globe, the action one of attempts to contain, invade, or explode a closed Communist world: 'the Iron Curtain,' the Berlin Wall. The globe itself was seen as a closed whole, a single scene of capitalist/communist struggle from which the only escape was the technological utopia of space travel. The US reconceived itself as the manager, either directly or by proxy, of the entire global political, economic, and military scene (Baritz, 1985), justified by an ideological opposition between 'freedom and slavery' (Ambrose, 1985). But this principle was belied by 1950s social conformism and its totalizing modernist obsession with planning, rational action, Keynesian economic control, and military power. Even as American leaders committed troops to seal off the Communist world in Vietnam, the social movements of the 1960s were exposing poverty, inequalities, and savage oppressions in the land of freedom. The ideology of apocalyptic struggle within a closed world, in part, maintained an external focus on extreme contrasts, diverting attention from cracks in the façade of liberal politics.

Computers played an important role in the developing discourse of the closed world. They were a key factor in the massive increases in the speed and scale of warfare, in air defense, command-and-control systems, satellite surveillance, and 'smart' weapons such as guided missiles, cruise missiles, and advanced jet aircraft. They were also of immense symbolic importance in the ideological worlds of the Cold War and the Vietnam War, representing total oversight, exacting standards of control, and technical-rational solutions to complex problems.

Paul N. Edwards

Turing machines and cyborgs

In 1950 Alan Turing, the mathematician who invented the theory of digital computation, devised an 'imitation game' in which a computer is programmed to simulate human thought processes (Turing, 1950). A person, communicating through a terminal, tries to distinguish between the computer and another person by interrogating them both—the Turing test for machine intelligence. Turing believed that within fifty years it would be possible 'to program computers . . . to play the imitation game so well that an average interrogator will not have more than 70 percent chance of making the right identification after five minutes of questioning.' At MIT in 1991, forty-one years later, computers fooled five out of ten judges in a limited turing test restricted to a single area of informal knowledge such as wine-tasting or romantic love (Markoff 1991).

Another of Turing's predictions received far less attention, though it is in many ways more profound:

> The . . . question, 'Can machines think?' I believe to be too meaningless to deserve discussion. Nevertheless I believe that at the end of the century the use of words and general educated opinion will have altered so much that one will be able to speak of machines thinking without expecting to be contradicted (Turing, 1950:456).

Here Turing was clearly right. Even then, computers we would now think of as pathetically primitive were known in the popular press as 'giant brains.' By the late 1980s 'expert systems,' 'artificial intelligence,' and 'smart' and even 'brilliant weapons' were part of everyday vernaculars. Within subcultures, such as computer hacking, highly articulated descriptions of the computer as a self with thoughts and desires, and of the human mind and self as a kind of computer, were commonplace (Turkle, 1984).

Turing thus predicted the emergence of a language of intelligent machines: 'cyborg discourse' (Haraway, 1985; Haraway, 1992; Edwards, forthcoming). This discourse is primarily concerned with the psychological and cultural changes in self-imagining brought on by the analogy between computers and minds. Artificial intelligence and cognitive science are part of this discourse, as are hacker communities and cyberpunk science fiction (Turkle, 1984; McCaffery, 1991). While closed-world discourse is built around the computer's capacities as a tool of analysis and control, cyborg discourse focuses on its mind-like character, its generation of self-understanding through metaphor (Lakoff, 1980; 1987).

These discourses are not purely intellectual or linguistic phenomena. The computer metaphor in psychology had sources in the military quests for automation of processes subject to human error and for integration of humans into combat machines. World War II and the ensuing Cold War produced intense, largely unopposed pressures for automation and integration in military systems. Integrating humans into anti-aircraft weapons, and refining communications systems through psychometric studies of the 'machine in the middle' of the communications circuit, were first steps toward full-blown 'device-independent' theories of intelligence, language, and thought (Wiener, 1958; Gardner, 1985).

At a press conference early in the 1991 Persian Gulf War, General Schwarzkopf played videotapes of computer-controlled, laser-guided bombs destroying buildings in Baghdad. A worldwide television audience experienced the joining of cyborg subjectivity with the politics of the closed world. As we rode the eye of the bomb to the white flash of impact, we experienced at once the elation of technological power, the impotence and voyeurism of the passive TV audience, and the blurring of boundaries between 'intelligent' weapon and political will. The dazzling—and terrifying—power of high-technology warfare displayed in the Gulf became an emblem for America's waning global hegemony. It was the cyborg as the psycho-logic of closed-world politics.

This moment is an icon for my central argument: in the computer age, theories, beliefs, and fictions about mind, intelligence, and selfhood are in part *political* constructs. They reflect a history involving new forms of warfare, militarism, a pervasive technological system, and global capitalism and its culture. So, too, the political constellation of the post-WWII era involves the subjectivity of mental machines.

Cyberpunks in cyberspace: computers, politics, and subjectivity in the 1980s

The early 1980s marked two key events in the history of computing: the introduction of powerful, low-cost desktop computers, and of commercial artificial intelligence software in the form of 'expert systems' (Feigenbaum and McCorduck, 1983; Feigenbaum, McCorduck et al., 1988). Direct experience of computer use soon became almost ubiquitous for middle-income Americans. Expert systems, hyped to the hilt, brought the notion of AI into everyday parlance and, seemingly, everyday use. By the early 1990s neural networks and virtual reality were receiving the same kind of mass-media attention.

The first half of the 1980s was also the height of the second Cold War (Halliday, 1986). Ronald Reagan's administration was marked by a resurgence of anti-communist rhetoric and major increases in military spending. The Pentagon attempted to severely restrict trade and scientific communication in 'defense-sensitive' areas, including computer science. Reagan ordered toy-war skirmishes in Grenada and Libya designed to flex American muscle on the global stage and, in 1983, proposed the Strategic Defense Initiative (SDI, or 'Star Wars'), a total space-based nuclear missile defense.

Reagan's was also the most popular peacetime Presidency in history.

Star Wars pre-empted the powerful Nuclear Freeze movement that had threatened to steal the thunder from Reagan's Cold War revival. The most advanced computers and software ever constructed would be the core of the SDI, channeling vast new Pentagon funding into computer research. The lesser known but related Strategic Computing Initiative, a major and controversial program in advanced computing and artificial intelligence of the Defense Advanced Research Projects Agency, was announced that autumn. Simultaneously, revelations emerged of a long, secret history of computer failures in NORAD nuclear early warning systems (Borning, 1987). This news intensified public fears of computer-initiated nuclear holocaust. In 1984 Computer Professionals for Social Responsibility was founded around opposition to aspects of Star Wars and Strategic Computing, marking the organized politicization of computer experts.

At least until the middle of Reagan's second term, anxiety about nuclear war and ideological polarization with Communism reached heights unseen since the late 1950s. Reagan's 'peace shield' was an ultimate high-tech version of the closed world. Part of what made it remarkable was the strongly positive public response to an idea disowned by most scientists as completely unworkable.

In the science fiction books and films of the 1980s, the closed world of computer-controlled global military power and the image of the computer as a cyborg, an intelligent being, merge to produce graphic images of subjectivity in the world of the very-large-scale integrated circuit. A number of archetypal figures appeared—human and mechanical—including hackers, crackers, phone phreaks, artificial intelligences, cyborgs, robots, and androids (Levy, 1984; Hafner and Markoff, 1991; Turkle, 1984). Their common ground was the sense that the closed world within the computer might be entered by humans, and that computers might become aware of the world outside—that the closed world might expand to such enormous proportions that it could encompass or even replace the real world.

'Star Wars' itself took its nickname, of course, from the film trilogy (1977, 1980, 1983), which introduced the largest movie audiences in history to the 'droids' C3P0 and R2D2 and the cyborg Darth Vader. They also introduced the Death Star, a planet-sized military spaceship wielding a planet-destroying death ray—a sort of ultimate closed world image.

2010 (1984), the sequel to Stanley Kubrick's dark masterpiece *2001: A Space Odyssey* (1968), explained Kubrick's killer computer HAL as the victim of mental illness. In *2010* HAL is cured by the nerdy but mystical Dr. Chandra, who erases HAL's traumatic memories. HAL becomes a hero, sacrificing himself for the human crew. At the same time, major plot tensions are the relationships between the Soviet and American members of the mission, constrained by military secrecy, and the development of a superpower crisis on Earth that threatens to erupt into nuclear war.

A central scene of Ridley Scott's film *Alien* (1980) features treachery by an android. Part of its terror lies in the fact that the android remains indistinguishable from his human colleagues until he is unintentionally dismembered during a fight. In this moment his lack of concern for his colleagues earlier in the film suddenly comes into sharp relief, the result not of a scientist's stereotypical coldness, but of the lack of emotion stereotypical of machines. The aliens are terrifying because they are simultaneously so Other and so (in appearance) Just Like Us.

War Games (1983) fictionalized factual news about teenage hackers and phone phreaks, break-ins to Pentagon computers over public telephone lines, the NORAD computer breakdowns, and artificial intelligence. An intelligent military computer egged on by a teenage hacker who thinks he is playing a computer game, brings NORAD nuclear forces to the brink of DEFCON

1—all-out nuclear engagement. The scene under Cheyenne Mountain is much reminiscent of the one fifteen years earlier inside the Infiltration Surveillance Center in Thailand.

Walt Disney's *Tron* (1982) provided a breathtaking, romantic vision of what would soon come to be called 'cyberspace' or 'virtual reality,' a surrogate sensory world inside the computer, while demonizing faceless corporate power. This theme was continued in William Gibson's extraordinary novel *Neuromancer*, the flagship work of cyberpunk science fiction (Gibson, 1984). *Neuromancer* introduced the cracker as outlaw anti-hero. In its near-future world, most of Earth's computers have been linked together in a gigantic network. People enter the network through 'cyberspace,' a virtual-reality visual grid-space, a 'consensual mass hallucination.'

Cyberpunk evolved into a disciplined, highly articulate school of science fiction. It linked a postmodernist aesthetic of decadence and fragmentation with computerization, mass-media artificial experience, biotechnology, multiculturalism, and a dark political future of massive urbanization and militarized corporate hegemony (Sterling, 1986; McCaffery, 1991).

To Case, *Neuromancer*'s main character, cyberspace is home. When Case finally re-enters cyberspace after a prolonged absence, the sensation is pure poetry:

> Please, he prayed, *now—*
> A gray disk, the color of Chiba sky.
> *Now—*
> Disk beginning to rotate, faster, becoming a sphere of paler gray.
> Expanding—
>   And flowed, flowered for him, fluid neon origami trick, the unfolding of his distanceless home, his country, transparent 3D chessboard extending to infinity. Inner eye opening to the stepped scarlet pyramid of the Eastern Seaboard Fission Authority burning beyond the green cubes of Mitsubishi Bank of America, and high and very far away he saw the spiral arms of military systems, forever beyond his reach.
>   And somewhere he was laughing, in a white-painted loft, distant fingers caressing the deck, tears of release streaking his face (Gibson, 1984: 52).

No one and nothing living escapes entirely unaltered in the cyberpunk world. Plastic surgery is ubiquitous, become a form of personal expression. Case's partner Molly has four-centimeter scalpel blades implanted in her fingertips which she can extrude, at will, like cat claws. Her nervous system has been amped up to give her lightning reflexes. Mirror lenses implanted into her face form permanent sunglasses that completely conceal her eyes.

If physical identity is a matter of choice in *Neuromancer*'s world, so is subjective experience. Psychoactive drugs are only a start. Some people have jacks installed in their brains which accept 'microsofts,' or chips, that extend their skills or change their personalities. The technology of 'simstim' lets one person's sensory experience be recorded and piped directly into the mind of another. Case and Molly use this as a communication device: as she carries out her part of their 'run,' Case can flip in and out of her sensorium at will, experiencing directly whatever she is seeing and doing. Ordinary people use simstim as a kind of super-duper television, plugging in simstim cartridges as we would insert a videocassette.

Even the body is optional and problematic. The Dixie Flatline is the recorded mind of a dead man, who exists now only in cyberspace. The ex-Special Forces soldier Armitage, by contrast, is a shell of a man whose personality has been taken over by the artificial intelligence Wintermute, a creature of cyberspace living in the real world.

Cyberspace means dispensing with 'meat things' in favour of a computer-generated landscape. For Case, this closed world is a better place to live, perhaps because conversion of the green world into a closed world is complete in *Neuromancer*'s future. All Earth scenes take place either indoors or in dense, grim urban cityscapes, mostly at night. Only when we reach the space stations Zion and Freeside do we encounter green spaces—but as inverted, artificial ecosystems on the inner surfaces of artificial moons.

Here the victory of the closed world over the green world is tightly linked with the expansion of capitalism. If everything is optional—the body, experience, culture, reality itself—everything is also for sale. Military power is still important, and military computers are a major presence in cyberspace. But transnational corporations replace nation-states as the central units of large-scale social organization, and the driving force behind almost every character is 'biz,' as Case calls it. The closest approach the novel offers to transcendence of this state is its Rastafarian characters, who listen to the voice of Jah from the refugee green world of the Zion Cluster space station.

Paul N. Edwards

The Terminator

The epitome of the intersection of closed world and cyborg discourse was James Cameron's film *The Terminator* (1984). *The Terminator* opens in Los Angeles in 2029 A.D. amidst post-holocaust rubble and smoke. An all-out nuclear exchange had been initiated by the 'Skynet computer built for SAC-NORAD. . . . They say it got smart. A new order of intelligence. Then it saw all people as a threat, not just the ones on the other side.' The few remaining humans eke out a miserable existence in grimy underground bunkers, emerging only at night to battle robot killing machines that are now the masters of the planet. To finish off the human resistance, the machines send a cyborg back in time to the pre-holocaust present. The Terminator's mission is to find and kill Sarah Conner, mother-to-be of the future resistance leader John Conner. But the resistance is also able to send a soldier, Kyle Reese, to warn and protect her.

The Terminator murders the first two Sara Conners in the L.A. telephone directory, then comes looking for the third. But Reese is already following her. When the Terminator attacks, Reese shoots it many times with a shotgun as close range, but this stops it only for a few seconds. The plot from this point on is the standard horror-movie script about a scared, helpless woman pursued by an unstoppable monster/man, rescued by a (male) good guy using ever-escalating violence. After many narrow escapes and Kyle's eventual death, Sarah finally destroys the Terminator by crushing it in a metal press inside a deserted automated factory.

Arnold Schwarzenegger plays the Terminator with a kind of terrifying mechanical grace. Completely devoid of emotion, within seconds of his appearance on the screen he kills two young men for their clothes. He has a seemingly symbiotic relationship with all kinds of machines: for example, he starts cars by merely sticking his fingers into their wiring. When shot, he sometimes falls, but immediately stands up and keeps lumbering forward. We see him dissect his own wounded arm and eye with an X-Acto knife, revealing the electro-mechanical substrate beneath his human skin.

The Terminator's computerized mind proves equally alien. At certain points we see through his camera-like eyes: the scene becomes graphic and reddened, like a bit-mapped image viewed through infra-red goggles. Displays of numbers, flashing diagrams, and menus of commands appear superimposed on his field of vision. He speaks and thinks with formidable precision. But he is also a totally single-minded, mechanical being. Kyle warns Sarah that the Terminator 'can't be reasoned with. It doesn't feel pity, or remorse, or fear. And it absolutely will not stop—*ever*—until you are dead.' The Terminator blends a perverse, exaggerated masculine ideal—the ultimate unblinking soldier, the body-builder who treats his body as a machine—with images of computer control and robotic single-mindedness, complete with the alien subjective reality provided by the Terminator's-eye sequences.

The film's main theme is the idea of an apocalyptic struggle to save humanity from a world of self-aware computers and autonomous machines. But in an unusual contemporary twist, Sarah Conner begins the film as a very ordinary waitress whose major purpose in life seems to be trying to get a Friday night date. Resentfully, under the relentless pressure of the Terminator's pursuit, she is forced to learn about the threats the future holds and her role as the mother and teacher of the future saviour. She bandages Kyle's gunshot wound. Under his tutelage she learns to make plastic explosives, as well as the importance of resistance, strength, and fighting spirit. At one point she saves the wounded Reese, ordering him to his feet in a voice that rings with determination. She, not Reese, finally destroys the Terminator. In the end she is transformed into a tough, purposeful single mother—pregnant by Kyle—packing a forty-four, driving a jeep, and heading off into the oncoming storm as heroically as any cowboy.

We thus meet a single mother as a new kind of heroine: the progenitor and trainer of a race of soldiers fighting for humanity against machines. When Sarah asks Kyle what the women of the future are like, he replies tersely, 'Good fighters' (one of his future combat partners is female). Women no longer shriek helplessly in the face of violence: they emerge as men's armed allies in the militarized future. The subtext is about arming women for a new role, outside traditional contexts of marriage and male protectorship. The message is also that women are the final defence against the high-technology, militaristic masculinity represented by the Terminator—not primarily because they harbor traditional connections to emotion and nature, but because they are 'good soldiers.'

The social reality of 1984 held extraordinary resonances with *The Terminator*'s themes. Reagan's Cold War rhetoric, the Nuclear Freeze movement, the NORAD computer failures, and the SDI created a highly charged context for the theme of computer-initiated nuclear holocaust. In addition, a rising tide of robot-based industrial automation, a new wave of computerization in workplaces based on personal-computer technology, and the Strategic Computing Initiative's controversial proposals for autonomous weapons matched the film's theme of domination by intelligent machines.

With respect to gender issues, the film took its cue from two social developments. First, the women's movement had begun to establish and legitimize more independent roles for women. The highest rates of divorce and single motherhood in history gave a special urgency to this search for new social identities. Second, women had become increasingly important as soldiers, filling ten to thirteen percent of all US military jobs by 1985, with serious proposals in Congress to increase the ratio to fifty percent in the Air Force. So the film finds its model for the future of womanhood in single motherhood and the armed forces.

The iconography of closed-world discourse is omnipresent in *The Terminator*. The Skynet computer is 'hooked into everything,' enabling it to become intelligent and initiate a nuclear holocaust using its central control. Almost all of the action occurs either indoors, inside vehicles, on urban streets and in alleyways, primarily at night. Almost no natural objects or landscapes appear in the film. Scenes from the world of 2029 A.D. take this imagery to a maximum; nothing remains above ground but the rubble and twisted girders of blasted buildings and charred machines. Human dwellings are underground, dirty, furnished with the burned-out hulks of television sets, now used as fireplaces. Only two scenes in the film occur in a natural setting: the few hours Sarah and Kyle spend resting in a wooded area, and the final scene in which Sarah drives off toward the mountains of Mexico. Thus, in a pattern characteristic of closed-world drama, the green world is the final refuge—when there is one—from apocalypse.

Cyborg imagery also pervades the film. The cyborg is a marginal figure: a man who is a computerized machine; a living, flesh-and-blood organism whose core is a metallic, manufactured robot. He seems to be alive, but he cannot be killed. He talks, but has no feelings. He can be wounded, but feels no pain. We learn that the Terminators were created to infiltrate the bunkers of the resistance by impersonating humans. Dogs, however, can sense them. Dogs, of course, like coyotes, are marginal figures of another sort, connecting humans with the animal, the natural, and the wild—links with the green world.

The Terminator is a caricature of the military ideal: he follows his built-in orders unquestioningly, perfectly, sleeplessly, and has no other reason for existence. But Kyle, too, has an intense single-mindedness about him, likewise born of military discipline. He speaks of an emotionless future, where humans, like the machines they fight, live a permanent garrison lifestyle. He dismisses these horrors with a disdainful 'Pain can be controlled.'

The Terminator is the enemy, but he is also the self, the military killing machine Kyle, too, has become—and which Sarah herself must become for humanity to survive. Reese and the Terminator are twisted mirror images: humans have built subjective, intelligent military machines, but are reduced to a militaristic, mechanical, emotionless subjectivity in order to fend off their own products.

The fictional world of *The Terminator* draws our attention to the ways closed-world and cyborg discourses are historically and conceptually linked. Just as facts—about military computing, artificial intelligence, nuclear weapons, and autonomous machines—give credibility to fictions of mechanical subjectivity, so too fictions—visions of centralized, remote control; clean, automated war; global oversight; and thinking machines—give coherence to the facts of an increasingly computerized world.

Conclusion

Cyberspace already exists, of course (Benedikt, 1991; Dertouzos, Cerf et al., 1991). It is one of the fictional constructions, the narratives of self, other, and reality, that is shaping our factual experience here and now. It is already a major preoccupation of millions (see Baym, this volume; Taylor, Kramerae 1993, Baym and Ebben). In the subjectivity of these fictional visions, artificial minds are both foreign and friendly, familiar and strange. The human mind has become, equally, an artificial product, a programmable computational object. The experiential quality of cyberspace includes anxiety about boundaries and borders; voyeuristic fears and caffeinated ambitions about power, love, sex, nature, and nuclear holocaust in the hands of machines; and the real-life on-line experience of disembodiment and abstraction from geographical space and real time.

There is much more going on here than in the well-known love-hate relations of previous ages with their machines. In the computer, human beings confront questions not only about their own changing roles but also about what their creations think, whether and what they feel, and whether they deserve rights, compassion, and even love as well as responsibilities. This new subjectivity—in concert with other scientific reconstructions of human nature such as genetic engineering—also involves fundamental transformations of gender identity, with troubled reconstructions of traditional relationships among gender and rationality, intelligence, emotion, embodiment and physical strength, war and peace.

The political and historical dimensions of this experience are usually ignored in the rush to consider philosophical and ethical issues. Cyberspace, exciting as it is, does not escape its origins in the quest for centralized, sanitized power and control through automated military force. Even should the military motivations recede, there is the risk that the green world and our bodily links to it will be consumed by the rationalism of the closed world, replaced by hyper-realistic simulation, artificial experience, and the language of 'systems' and 'management' that has already gone a very long way toward destroying the spiritual heart of the environmental movement.

I welcome the exhilaration that comes from turning our abstractions into sensory experience, the poetry of *Neuromancer*, and I think we should not be afraid to face the contradictory and paradoxical pulls that draw us into cyberspace even as we struggle to save our green planet. But I worry about the loss of grounding—that perfect green-world metaphor—when we become cyberpunks: when we step through the looking glass into an artificial world we cannot or will not leave. Where will Sarah Conner's jeep end up? Who will stop the next generation of Terminators? The militarized history of cyberspace may serve us well, in the New World Order, as a cautionary tale.

Connecting cultures: Balinese character and the computer

Dianne DiPaola Hagaman

Abstract

Gregory Bateson and Margaret Mead intended to use a combination of text, still photographs, and motion picture film in the report of their study of character development in Bali, but found this technically impossible. Multimedia computational devices have now made it possible to do what they could not do, making the three media (in Latour's terms) 'combinable on a flat surface.'

We were compelled to economize on motion-picture film, and disregarding the future difficulties of exposition, we assumed that the still photography and the motion-picture film *together* would constitute our record of behavior. (Notes to the Photographs, in Bateson and Mead, 1942 (italics Bateson's))

If inventions are made that transform numbers, images and texts from all over the world into the same binary code inside computers, then indeed the handling, the combination, the mobility, the conservation and the display of the traces will all be fantastically facilitated. When you hear someone say that he or she 'masters' a question better, meaning that his or her *mind* had enlarged, look first for inventions bearing on the mobility, immutability or versatility of the traces; and it is only later, if by some extraordinary chance, something is still unaccounted for, that you may turn towards the mind. (Latour, 1986 (italics Latour's)).

The Bali research

Gregory Bateson and Margaret Mead arrived in Bali in March of 1936 to study the relationship between forms of social organization and types of temperament or character structure. They had developed a complex theory about the way societies emphasized one or another of the temperamental types available in the human organism, and a typology of such types (divided by gender) and the situations that went with them.

> What if human beings, innately different at birth, could be shown to fit into systematically defined temperamental types, and what if there were male and female versions of each of these temperamental types? And what if a society—by the way in which children were reared, by the kinds of behavior that were rewarded or punished, and its traditional depiction of heroes, heroines, and villains, witches, sorcerers, and supernaturals—could place its major emphasis on one type of temperament, as among the Arapesh and the Mundugumor, or could, instead, emphasize a special complementarity between the sexes, as the Iatmul and the Tchambuli did? And what if the expectations about male-female differences, so characteristic of Euro-American cultures, could be reversed, as they seemed to be in Tchambuli . . . (Mead, 1972: 216)

Having placed the societies they already knew in that typology, they could now choose cases to fill in its missing cells.

> We had chosen Bali with knowledge and forethought as the culture we wanted to study next in order to obtain material on one temperamental emphasis we had only hypothesized must exist. We had seen just enough material in films and still photographs, had heard just enough of the music studied by Colin McPhee, and had read just enough in Jane Belo's careful records of the ceremonies with which the Balinese greeted the terrible disaster of the birth of twins to assure us that this was the culture we wanted to work on. (Mead, 1972: 224)

During their two years of fieldwork they took 25,000 still photographs and shot 20,000 feet of 16mm motion picture film. They usually worked together: Mead made verbal notes and Bateson photographed moving pictures and stills.[1] Their Balinese secretary, Made Kaler, kept a record in Balinese. The time and date were written on each role of film when it was placed in the camera and again when it was removed. In this way the images could be matched with the verbal records whose time was also recorded. They did not make sound recordings, relying instead on musical recordings made by others. (Bateson and Mead, 1942:49 and Mead, 1972:231)

Balinese Character: A Photographic Analysis, the book Bateson and Mead published in 1942, contains 759 of the still photographs, reproduced in one hundred Plates. Each Plate consisted of two facing pages. One page contains from four to thirteen photographs, and its facing page a general statement of theory, a description of the context in which the photographs in the plate were made, and detailed captions for the individual photographs (Figures 1 and 2). Bateson and Mead never solved the problem of incorporating the motion picture film,[2] or of making it convenient for readers to follow the multiple paths through the data their careful cross-referencing made possible.

Because the technical apparatus they needed to use motion picture film and still photographs together is now available, it is useful to examine their methods and their reasons for adopting them, and to examine the implications of their methods of analyzing and presenting ethnographic work.

Why they took photographs in the first place

In the introduction to the book, Mead says the methods she and Bateson had used separately in previous work seemed inadequate to describe the aspects of culture and behaviour they were studying: '. . . from 1928 to 1936 we were separately engaged in efforts to translate aspects of culture never successfully recorded by the scientist, although often caught by the artists, into some form of communication sufficiently clear and sufficiently unequivocal to satisfy the requirements of scientific enquiry.' (Bateson and Mead, 1942:xi).

Using their own past work as examples, Mead outlines the specific dissatisfactions she and Bateson had with conventional methods of describing phenomena, conventional ways of doing and presenting fieldwork. Of her three previous books, she says:

> As no precise scientific vocabulary was available, the ordinary English words were used, with all their weight of culturally limited connotations, in an attempt to describe the way in which the emotional life of these various South Sea peoples was organized in culturally standardized forms. This method had many serious limitations: it transgressed the canons of

Dianne DiPaola Hagaman

precise and operational scientific exposition proper to science; it was far too dependent upon idiosyncratic factors of style and literary skill; it was difficult to duplicate; and it was difficult to evaluate.

Most serious of all, we know this about the relationship between culture and verbal concepts—that the words which one culture has invested with meaning are by the very accuracy of their cultural fit, singularly inappropriate as vehicles for precise comment upon another culture (Bateson and Mead, 1942).

Of Bateson's work:

Parallel with these attempts to rely upon ordinary English as a vehicle, the approach discussed in *Naven* as being developed—an approach which sought to take the problem one step

Plate 16

VISUAL AND KINAESTHETIC LEARNING II

Teaching by muscular rote in which the pupil is made to perform the correct movements is most strikingly developed in the dancing lesson.

Mario of Tabanan, the teacher in this sequence, is the dancer chiefly responsible for the evolution of the *kebiar* dance which has become very popular in Bali in the last twenty years. The dance is performed sitting in a square space surrounded by the instruments of the orchestra, but though the principal emphasis is upon the head and hands, the dance involves the whole body, and Mario has introduced a great deal of virtuosity into the difficult feat of rapid locomotion without rising from the sitting position. The chief faults in the pupil's dancing are that he dances only with his head and arms, and does not show the disharmonic tensions characteristic of the dance.

This sequence of photographs illustrates two essential points in Balinese character formation. From his dancing lesson, the pupil learns passivity, and he acquires a separate awareness in the different parts of the body (cf. Pl. 20, fig. 4).

1. The pupil dances alone while Mario watches in the background. Note the imperfect development of the pupil's finger posture.

2. Mario comes forward to show the pupil how it should be danced.

3. Mario urges the pupil to straighten up the small of his back. Note that this instruction is given by gesture rather than by words.

4. Mario's hand position and facial expression while demonstrating (cf. Pl. 22).

5. Mario takes the pupil by the wrists and swings him across the dancing space.

6. Mario makes his pupil dance correctly by holding his hands and forcing him to move as he should. Note that Mario is actually dancing in this photograph, and that he postures with his fingers even while holding the pupil's hands. The position of Mario's left elbow in these photographs is characteristic of the tensions developed in this dance.

7. Mario even assumes the conventional sweet impersonal smile of the dancer while he moves the pupil's arms and holds the pupil tightly between his knees to correct his tendency to bend the small of his back.

8. Mario again tries to correct the pupil's tendency to bend his back.

I Mario of Tabanan teaching I Dewa P. Djaja of Kedere.

Tabanan. Dec. 1, 1936. 3 O 11, 13, 14, 17, 21, 22, 23, 25

Figures 1 and 2 'Plate 16, Visual and Kinaesthetic Learning II', from Gregory Bateson and Margaret Mead, *Balinese Character*.

further by demonstrating how such categories as ethos, there defined as 'a culturally standardized system of organization of the instincts and emotions of individuals,' were not classifications of items of behavior but were abstractions which could be applied systematically to all items of behavior.

The first method has been criticized as journalistic—as an arbitrary selection of highly colored cases to illustrate types of behavior so alien to the reader that he continues to regard them as incredible. The second method was branded as too analytical—as neglecting the phenomena of a culture in order to intellectualize and schematize it. The first method was accused of being so synthetic that it became fiction, the second of being so analytic that it became disembodied methodological discussion.

In this monograph we are attempting a new method of stating the intangible relationships among different types of culturally standardized behavior by placing side by side mutually relevant photographs. Pieces of behavior, spatially and contextually separated . . . may all be relevant to a single discussion . . . the same emotional thread may run through them. To present them together in words, it is necessary either to resort to devices which are inevitably literary, or to dissect the living scenes so that only desiccated items remain (Bateson and Mead, 19452:xi–xii).

They settled on photographs and motion-picture film as ways to expand their descriptive vocabulary, not as a replacement for other tools, but as an additional tool. They saw different media as different ways of getting at the same thing, enabling different kinds of describing, expressing, and knowing.

Additional forms would allow them to describe behaviour more *precisely*, to use the word Mead repeats three times in two paragraphs of the Introduction to define the kind of language proper science requires. What qualities, for their purposes, make a description more precise?

A more precise description requires a form that conveys an interconnected sense of the wholeness of experience, preserves a kind of *simultaneity*, presents simultaneously events that had occurred simultaneously, not isolating elements but making the view more systemic. It requires a form that *records fine detail*, the images being detailed and complex enough that many more connections and greater understanding can be extracted from them than written notes can itemize.

They valued the potential of images for describing, simultaneously, specific and minute details of surface, gesture, and spatial relationships, and their alterations over time, because, for their purposes and according to their theory of knowledge, stringing these aspects of events out linearly in text would be a distortion.

Plate 16, 'Visual and Kinaesthetic Learning II' (Bateson and Mead, 1942:86–7), for example, contains a sequence of eight photographs of a dance lesson: teacher and students surrounded by the orchestra. The master guides the student visually and kinesthetically, not verbally. The plate helps Bateson and Mead establish two important points about Balinese character formation. 'From his dancing lesson, the pupil learns passivity, and he acquires a separate awareness in the different parts of the body.'

Each image in the plate establishes relative spatial and size relations rapidly. The images give us detailed nuances of facial expression, body tension and position, and often the physical location and larger context of other people, the musicians, the instruments. simultaneously 'frozen' at a particular moment.[3] It's all there at once, eight images combined on the flat surface of the page for the viewer to study individually and compare with one another.

The emphasis on portraying relationships simultaneously also determines, in part, the composition of the individual images. Bateson composed many of the photographs, we can see, so as to 'preserve the wholeness of each piece of behavior.' Particular aspects of a scene that interest him are seldom isolated in the frame by such compositional devices as selective focus. On the contrary, he apparently made no attempt to exclude background detail, or the heads, arms, legs, and other body parts of anyone who happened to walk by from the frame. In fact, the notes sometimes say whose head or foot it is. These 'accidents' only enhanced the value of the image as data.

Putting photographs and film together

After returning to the United States for further analyses of the material and arrangement of it into a presentable form, the 'difficulties of exposition' could no longer be 'disregarded' as Bateson and Mead confronted the impossibility of presenting the two formats together. They had hoped to use the film and the still images together, both in their analysis and in its later presentation. In the

1930s, when the work was produced, they couldn't do it. The technology at the time being what it was, no common format existed in which the two media could be combined. In his 'Notes to the Photographs' in the book, Bateson expresses disappointment that some plates are, in his view, inadequate because they lack particular images that were recorded on motion-picture film. 'The present book is illustrated solely by photographs taken with the latter [still camera], and as a result, the book contains no photograph of a father suckling his child at the nipple, and the series of kris dancers (Pls. 57 and 58) leaves much to be desired.' (Bateson and Mead, 1942:51).

Vaguely aware of this problem while in the field, they had conducted their research as if today's computer imaging technology—which makes it possible to digitize photographs and film (still images and moving images) and present them together, along with sound and extensive text, in the same piece of work (together on one flat surface)—was available to them in 1936, which it was not.

It might seem odd, or even naive, for Bateson and Mead to have ignored these problems, until you consider the degree to which they invented their photographic methods of record and description in the course of doing the research.

> When we planned our field work, we decided that we would make extensive use of movie film and stills. Gregory had bought seventy-five rolls of Leica film to carry us through the two years. Then one afternoon when we had observed parents and children for an ordinary forty-five minute period, we found that Gregory had taken three whole rolls. We looked at each other, we looked at the notes, and we looked at the pictures that Gregory had taken so far and that had been developed and printed by a Chinese in the town and were carefully mounted and catalogued on large pieces of cardboard. Clearly we had come to a threshold—to cross it would be a momentous commitment in money, of which we did not have much, and in work as well. But we made the decision. Gregory wrote home for the newly invented rapid winder, which made it possible to take pictures in very rapid succession. He also ordered bulk film, which he would have to cut and put in cassettes himself as we could not possibly afford to buy commercially the amount of film we now proposed to use. As a further economizing measure we bought a developing

tank that would hold ten rolls at once and, in the end, we were able to develop some 1600 exposures in an evening.

The decision we made does not sound very momentous today. Daylight loaders have been available for years, amateur photographers have long since adopted sequence photography, and field budgets for work with film have enormously increased. But it was momentous then. Whereas we had planned to take 2,000 photographs, we took 25,000. It meant that the notes I took were similarly multiplied by a factor of ten, and when Made's notes also were added in, the volume of our work was changed in tremendously significant ways. (Mead, 1972:234).

They had very specific reasons for using visual materials and anticipated they would be significant to their work. But the details of the subject matter, composition, and other particulars of making and using the images were worked out in the field: one afternoon Bateson used the camera in a way they didn't anticipate. They were innovating and experimenting, and they knew it.

Photographs as descriptive records from which to form hypotheses

We treated the cameras in the field as recording instruments, not as devices for illustrating our theses. (Bateson and Mead, 1942:49).

Bateson and Mead saw still photographs and motion-picture film as forms of description. As descriptions, photographic images have all the limitations of viewpoint, selectivity, and contextualization of other kinds of description: verbal accounts, tape recordings, drawings. Images are finely detailed maps of selected 3D space at a particular place and instant in time or in the case of film, over a specific period of time, mapped point for point onto a 2D surface. These maps can be carried to distant places and studied at later times, an activity that necessarily attaches a more complex notion of time to the image.

But what images describe—their meaning, what they 'show'—is an interpretation. Bateson and Mead did not take that meaning to be self-evident. Rather, they considered the connections, explanations, and interpretations the photographs suggested as hypotheses to be explored further, as they directed the photographing more specifically to the new ideas and connections suggested by earlier images.

Plate 54, 'Girls' Tantrums' (Bateson and Mead, 1942: 162–3), contains thirteen photographs, the first two of the same incident, a tantrum in the road, photographed early in the fieldwork. In the first photograph, a young girl is shown screaming, with 'her hands raised to her head in a posture closely related to those of the boy in PL.53.' In the caption to the second photograph, Bateson points out that this particular image 'gave us the first clue for the formulation that the Balinese mother avoids adequate response to the climaxes of her child's anger and love.' The photograph shows the young girl clinging to her mother's legs. The mother's response is 'negligent and relaxed . . . her arm scarcely in contact with the girl's sling cloth.'

Bateson and Mead didn't look at this photograph and state a theory, citing the photograph as evidence. For them, photographs don't prove a hypothesis, they provoke further tests of it. The distinction is important. They used the image as data rather than as a self-evident proof. The details of the photographs suggest a general theory or principle. If the principle is in fact general, I will find other versions of it when I return to the field. If I don't, further details will suggest a reformulation.[4]

This method of using photographs required them to study and compare images in the field. Plate 23, 'Hand Postures In Arts And Trance' (Bateson and Mead, 1942:100–01), for example, contains eight photographs. The photographs show Balinese artists, unlike Occidental artists, accentuating the sensory function in their left hand. Bateson writes that, because this point was not noticed in the field, where they could have checked it further, it 'therefore cannot be stated definitely or backed up by native statements.'

To test their hypotheses about temperament and culture, where did they point the camera? Their practice was initially guided by such assumptions as these:

> . . . that parent-child relationships and relationships between siblings are likely to be more rewarding than agricultural techniques. We therefore selected especially contexts and sequences of this sort. We recorded as fully as possible what happened while we were in the houseyard, and it is so hard to predict behavior that it was scarcely possible to select particular postures or gestures for photographic recording. In general,

we found that any attempt to select for special details was
fatal, and that the best results were obtained when the photography was most rapid and almost random. Pls. 71 and 72
illustrate this; the photographer assumed that the context was
interesting and photographed as far as possible every move
that the subjects made, without wondering which moves might
be most significant. (Bateson and Mead, 1942:50).[5]

But within these broad outlines, the question remained: where
do you point the camera? Though Bateson and Mead continued
to have differing opinions about that, in *Balinese Character* they
did it Bateson's way. He believed in pointing the camera at what
he thought was important, and he used the camera to help refor-
mulate what he and Mead thought important or relevant.[6]

Eventually, they pointed the camera at sequences of behaviour
as a way to closely describe such unfolding interactions as
exchanges of glance and gesture. They compared sequences of
images from similar events, (eg, mothers teasing older child with
a younger sibling or borrowed baby) with each other, and
sequences from one area of social life with sequences from other
areas (eg, mother teasing older child, cremation towers being carried to the cemetery, young girls dancing in trance, and artist's
paintings of their dreams). From these diverse areas of cultural
activity and behavior, they arrived at more general relationships
(eg, the Balinese systems of hierarchy and respect).

: . . because of the density of the population and the richness
of the ceremonial life, we were able to put together many new
kinds of samples. We had not one birth feast but twenty;'
fifteen occasions, all carefully recorded, when the same little
girls went into trance; six hundred small carved kitchen gods
from one village to compare with five hundred from another
village; and one man's paintings of forty of his dreams to place
in the context of paintings by a hundred other artists. (Mead,
1972:235).

In all, then, they worked at four levels: the individual photograph; the individual interaction described in a sequence of photographs or a segment of motion picture film; the comparison of
a collection of sequences, each taken of a similar exchange, but at
different times and places, involving the same individuals or not;
and comparison of collections of sequences, describing different
aspects of the culture which might seem superficially separate.

Some logistical problems Bateson and Mead worked with, and how those problems have been altered by technological developments

Logistical and practical problems arose in connection with three separate activities: making and analyzing the images in the field; moving the materials to New York where they are analyzed again, and shown to other people, though the researchers can no longer return to the original site to 'check up a point,' as with Plate 23; finally, editing, summarizing, and combining (recontextualizing) images for a final presentation. Each kind of problem could be solved differently and more efficiently today through the use of digital technology.

Bateson and Mead cut and developed their film in the field, then had their negatives printed and enlargements made and returned to them. Today, skipping the step of printing entirely, one can scan negatives directly into the computer so that they are quickly accessible for study and comparison. Going further, one could use a digital still camera and avoid the use of film altogether. Motion picture film, and video (which was not available to Bateson and Mead), can also be digitized directly into a computer. Digital video cameras, when they are available, will cut out the conversion step.

Bateson complained about the problems of sorting through all the materials when they got back to the United States, and the difficulties of sizing and laying out such a large collection of images for a final printed product.

> Selection by size was more distressing. Each plate was to be reproduced as a unit and therefore we had the task of preparing prints which would fit together in laying out the plate. Working with this large collection of negatives, it was not possible to plan the lay-out in advance, and therefore, in the case of the more important photographs, two prints of different sizes were prepared. Even with this precaution, the purely physical problems of space and composition on the plate have eliminated a few photographs which we would have liked to include. (Bateson and Mead, 1942:51).

Computers would have solved many of these problems, providing a flat surface on which the various media Bateson used could be viewed together, stored electronically so that specific pieces can be rapidly located, all this contributing to a more efficient sifting of material, and facilitating the analytical process of comparing and combining images.

A simple example of a computer solution is the size of images. Bateson regretted the small size of the photographic reproductions (the consequences of the economics of book reproduction). But size became a constraint because the readability of an image at a small size became a criterion by which they chose images. So reading in the computer, by allowing viewers to increase the size of a particular image at their discretion, would be an advantage.

Back in the United States, Bateson and Mead asked other researchers from other disciplines to view and comment on the material, after the field work was over but before publication. Mead talks about researchers picking details out of the filmed sequences ('When we showed that Balinese stuff that first summer there were different things that people identified—the limpness that Marian Stranahan identified, the place on the chest and its point in child development that Erik Erikson identified.') (Bateson and Mead, 1976:40). Today, such collaboration and consultation might well take place (if not now, soon) while they were still in the field by sending visual materials via Internet to New York (or any other part of the world) for other researchers and collaborators to examine.

Bateson and Mead analysed their field materials, and presented the photographs and text as a rich, layered work. Mead describes the form of the book as an experimental innovation (as it certainly was). Readers then make the connections and relationships the text points out, or follow other paths of association, of potential interest but not pursued by the authors, such as tracing one person through a series of plates (the readers thus making their own paths).

Bateson and Mead expected readers to use their formal innovations. They wanted readers to explore the plates for themselves. They cross-referenced images and provided additional information so that readers could create their own combinations of the materials.

Cross references from one photograph to another and from one plate to another have been inserted often, and such insertions often carry implicit generalizations like those implicit in the juxtapositions. To enable the reader to explore the plates for himself, a random supply of cross references is given in the

Glossary and Index of Native Words and Persons. As far as possible, native words have been kept within parentheses. They are provided for the use of readers already familiar with Balinese language and custom, and the ordinary reader need pay no attention to them unless he wishes to set side-by-side the various photographs connected with one ceremony or native concept. . . . Similarly, it is possible from the names of identified persons to obtain an over-all view of some of the most photographed individuals, such as I Karba, I Karsa, I Gata, and their respective parents. (Bateson and Mead, 1942:53).

What Bateson and Mead wanted to accomplish by combining stills and film can be done today in *hypertext*. A basic characteristic of hypertext is cross-referencing (as in an encyclopedia, where the end of an entry directs you to 'see' related items). Hypertext can be created without a computer, but a computer makes it easier to write and to read. The integration of a variety of media (film, stills, sound) in one document, however, *is* tied to the computer.

What would a hypertext *Balinese Character* look like? How would it work? In a straightforward translation you would select a cross-reference Bateson and Mead had designated not by turning to the indicated page, but by clicking on the reference with your mouse. The designated image(s) would appear for comparison and study. What appeared might be another photograph, a text, motion-picture film, or a recording of a gamelan orchestra (such as Bateson and Mead used in the film *Trance and Dance in Bali*.)

Bateson and Mead often divided the recording of data, as mentioned above, between film and still photographs. This created problems when they wanted to discuss materials recorded in the two different ways. For example, Plate 42, 'A Bird on a String,' (Bateson and Mead, 1942:138–9) contains twelve photographs of a boy playing with a tiny living bird on a bark string. But the still photographs represent only about half of the entire sequence: 'The whole sequence, as recorded in M.M.'s notes, lasted about 15 minutes, but of this period only about 7 minutes was recorded with the camera. At this point the film in the still camera finished, and the remainder of the sequence was recorded with the motion-picture camera.' The second half, on motion-picture film, is thus unavailable in the book, but would be available in a computerized hypertext.

Latour: Immutable, combinable mobiles

Two of Bruno Latour's ideas about knowledge, representations, and power have implications for our understanding of *Balinese Character*, and for creating and presenting work using electronic imaging technologies, 1) A 'shift in thinking' occurs when people put knowledge into the form of 'immutable and combinable mobiles;' and 2) 'experts [unlike novices] assemble materials in such a way as to make relationships apparent.'[7]

For Latour, representations ('inscriptions') become sources of greater power when they are mobile (can be moved from place to place), immutable (do not change when they are moved), and combinable with one another (when their size can be 'averaged,' their internal relationships remaining consistent) in order to make comparisons.

Such representations become inanimate allies in 'agonistic' encounters in which it is not the antagonists' abilities that matter but the new understanding the juxtaposition of representations allows: an 'average mind . . . will generate totally different output depending on if it is attending to the confusing world or to inscriptions. . . . It is because all these inscriptions can be superimposed, reshuffled, recombined, and summarized, that totally new phenomena emerge, *hidden from the other people from whom all these inscriptions have been exacted.*' (Latour 1986:11, my emphasis).

To put what we have been discussing in Latour's terms, the computer screen becomes a 'small laboratory' in which previously uncombinable forms or media, such as film and still photographs, may be combined and recombined. This creates the potential for an analytic result which is more than a sum of the parts, identifying relationships (patterns or contrasts) which are visible only because you have combined immutable mobiles. The newly visible relationships drawn from these materials result in a shift in conceptualization, a reformulation of the structure of what you're looking at. This is the 'totally different output' Latour speaks of, which occurs as a result of the manipulation of the laboratory setting.

New knowledge, a new way of seeing the world, results from having an efficient pictorial language and being able to recombine inscriptions gathered from different times and places. Anything that improves this combinability is favoured historically because it creates this advantage in power and knowledge.

For the same reason, anything that accelerates the mobility of traces without transformation will be favoured too.

But inscriptions by themselves are not enough. Latour describes Darwin and other naturalists (using them to exemplify the problems of everyone who gathers data) as being 'swamped' in specimens (like Bateson complaining about wading through all the Bali materials once he got back to New York). Having turned things into paper (including photographic images), the analyst now must reduce the amount of paper. A 'deflating strategy' is needed. Latour emphasizes what he calls the 'construction of cascades,' in which people working with information turn more paper into less paper.

For Latour, good theories, unlike bad ones or 'mere collections of empirical facts,' provide 'easy access to theory' by assembling materials in one place where 'relations between them and hence the answer [the analysis] could essentially be read off from it. Experts [unlike novices] assemble materials to make relationships apparent.' *Balinese Character*'s presentational strategy makes the relationships between temperament and culture apparent: the photographs, the words, and their arrangement are the analysis, in the sense that their theoretical import can be 'read off' the pages. The analysis embodies the theory in just the way that Mead says the Balinese 'embody that abstraction which (after we have abstracted it) we technically call culture.' (Bateson and Mead, 1942:xii).

Mead and Bateson's purpose was agonistic in the Latourian sense. They wanted to make an argument about 'how character is formed from early childhood to harmonize with values implicit in culture' (Bateson, 1972:123) and convince others they were right, thus enrolling them as allies. As Bateson said about the research in Bali, 'we assumed that the still photography and the motion-picture film *together* would constitute our record of behavior.' The combined media would have allowed stronger support (in the form of inanimate allies) for their theories, making a more 'expert' arrangement of 'allies' possible.

For Latour, the study of signs by themselves obscures the understanding of power. You must study the process that enabled those signs to be where they are, how they are, doing the work they're doing. 'The scale of an actor is not an absolute term but a relative one that varies with the ability to produce, capture, sum up and interpret information about other places and times.' How to dominate on a large scale? 'The name of the game is to accumulate enough allies in one place to modify the belief and behavior of all the others.' (Latour, 1986:29 and 31). If visual representations can define a culture (for instance, define what kind of people the Balinese are), then a nationwide magazine such as *National Geographic* is a large-scale actor and an ethnography in hypermedia can become a bigger actor than a book.

Latour points out that, in the case of natural science laboratories, increasing research costs mean that very few scientists can engage in the 'proof race.' The social science proof race is quite different. Increasingly, though of course not universally, the new imaging technologies, which make using combined media and hypertext structures less of a tsimmes for anthropologists, are available to 'the other people from whom all these inscriptions have been exacted' and from whom they were 'hidden.' This makes it possible, at least in principle, for the people social scientists study to construct a counterargument, should at least some of them have access to the appropriate tools and so desire.[8]

Furthermore, the *relative* inexpensiveness and ubiquity of electronic media and instruments (eg the expense of buying a camcorder and making a video compared to the expense of making a motion picture film) takes visual media out of the hands of 'professionals' or specialists (and their conventional ways of picturing and deciding what's worthy of picturing) and increases the number of people who control them.

Conclusion

Bateson and Mead believed that visual materials were necessary to the full investigation of such subtle relationships as that between temperament and culture. Still photographs and motion-picture film gave them a vocabulary with which to identify and describe those relationships. They intended, though they didn't have the language Latour later provided, to combine the variety of materials they had gathered ('combinable, immutable mobiles') in such a way as to provide a compelling demonstration of their analysis, one in which the conclusions could be read off the presentation. They displayed photographs and text together, but could not incorporate the motion picture film, so integral a part of their evidence, with those other materials on one flat surface. In that sense, the construction of what Latour calls the nth+1 cascade, the combination that reduces the bulk of what is to be handled, was impossible for them. Digital imaging and computer-based hypertext today make their vision attainable in ways they did not foresee but would have loved. I hope I'm not too presumptuous in assuming that Gregory's response to these new developments would have been, 'Yes, now I can really get busy.' And Margaret's would have been, 'It's about time, for God's sake.'

Notes

1 Some of the motion-picture filming was done by Jane Belo.
2 A number of films were eventually made: *A Balinese Family, Bathing Babies in Three Cultures, Childhood Rivalry in Bali and New Guinea, Karba's First Years,* and *Trance and Dance in Bali.* From series Character Formation in Different Cultures, produced for the Institute for Intercultural Studies, released in 1951 by the New York University Film Library. All are 16 mm, black and white, sound.
3 Which is not to say that these relations are described 'objectively.' For example, different focal lengths affect the apparent relative space between and size of elements in the frame from foreground to background.
4 This way of using visual materials, uncommon even in anthropology, is the opposite of the practice of the news media, in which the analysis (what the 'story' is) is determined before the images are made. (Ruby, 1973, and Hagaman, 1993)
5 Pls. 71 and 72 are titled, respectively, Sibling Rivalry III and IV. Each plate contains six photographs from the same sequence of a mother playing a 'game' which 'consists of putting the new baby in the knee baby's lap and urging the latter to treat the rival as "younger sibling." '
6 See Bateson and Mead, 1976, for an amusing debate in which the two state their respective positions.
7 See Latour, 1976.
8 Jay Ruby has given a number of examples of social science 'subjects' creating and presenting their own analyses of their societies and cultures by means of these technologies. See Ruby, 1991.

Information systems strategy, a cultural borderland, some monstrous behaviour

Mike Hales

Abstract

Does it help to think 'culture' when addressing multinational practices of information systems strategy? This paper says it depends on where you stand yourself, what you're attempting to articulate, and whether you can address topographies and systematic violations as well as meanings and situated actions. Discussing an actual case of organization-development consultancy, and seriously mixing its metaphors, the argument uses: a (materialist) distinction between meanings and powers, to suggest that the culture disciplines may not give sufficient help in producing actual change; 'terrain', to voice the possibility that computer systems strategy work may be done monstrously; and 'theatre', to invoke the construction of research-and-development borderlands which have as their harvest not only meanings but also (unacademic) powers.

Antoine Artaud wrote tracts describing . . . another theatre . . . working like the plague, by intoxication, by infection, by analogy, by magic; a theatre in which the play, the event itself, stands in place of a text. (Brook, 1990:54).

[Artaud] was always speaking of a complete way of life, of a theatre in which the activity of the actor and the activity of the spectator were driven by the same desperate need. . . . [I]t is easier to apply the rules to the work of a handful of dedicated actors than to the lives of the unknown spectators who happen by chance to come through the theatre door. (Brook, 1990:60–61).

This chapter emerges from a current project with a multinational, here called 'ABC Global'. ABC designs, manufactures and installs computer-based systems via 100-or-so local companies.

Our project centres on the articulation of ABC's strategic intention to use new, bought-in software packages to support administration of the order process in local companies, on divisions of labour in information systems development, and on the implications of the strategy for managers' competences.

We are a team of consultant-researchers based in a business school's centre for research in innovation management. I am the member most involved in 'culture' as an approach to power and computing technology. My colleagues spend more of their time in organization development, group facilitation and training, and research in total quality management and supply chain management. In disciplinary terms none of us are culture professionals, and as Raymond Williams suggests, 'culture' is one of the two or three most complicated words in English (Williams, 1976:72). So why and how are we concerned with cultures of computing?

ABC Global is tantalized by a principle stated by Percy Barnevik, chief executive of ABB: 'We'd rather be roughly right and fast, than exactly right and too slow.' Knowing this slogan, ABC managers sometimes joke that ABC is good at being '*exactly . . . wrong*'. It's the legacy of an engineering view of the world married to a hugely centralized bureaucracy. ABC would love to change, has stated that in the future it will move differently, but isn't comfortable in the movement. We feel sure that 'being roughly right and fast' will depend far more on language and meaning, and the self-conscious management of languages and meanings, than on precise engineering of systems and procedures. We suspect that to achieve its stated commercial aims, ABC needs to learn to manage the reproduction of its culture; and we know that this notion is deeply contradictory.

We also are inclined to adopt 'roughly right and fast' in our own intellectual practice, which creates difficulties positioning what we do on academic terrain. This is not the usual difficulty, of the complexity and competitiveness of the academic economy—although in fact we find ourselves moving in and out of anthropology, cultural studies, sociology, feminist theory, organization theory, the 'postmodernism' debates and information systems research. Rather, it's the special difficulty of being primarily oriented to reflective and interpretative *action* (producing durable and coherent changes in practices) rather than tradable, publishable understandings. This makes us monsters—lacking the wisdom of centaurs, as strange as cyborgs, more substantial than chimeras.

These days 'cultural' approaches to computing technologies are rather high-profile—for example, in academic and industrial discourses around participatory design, computer supported cooperative work (CSCW) and groupware. Having played the culture hunch for years (Hales, 1980) I have to see this as a good thing. But these approaches still seem part of a activist's problem, rather than an activist's solution, in three respects.

Firstly, they are professionalized, in academic, disciplinary terms. This naturally produces the perception that other approaches to cultural phenomena must be 'unprofessional'. Such a construction of legitimacy constitutes difficulties for action-oriented researchers whose problems are produced in unacademic practice. As a signifier of discipline and professionalized intellectual location, 'culture' seems too weak to characterize what it is that we work in this borderland. Monsters, we find, are *undisciplined*.

Secondly, the emergent computing-related discourses of language, communication and meaning (eg, in CSCW) persistently fail to attend to power—or as I would prefer, *multiplicities* of powers. Powers are what must be worked when practical changes are intended, so discourses in which 'power' is marginal or suppressed don't help a lot to organize such work.

And thirdly, academic discourses operate (by definition, as *professionalized* practices?) with rationalist mythologies. But rationalist modes of power constitute only a small subset of those active in any actual domain, academic work included. Thus academic approaches to culture and technology are prone to fetishize speech action, bracketing-out 'action' in larger historical and materialist senses and also, at a different level, restricting their own legitimate interventions to 'talk' or talk-surrogates. We sympathise with our fee-paying ABC clients, who want to see some action (from us, and from others as a result of what we perform) rather than just to talk and 'understand'. So we find ourselves poorly served by discourses in which communication or interpretation hogs the limelight, when what we need is theory of human action, and specifically, theory of theorisers' *practice*.

Information systems strategy—The project with ABC

Our contract with ABC requires us to research, design and pilot a management development programme for top-400 managers in

ABC local companies.[1] Several clients make up ABC's project steering group, and we have a complex—and continually negotiated—set of terms of reference. There are three main stakeholders. The project originated with information systems (IS) policy makers. They told us a strategic future-tale: of ABC adopting standard, bought-in, MRPII systems for sales-order process administration, and of a smallish window of opportunity within which many local companies, undertaking replacements or first-time installations of such systems, could be enrolled as subscribers to the global standard. The strategy requires local senior managers to accept ownership of both administration systems and IS projects. This is something of a poisoned challenge because, owing to capacity constraints, these local, business-led, standard-system installations must be faster and slimmer than previous, IS-led, custom-build projects. Managers may not yet see the iceberg, but they can read 'Titanic' on the boarding pass.

The strategy extends from computer systems into the business processes that the systems are intended to support. This brings in a second set of stakeholders, responsible for developing process- and customer-oriented management across ABC. Finally, the strategy requires line managers to be accountable for the disposition of resources both within IS projects and within the new working divisions of labour that operate afterwards; this brings in stakeholders responsible for competence development in management cadres, and in particular for developing cross-functional working as a managerial style.

As the supplier in this contract we engage with a number of cultural domains. The project's structure gave us four major 'slices' through ABC cultures.[2] Combining these we could generate a pretty complex map of cultural 'places' in ABC. It confirmed our prior assumption that 'cultural' differences (lifeworld differences between differing locations in the division of labour) were an important reality. Briefly, here are the four slices.

1. Corporate-level negotiations

Negotiations with the clients were an early and persistent source of cultural insight. Our steering group includes senior managers from an established occupational sphere (IS), a marginal one (organization development/management development) and a rising one (process management). If it weren't for our project, and our own insistence that it is about organization development, these people wouldn't be working together. Thus even at this formal level our project is a borderland. We have substantial cultural problems in this setting, including the arms-length norms of senior management action in ABC and customer-contractor relations in consultancy—*I give you a spec, you perform it; I'm not looking for challenges, just promises and results*—and policy-level work organization—*this is my change initiative, my policy patch, that one's yours*. We've been seeking ways to shift this steering-group culture.

On another level, in the ritual tableaux of budget-governed life (project presentations, evaluation meetings, steering group meetings) we perform role-plays requiring a considerable cultural facility. In this highly political context we begin to see drama as the most central 'cultural' mode. We continually position our own project in the action space of senior ABC managers, and try to transform *their* space in accordance with our explicit brief for change. Work on such symbolic and dramatic materials predated the project start.

2. *Professional domains*

We soon encountered the privileged nature of 'design' in ABC. 'Process management' is a powerful totem in the sales-order process domain (our process-producer paymasters) but the engineering design tribes (the product-producers—software engineers) clearly have the bigger magic. Thus, in our fieldwork interviews we got many stories about how the quality of available tools falls off as you pass through the boundary objects at the design/sales-order interface. For example, system installers and marketing people must articulate ABC's powerful standard modules of functionality into configurations of working stuff that suit specific customers' needs and sites; this is 'dimensioning'. Stories were told of dimensioning tools that were *poorer, less suited to their users and less cared for* than engineers' software-producing tools. In the marketplace, ABC trades on the technical excellence of what designers produce; but workers downstream, picking up design's boundary objects, are obliged to struggle with poor tools in order to put ABC in a position to actually get revenue.

Finance is privileged too. There is a clear tendency for finance functionality in the new applications to be configured in support of 'the centre': conventional financial accounting practice (profit reporting, say) rather than management accounting practices and the needs of operating units (say, activity-level costing of mainte-nance work). Even partisans of local managers' information needs would typically privilege the reality of established finance professionals (who *know what they're doing* and thus may legiti-mately be asked what they require of a system) over that of most actors in supply operations (who *don't know what a good process looks like* and therefore will only clog up the analyst's project file with incoherent *wish-lists* if you ask them what they'd like a new system to do). Such a reading of the situation re-enacts the pow-erful centrality of finance as capital. Finance people's ancient and mysterious knowledges are 'more real' than those of staff in newly-formed companies, or marginal and emergent professional groupings such as marketing and logistics.

3. Countries/companies

Differences between countries and companies were sometimes substantial. For example, we saw how a long-established Danish company operated in 'discursive', semi-participatory ways while evolving a requirements specification for an integrative system; this was impossible for an English company overshadowed by a previous merger and present managerial terror. In Hungary, ingrained petty patterns of coupon-clipping Eastern-bloc bureau-cracy reproduced themselves within a new joint venture company, in the face of the Mother Company's desire to introduce new daughters to world-standard 'improved' processes. Here were serious issues for us, given that our management programme must assist old and new companies worldwide.

4. Layers of formal organization

Hierarchy was recognized in the brief, in that IS strategists accepted that requirements must deal with 'strategic', 'opera-tional' and 'transactional' needs. We treated this layered *func-tional* analysis as a social-group or *lifeworld* classification, interviewed layered samples of staff and found—no surprise—that people in 'lower' layers had different perceptions of informa-tion systems, projects and strategies. How to surface questions with Top-400 managers: Who sees the order process MRPII sys-tem? who acts with it? who owns or ought to own the configured functionality of such a system? Answers include: top managers, who pass through a company doing the managerial Grand Tour, making their mark on balance sheets; operational managers, who get their arses kicked when customers' orders go askew and costs aren't controlled; and clerks who spend workdays at terminals, and evolve sophisticated work-arounds to get the goods to the customer. How to recognize and negotiate such differing usages and claims to ownership?

We have tried to do our ABC work as ethnographers and even ethnomethodologists, of a sort. We may have learned them from versions of political activism rather than academic disciplines,[3] but we end up trying to honour basic ethnographic principles such as: work in the natural surroundings of the people you're attending to; speak in their terms not for them; describe rather than judge 'strange' practices—they do make sense, but you can't yet see it; pay serious attention. And because we found that the uniform and smooth descriptions of our schools and universities wouldn't support real work,[4] we strive for conceptually dense and heterogeneous theorizations which acknowledge necessary gaps between persons, places, times and things (Rutledge, Shields and Dervin, 1993).

However, we simply must do it fast. For example, in pairs we conducted fieldwork in four local ABC companies, spending three days and interviewing 20–30 people in each, in singles and groups, and presenting our 'ethnography' as a poster exhibition for the management team during the last half-day. Posters were developed from live notes, fresh or brought-forward diagrams, and night-before collages of sticky-notes on the hotel bedroom wall. They were all that we took away. A pretty thin record, far from the 'thick' data of ethnographic studies; but this was our design, and indicates how our workings persistently depart from canons of disciplined cultural study.

A cultural borderland and monstrous behaviour

The University team treats this as a 'culture project'. We expected to find many culturally differentiated locales in a complex organization like ABC (a locale is a social 'space' in which actors move, not necessarily a spatially contiguous domain) and presumed that working these differences—doing things with culture—would be a primary aspect of our contribution to ABC. We expected that, because of their instrumental orientations, the dominant managerial and professional groups in ABC would be blind to cultural processes (meaning-centred processes) and believed that this was likely to damage managers' capability in complex, distributed, changing situations. Thus we presumed that a primary requirement for the management programme was to enable managers to develop new modes of speaking of systems development. We saw these new language games as *about* language as well as about computing apparatuses and data.[5]

However, language is not the only level at which our action is pitched. And understanding—the natural term of reference if we're working in a language-centred, hermeneutic mode—is not necessarily the key term in our own understanding. When we started the project we thought that, for ways of speaking to seem appropriate, *places for speaking* must be considered, and we therefore undertook (between ourselves) to enable some other things to be said and heard and to create some new places for speaking and hearing. We intervened.

We asked questions, the basic form of an interviewer's intervention. Some were open ended, in the sense that they were not strongly leading or framed in our own technical terms. We hoped they would seem legitimate to our interviewees, attentive rather than intrusive. For example: 'As a manager, what measures do you find you use in monitoring the activities you manage?'. Other questions called for free association, an image rather than a structured, formal statement. For example, we often used a metaphor game to open a group interview session: 'The X information system which I use is like a. . . .' These latter questions were odd, broke through ABC normality, and produced some discussions that otherwise would have been unlikely. For example, a programmers' time-logging information system became *a tall, confusing building with poor signposting*, and *an octopus*; an ABC local company became *a bus being driven down a pot-holed road*; a logistics management system became *a lorryload of sand dumped on the front lawn* delivered to users when what they sought was *a bucketful*. Such things are not usually said to people coming from head office to talk IS policy.

Here was not only a differently cued investigator/interviewee language game, but also a different social mode of talking about ABC and information systems *between interviewees*. The metaphors grew and were retold in novel group settings, drawing together people who wouldn't otherwise talk in such a way. Our investigation was creating (temporary) places for different language games. Our aim was partly to test what ABC's people would accept (generally they were comfortable with free-association gambits and cooperated willingly in unfamiliar mixed-group settings). But we also demonstrated to managers that interventions of this 'cultural' (meaning-focused) kind, as distinct from instrumental exercises, *can* produce valid knowledges. We showed our sponsors that a cultural-intervention strategy was a practicable interpretation of the project brief, acceptable to ABC companies, and ordered, efficient and effective in producing understandings unavailable through normal ABC policy processes.

Thus we constructed the project as a borderland—a terrain which articulates with ABC normalities but also is *strange*. It connects multiple intra-organizational locales in unfamiliar ways (eg, less proprietorial or judgmental) and also introduces practices from other places. Some of these introduced strangenesses are recognizable as ways of thinking or working within academic theory or methodology. However, we had learned them, and worked with them in ABC, mainly as practitioners in *interventionist* traditions: the worker-writers' and oral history movements, community planning and development, adult non-vocational education, advocacy, consciousness-raising groups, counselling and group facilitation. 'Intervention' sits awkwardly with the 'helping' values of these traditions. I mean to imply that the abnormally disciplined disinterestedness of a skilled helper—and the source of the 'help'—is an interested and disruptive intervention in the differently interested modes of 'normal' practices. In ABC our intervention, similarly, was *to produce breakdowns*, to manage the production and partial resolution of breakdowns in normal ABC speakings and hearings.

A borderland exists because we were given control of some organizational resources. Mostly, these were small amounts of staff time spent in meetings called and managed by us. To maintain this borderland requires a live weaving of ways of behaving both familiar *and* strange to ABC people: familiar enough to be performable but strange enough to challenge and fascinate. The management programme should similarly be a borderland, larger and more durable, maintained in a distinctive strangeness for a year or two within ABC.

We place ourselves into ABC as monsters: academics in 'practical' cultures, activists in a bureaucracy, poets in a world of technicians. We operate with academic theories of human action and academic investigative methods; as humanist, socialist and feminist adventurers; in the heartland of capital not quite brave enough yet to be postmodern; and whose senior managers are perfectly capable of shooting a messenger. On any of these counts we run the risk of being rejected by ABC. We must maintain this danger rather than go native because we believe that the aura of breakdown that we carry *is* our contribution to ABC's goals. We will not resort to trading simply in the obvious in order to get to the close of our contract.

Working 'culture'

Nor will we resort to trading 'cultural' material in the complex ways that disciplined academics do. But what meanings *have* I been exploiting in 'culture'? What have I been doing with them? What troubles do they bring?

First, 'culture' is a theme which can help to constitute rigorous approaches to power and technology. As an intellectual theme, however, 'culture' is a signifier of discipline and professionalized intellectual location. Culture professionals appropriate the discourses of 'culture' as their own career capital, and through the symbolic violence intrinsic in professionalism (Bourdieu, 1991) they constitute others' workings of this territory as both undisciplined and unprofessional. Monsters must be *undisciplined*—and for this privilege they suffer.

Second, 'cultural' processes are important in computer-related contexts: processes that work meaning, constitute meaning in actions and things, produce and distribute meaning. Here we are close to Clifford Geertz: 'Believing that . . . man is an animal suspended in webs of significance he himself has spun, I take "culture" to be those webs, and the analysis of it to be therefore not an experimental science in search of law but an interpretative one in search of meaning' (Geertz, 1973:5). This construction of problems by culture professionals is helpful, but also establishes difficulties for theorist-activist monsters. For example, in adopting Geertz's position Czarniawska-Joerges is driven to add: 'a gloss saying that woman is an animal suspended in webs of significance she herself has *not* spun' (Czarniawska-Joerges, 1992:52). Activists must focus on the differential powers of different actors. This materialist interest is easily marginalized even in Geertz's realist tradition of cultural anthropology.

In ABC we are concerned with attempts to *shift* webs of meaning in organizational practices, and with the powers and entrapments that subsist in attributions of significance. In struggling theoretically we find that meaning (ie, recognizing the constitutive human and managerial significance of languages and lifeworlds) must be distinguished from significance (ie, recognizing the equally primitive status of power). There are many powers, and the reference includes much more than just signification. Activist monsters need to make a materialist distinction, between the powers of the meanings centred in my practical locus and the powers of the meanings centred in yours.

Third, 'cultures' can be the worlds of signification of specific social groups or practices—the culture of finance, for example. This interpretation extends to a *situational* concern with cultural 'places' in ABC—locations in which 'what we do here' makes different senses, especially in relation to artefacts (such as MRPII systems) which are intended to 'stabilize' action and afford constrained knowledges. Extended further, we can see meaningful 'leavings' and deposits—notably computing artefacts—as boundary markers of struggles to gain symbolic and material holds over others' lives; we are now on the terrain of *ideology* and *hegemony* (Eagleton, 1991). Further (drastic) extension—helped by feminist theoretical work (Nicholson, 1991)—gives us a focus on systems of meaning which not only greet us as we awake each day but also pursue us into dreams, forming alliances with systems of terrible need; this is the post-structuralist ground of power and the force of *desire*. Most of the situation-oriented work on computer system design stands some way off from such (Nietschian?) traditions; activists need them, however.

Finally, 'culture' can be a selfconscious, specialized, modern mode. Within this frame power becomes 'the literature', 'the canon', the selective tradition, 'art' (Eagleton, 1983; Williams, 1961; Williams, 1981). Cultural producers require theory which assists voicing, text-working, forging meanings, articulating working understandings, performing educational programmes. In ABC we begin to see drama and performance arts (and not, say, writing or conversational dialogue) as the 'cultural' mode most central to implementing an IS strategy.

Monsters can't afford to be picky. In foraging we range across all of these fields of 'cultural' interpretation; it's all grist.

Mike Hales

Bodies, meanings, 'earthmoving', 'performing'

Two persistent metaphors of our work with ABC are linked: terrain (borderland) and (dramatic) performing. The link lies in taking seriously both meaning and the fact that all speakers and hearers, all writers and readers of technology texts, are embodied, are corporeal. Humans are located in physical spaces (buildings, continents) and multiple historical-institutional spaces (countries, households). Humans are located in the cultural spaces of professions, projects, careers, lives. None of these realities is available without the others, and (management commonsense notwithstanding) the domain of management is constituted by all of these at once.

This dual interpretation means that 'management development' requires not merely some *talk* with managers, but also a differing *organization* of bodies, materials and voices. The practical questions concern on one hand the scale of resources that we as outsiders are able to enrol, and on the other, the legitimacies that we as 'researchers' may be able to mobilize in articulating our actions. The research contribution itself is managerial.

Attention to both talk and the material organization of bodies and voices gives us our theatre metaphor. We build a set, mould masks and sew costumes, we script an action and block some moves, we perform—all of these at once, and two matinees at weekends. Whether or not a performance *looks* like a dance—it may need to look like monologue, farce, whatever—*producing* a performance always is. We tend to Brecht (maybe Artaud) rather than Stanislavsky. In order to be heard and seen we pay attention to the construction of theatres of action. In these spaces we go outside the obvious with people, and require them, if we can, to suspend their disbelief.

Such work is labour for an emergent institution. The labour consists of picking up pieces of ABC terrain and walking them to where they can be re-articulated with other bits of landscape. Activist monsters are *part of* as well as *on* a terrain. They move terrain by simultaneous de- and re-construction: become part of it, walk in other directions, pull the net along, snip some strands behind. These monsters stitch culture into new configurations with their own bodies and leavings; contours are shifted. The practice is a kind of cultural earthmoving. It's heavy work.

I spend a lot of time carrying stuff backwards and forwards

114

between ABC worlds and academic worlds—offering myself up to interrogation by sociology, philosophy, information systems methodology. I don't know whether Sisyphus or Hercules/Augeas is the more appropriate analogy; and if that's the choice, what the hell? Is it possible, even in principle, for any *academic* tradition to take the embodied nature of humans seriously enough to have developed a political economy and geography of symbolic action?

The terrain/performance duality, and its bodily grounding of language, can be explored in another way through the ambivalence of 'doing things differently'. Take the meaning aspect first. Activists must attend to meanings because we're interested in what moves us humans, blocks us, orientates us. We need to know: *Why don't we do more things different?* What are the sources of witting and unwitting conservatism? Humans clearly need to work with—*within*—traditions, if their lives are to be meaningful and manageable; how can we do this, yet produce lasting change? How are we to perform tradition in modern (postmodern?) times?[6] In this connection 'Why don't we do more things different?' directs attention to dialogue. Dialogue enables us to interpret and value actions outside the normal, and may even build a determination to perform them.

Because humans are embodied, meanings carry across the skin-to-skin interface only through material entitites. We call these symbols. So, shifting from the hermeneutic to the body aspect, the question becomes 'Why don't we do more *things* different?' Meaning-carrying things. Inevitably, tiny things—movements of muscle or molecules of air, pigment and pixel material. But also many more extended and durable things—costumes, rooms, cities; trucks and telegraphs; utensils, machines, document collections, computer systems. Why don't we do (make, place, inscribe) any or all of these kinds of things different than they, repetitively and historically, are? As symbol-processing machines, computers can live at the skin-to-skin interface, as some of the things closest to ourselves; the same entitites can also be some of the largest, most extended and intractable artefactual things in our material world (Star, 1992).

Concluding reflections—Cyborg research and rigorous myth work

As 'action researchers' we must be interested in the powers that invest themselves in action, which are so invisible that they are called 'culture'—the waters that human fish breathe. We must have the capability to talk powers rather than just meanings, and especially, our own repertoire of powers as meaning-workers in ABC.[7] Powers lie in the conjunctions of meanings and materials, but in academic discourses 'culture' often seems weak, idealist rather than materialist.

Power and culture lead us to myth. We have a fascination—a horrified fascination?—with how people can work with diverging interpretations of systems and situations and yet still in some sense it 'works' (Star, 1993; Star & Griesemer, 1989). Things get done. One way or another computer systems get built and used and some kind of stability or pattern sets in. Myths get reworked or created to legitimate what turns out; indeed, what gets constructed is always system *and* myth. Users get dumped on, techies get blamed, boys find toys, women stay marginal. How do we do it? What are the 'cultural' processes that produce and reproduce patterns through all the change? And how may we intentionally produce change that sticks? Karl Marx surely would have said: Academics have interpreted myth in various ways; the point for cyborg researchers, however, is to *work* it.

Myth-working might well be treated as performing in the dramatic sense. Modes ranging from storytelling (Hales, et al., 1994) through Situationist happenings to revolution might be studied for their specific dramatic rigour. This notion feels comfortable, dangerous, interesting; I look forward to a day when information system designers study Brecht and Piscator, or Peter Brook's *The Empty Space*, and job ads for business analysts and software project managers request 'at least three years street theatre experience'.

Just who do we think we are, to behave in the undisciplined ways I have illustrated and advocated? We are perhaps not cyborgs—in our ABC work we are not directly articulating 'technology' in the sense of computing artefacts—but we do operate within the reality incited by Donna Haraway's poem-like socialist-feminist manifesto, which presents activism as cyborg action (Haraway, 1991). Like her, we find we are monsters simply by engaging in struggles to become more human. It has become monstrous to treat consultancy, management, design or research as if they were *primarily* human ventures. Like Haraway, we accept that culture is where humans become deeply un-natural, and radical strangeness becomes both possible and necessary. The incompletely determined relationship between meanings and materials affords both danger and wonder, and constitutes the powers that we alone, as humans, have.

Notes

1 More on the project appears in Hales (1994a, 1994b) and Hales, Marsh and Sang (1994, in press).
2 We anticipate that a fifth 'slice' of culture—gender—will also be important, given the clerical framing of many of the activities in the sales order process and the archetypal masculine-instrumental rationality of the dominant occupational cultures in ABC—engineering and finance. Our interview sample was roughly balanced but we had no substantial research mapping of male-female differences of viewpoint. However, there is an element in our proposed design which allows gendered differences to be surfaced and worked during the programme itself, in particular projects in local companies.
3 It was the New Left and feminism that taught us to attend to people's life-worlds, rather than ethnomethodology.
4 I did postgraduate work in a university whose motto is: 'Be still and know'. In such a world, to struggle to *be active and know* is monstrous.
5 Mike Robinson (Robinson, 1991) uses the concept of 'double-level' languages to analyse success and failure in CSCW systems. The distinction made here is similar, though I have argued (Hales, 1994) that a three-level model makes better sense. Self-conscious focus on and action through language is characteristic of much activity in CSCW.
6 Hales (1993) offers a critique of the 'human centred systems' movement concerning its neglect of this difficulty, and the naturalization of culture and tradition.
7 Powers to, powers over, stored powers, powers as effects of structures, powers as performances (Law, 1991); and always in the plural.

Making space: a comparison of mathematical work in school and professional design practices

Rogers Hall and Reed Stevens

Abstract

Research accounts of mathematical and scientific competence play a central role in ongoing efforts to reorganize education. At the same time, new technologies change the character of work in settings where these competencies are learned and used. Two contemporary research programs—(1) cognitive science studies of expert versus novice skill and (2) interactional studies of scientific and technical practice—produce sharply diverging accounts of what competence is and how it develops. Cognitive science has been broadly accepted as a template for educational change, while relevant interactional perspectives have had little impact. We propose a synthetic approach that draws on both programs, illustrated with a comparative study of mathematical practices in design work. Starting with scenes in which groups of designers collaborate to make space for others, we restore material and social aspects of their work settings in an exploration of discipline-specific forms of competence. Our continuing project is to reassemble competence in terms of: (a) people's local representational practices, (b) their trajectories of participation within and across institutional settings, and (c) their capacity for managing social relations of accountability.

Experts' schemata contain a great deal of procedural knowledge, with explicit conditions for applicability. Novices' schemata may be characterized as containing sufficiently elaborate declarative knowledge about the physical configurations of a potential problem, but lacking abstracted solution methods. (Chi, Feltovich, and Glaser, 1981:151).

Rule 7. Before attributing any special quality to the mind or to the method of people, let us examine first the many ways through which inscriptions are gathered, combined, tied together and sent back. Only if there is something unexplained once the networks have been studied shall we start to speak of cognitive factors. (Latour, 1987:258).

When does mathematics emerge in the heterogeneous work of solving design problems? What mathematical practices develop for working out solutions to these problems? How do new technologies intended to support work give structure to people's mathematical activity? We are early in a research project that approaches these questions by contrasting the fine-grained activities of people doing design work in very different settings.

We start by entering two scenes where people are hard at work designing space for others. People in each scene consider a design in progress, calculation helps them to determine whether their efforts will satisfy pre-existing conditions, and much of their work is mediated through computer-aided design (CAD) tools. Apart from these similarities, however, we visit very different worlds for doing design and using mathematics. By opening with excerpts from dense interactional work in these worlds, we call into question who these people are, how or why they do design work in different ways, and what kinds of competence we or they find valuable.

Scene 1

At our first site, ParkPlace,[1] designers work in teams of three to five people around clusters of tables in a large, open room. The room is noisy enough to make audio recording difficult, since people move freely across groups, trading local gossip and technical assistance. Computer workstations connected by a local area network crowd the side walls, where teams assemble to view and modify designs. All the workstations share a single printer, leading to long printing queues and occasional friction between design teams trying to produce paper documents.

The four team members we follow are experienced users of CAD layout tools with features for simulating the energy requirements of a housing structure under different environmental conditions. They have just been asked to revise the unit floorplan for an undergraduate housing complex in Seattle, Washington, for use in the colder climate of Duluth, Minnesota. Their client must limit the combined building and heating costs over a 25-year period, and the design brief gives quantitative information about average seasonal temperatures from both sites. We enter their work as Norm hands control of the CAD system over to Teri[2]. Ed and Susan stand behind, generating alternatives that trade material (eg, insulation) against long-range heating costs. Rob and Barb (observing, but not team members) eventually offer help with calculations, and the segment ends as team members reconsider design alternatives in light of a round of calculation. This tight cycle of activity—choosing an alternative, implementing and evaluating it, then returning to consider new options—is typical.

[T4, 6/8/93] 11:08:29 to 11:10:20

Norm: Yo Teri.

Teri:	*takes mouse*
Norm: Are we . . . Ok. Um, TRY to **make** the inside temperature **not** as, not as . . . hot. Make [it cooler. A little bit cooler.	*L hand to **Inside Temp.** in Analysis Window . . . then to **Slider palette***
Ed: [Forty two per month is times [twelve months . . .	*head down, doing hand calculation*
Susan: [Well it has to be hot enough for . . . when it's winter.	*stands*
Norm: Not THAT cool!	*watches Teri set temperature*
Teri: Hhhha.	*bumps inside temperature from 12 C° to 19° C*

Two lines of work have started: Norm, Teri, and Susan pursue a livable, but efficient inside temperature; meanwhile, Ed starts hand calculations to determine heating cost for the dormitory over twenty five years. It will be difficult to bring these lines back together, since every change at the interface requires a new series of calculations from Ed, who is already lagging behind.

Norm: Enough.

Teri: About [there? . . . It's, where is it?

Norm: [Now update values, go **to** update.	*R hand to* **screen**
Teri: So where is [it? *Oh*, ok.	
Norm:	[*R hand to* **Update values**
Susan:	*looks around, walks away*
Ed: Times [twenty five . . .	*looks at Norm, then screen*
Norm: [Nineteen. Thirty eight dollars per month?	
Teri: Isn't that [more?	*looks at Norm*
Ed: [Twenty five years . . .	
Norm: **Design** cost? Is . . . Alright, thirty eight.	*R hand,* **towards** *screen*
Teri: It's the same	
Norm: What's twenty-five times twelve?	*looks at Ed*
Teri: It **went** up! It was like, wasn't it thirteen [before.	*L hand to* **Heating Cost** *in Analysis Window*

Norm: [Two hundred and ˙
    fifty, wait. (3 sec) That's
    three hundred, three hundred
    MONTHS?	

Susan:	*returns and sits*
Norm: Woh!	

The CAD system delivers the projected cost to heat this structure for a month, based on an average seasonal temperature that Norm and Ed have calculated earlier. Teri struggles to determine whether heating cost is rising or falling as a result of changing inside temperature. Norm asks Ed for a partial calculation (ie, 'What's twenty five times twelve?'), but he then uses oral calculation to produce a twenty five year heating cost on his own.

Teri: **That'd** be like, thirty
    eight, that'd be like . . .
    about . . . a hundred
    thousand dollars!
	L hand to **Heating Cost**
	
	looking at Norm

Norm: A hundred thousand a, oh COOL! NO, no, no, no. Look, it's **only** eighty thousand.	*looks at Ed's calculation* *L hand points to **Heating Cost***
Teri: No, [**no** . . .	*L hand to **Heating Cost***
Rob: [Tell you what, you all holler stuff and I'll, I'll do calculations over here.	*all turn to R*
Barb: Rob? [Here's one I've got (a calculator).	*off camera*
Rob: [If you want to know a number . . . Oh, ok. Here you go.	*hands over calculator*
Norm: Ok . . . Thank you.	*picks up calculator*
Ed: If it's forty two . . .	
Teri: So, uh . . . you **do** thirty eight times . . . twelve.	*points at **Analysis Window***
Norm: Time . . . Oh, no, no, no. It's, [um . . . It's twelve times twenty five . . . Right?	*keys values into calculator*
Ed: [That's PER MONTH!	

As Norm and Teri begin reading values from the interface and entering them into a calculator, Ed drops his paper-and-pencil calculation and attempts to re-enter the conversation. He starts to offer a result (ie, 'If it's forty two . . .'), but it comes from an earlier state of this fast moving design!

Norm: I think it's three hundred. Yeh, I was right. Times thirty eight. (3 sec)	
Ed. If it's forty two dollars it'll be twelve [	*looks down at brief*
Norm: [AHHHH!	*sharp intake of breath*
Teri: See?	

Norm: It's WAY more. These [cheapskates! We're gonna **have** to make the design costs less.	*points to **Design Cost** in* *interface*
Teri: [I **know**. I wanna, do . . .	*hands frame **screen***
Susan: We need some (more winter) . . .	
Teri: How about [. . . This is a cheap college!	
Susan: [It's fourteen dollars over.	

In Duluth's colder temperature, the housing unit will exceed the client's budget. Susan watches intermittently and notices that they are not far from what the brief requires. The scene ends as the team, less Ed, considers how to lower building costs.

Teri: Maybe (littler windows).	*looks from calculator to screen*
Norm: How about we **make**, delete THAT door. We **don't** need two windows, I mean two doors.	*R hand to **door** in floorplan,* *then palm **up***
Susan: We don't (inaudible)	*leaning in*
Teri: We don't need that **many** windows either!	*R hand **sweeps** floorplan*
Norm: Yeh, alright. **Delete** a door.	*R hand points at **screen***
Susan: Why don't you just **take** away one window in each room?	*R hand points at **screen***

Scene 2

At our second site, OutBack, the work space is arranged in a series of semi-enclosed cubicles, each belonging to an individual, and workstations in these cubicles are linked through a local area

network. The cubicle we enter is quiet, though work is interrupted by intermittent phone calls and conversations with passing
coworkers. Again designers share a printer, this time housed in a
separate plotting room.

Jake and Evan return to a roadway design after several
months of working on different projects. Their earlier design
needs to be revised in light of new information about the development site, and the client has asked them to reorganize roadway
and site preparation in a phased plan of work. As we enter, Jake
and Evan are reacquainting themselves with the project.

[OB2 8/13/93] 5:01:40 to 05:08:34

Jake: I'm wary of just yankin'
the numbers off in five
minutes, and [I almost
feel that if we just

Evan: [Right. Refresh
ourselves or something?

Jake: Well almost just went   *folds sheets back, straightens*
through, right. Just at least   *those underneath*
look at the sections or
something. But . . . I don't
know.

Evan: OK (inaudible) (7 sec) I   *rolls out profile of road, points*
almost ALWAYS put a   *to **label** in top right*
label on them.
[20 sec. Later]
I remember you were, yeh,
you pretty much left it up to
me. You said, you know,
just . . . you know, get   *edge of R hand moves **along***
something, we went with a   ***profile***
MAX slope here, and that's
what I did, then I printed
what one of those.

Jake: Actually, I think **this** is   *little finger on **road** in profile*
even . . . Now thinking back
I think we went with MORE
than fifteen percent.

Evan: On this one?

Jake: Yeh. **Yeh**, hah . . . cause   *looks **up**, stands, and walks*
do you remember didn't we   *across room to get calculator*
find that fifteen percent just   *from desk*
wasn't gonna . . .

They discover an unusually steep road, and as the action continues (below) Jake takes a 'look' by reading quantities from scales along the vertical and horizontal margins of the profile view and using his calculator to find the slope.

Evan: I remember, I think I
remember being really
concerned about it.

Jake: **Let** me just look.   *L hand points to **margin** of*
Nhhhhha, forty two point   *profile while R hand keys in*
one minus . . . five . . .   *numbers*
Yeah, we went twenty
percent. (3 sec) [You
remember?   *writes 20% on profile near road*

   L hand traces across from
   margin as R hand writes
   numbers

Evan: [Ohh! Yeahaha, I
remember. (3 sec) I re . . .
ah remember not thinking
that they were too serious
about it, at that time.

Jake: (13 sec)   *Circles two margin quantities,*
   then keys these in to check the
   calculation.

Umm, nineteen and a half,   *glasses off, rubbing eyes*
whatever. (3 sec) Well that's
alright, we can just . . . note
that. (sighs) HAhh.

Evan: That's the city criteria?

Jake: Yeah . . . city design
guidelines. It's fifteen percent

max on, on uh . . . collector
roadways. Secondaries they
allow you to go steeper. I
think they actually allow you   *looks at E*
to go to twenty.

Evan: OK, OK . . . we::ll . . .

Jake: But that's alright.

With an anomalous roadway before them, the work to make
this situation 'alright' quickly gets complicated. Jake begins a
search for specific images across multiple documents. Indexing
these documents with outstretched hands, he gives a coordinated
reading of selected images in terms of how much dirt will need to
be 'cut' out of the existing site.

Evan: Yeh, I think we were   *R hand points up from **lower***
shootin' way up out of **there**.   ***right** of profile*

Jake: *(5 sec)* Yeah, this huh   *R hand points below road at*
road (laughing) is a, is a, a   *center of profile*
uh . . . STRETCH. You
know? (6 sec) It's gonna be
brutal man, twenty percent   *writes 400, 450 350, 500 below*
for . . . for ah . . . fifteen   *road at center of profile*
hundred feet (laughs)

Evan: Other**wise** you'd be up   *R hand to **upper left** in profile,*
here and **you'd** have to cut   *then **sweeps right** and then **left***
way across, [shhoo . . .   *above road*

Jake: [Ri::ght. (4 sec) **Well**   *R pencil to **top right** of profile*
you know what it was, is . . .
(4 sec) Ummm . . . up at this   *flips into stack for plan with*
end of the canyon . . .   *topo map*

We really wanted to   *L hand points above **concave***
avoid . . . the **slopes** are so   ***segment** of proposed road*
steep, we wanted to
avoid . . . getting into a lot
of cut . . . although that
doesn't **seem** right, cause we're *L finger **sweeps up** and down*
on that side of the low point.   *over road*   -

Where's the plan with the station? . . . What'd we do with that?

with Evan, flips up views from the stack, then pulls out a rolled document

Evan:

R hand circling over plan view . . .

You **want** to know about, this station, right?

*L hand to **road** at lower right of plan view*

Jake: Yeah. See like right here (7 sec)

layers profile and plan with topo

Like **right** at sixteen fifty or so . . . like right at **this** corner, we're actually gonna cut, we're gonna have to, hhnn . . . we're gonna have to . . . **take** down this side of this anyways, you [see that?

*L hand to profile **margin** then to **road** in plan*

*R pencil **shades** region above concave road in plan*

Evan: [(xx), yeh.

Jake first explains that they wanted to avoid 'a lot of cut' into an adjacent hillside. However, by orienting to topographic features in the plan view and coordinating this reading with a relevant section view, he⁻ realizes that even their anomalous grade will require cut and pursues a different explanation.

Jake: But, um . . . That will be like . . . **it's** just in this one area. So it'll be **somethin'** like this, you know, this.

*R pencil **erases** shading then draws a **dashed convex line** above concave road in plan*

But then **see here**, I think what was goin' on is, I think here,

*L hand to **top of hill** in profile*

This **is all** . . . trees, [right?

*R pencil **circles** roadway left of dashed area in plan*

Evan: [Um, hm.

Jake: And so the reason we did, we kept, see even at the top we're in ff, we're not in cut, on either side. And I think it was, was **because this is all trees** And if you get, if you cut even five feet **you're gonna chase** grade all the way up on both sides.

L hand remains at top of hill in profile
*R pencil **circles** same roadway in plan*

*R pencil **sweeps up then down** from roadway in plan*

Evan: Yeh.

R pencil beats table

Jake: And you're gonna **have to** grade the whole slope, or else put in a wall. (3 sec) So . . . I think that's what was driving this design, is **RIGHT when you drop** into this canyon you get into the trees on both sides.

*R pencil **hashes above** and below*

*L to **top of hill** in profile*

*R pencil **circles roadway** in plan*

Jake's new explanation frames the anomaly against a greater evil: they were 'gonna chase grade' up two hillsides and denude a forested canyon area. He then recapitulates for Evan.

[8 sec. Later]

Jake: We didn't, the real **key here** was to keep outa cut up at the high end of the canyon. And **also we were**, remember, if you look at the sections . . . The other thing is, um . . . Sort of again, I mean I'm gonna have to take some time and go over this with Ted but, you know, this, it was the same thing when . . . If you look at the sections, like **here** we're in a lot of fill. But let's look at **twenty three fifty**, because the **canyon's COMIN'** up HARD on both sides,

*R pencil taps **top of roadway** in profile*

*R pencil to **centre of roadway** in profile*

*R pencil below **centre of roadway** in profile*

*R pencil to **profile margin** . . . hands up in **sharp V** from table*

so **the actual** . . . area of grading is gonna be . . . **you**

know, not that significant. You [know what I'm saying?	*R pencil to* **roadway** *in plan with stations, then* **roadway** *in plan with*
Evan: [Right. Right, it's just, it's just a . . . right.	
Jake: **Cause it's gonna be** like this . . . BOOM.	*R pencil draws* **section view** *in plan with stations*
Evan: Quick fill.	
Jake: Right.	*unrolls section view*
Evan: Deep, but, not encompassing a lot of area.	
Jake: Right	*lays sections out*
Evan:	*points to section Jake just sketched*

Drawing a section view of the canyon, Jake shows that filling dirt below the roadbed is 'not that significant.' When Evan tentatively counters that fill will be 'brutal' (below), Jake strengthens the case and reminds him of their desire to preserve the existing hillside.

Jake: Right. See look **at that** . . . That's only (3 sec) a [hundred . . .	*R pencil sweeps* **horizontal axis** *of section*
Evan: [(laughs) **That's brutal**, huh? Well, I don't know . . . [maybe not.	*L hand* **below roadbed** *in section*
Jake: [(Yeh. (3 sec) Well, but . . . look at it THIS way. You can **have THIS** . . .	*R points below* **roadbed** *in section*
or you can **have THIS**. Big deal, right? Little bit **less fill** down here, and what that buys you is [at the **other end** . . . you're ripping down the **whole** side of the hillside.	*R draws* **new roadbed** *under proposed, then* **again for** *section below* *R pencil points* **up and out** *from table, then* **beats**

Re-embedding scenes from work

We have presented dense streams of talk and activity, without identifying the 'types of people' who produce them, to problematize images of competence from very different research traditions: cognitive science and interactional studies[3] of scientific and technical work. How can we follow the development of competence in relations between design activity, mathematics emerging in that activity, and forms of technology that give structure to both in different institutional settings? Our project compares a team of seventh graders at work on the design of living space (Scene 1) with a pair of civil engineers at work on the design of a large housing development (Scene 2).

Cognitive science and interactional studies of science and technology differ markedly in (1) where they locate competence in theory, (2) how they use people, problems, and activity to do this, and (3) what they hope to understand about how competence develops (ie, learning). To define competence in terms of *different mental structures* held by representative 'experts' and 'novices', cognitive scientists take individuals out of naturally occurring settings and compare their work on experimentally equivalent 'tasks'. Learning is operationalized as the acquisition of specific mental structures (eg, skills and strategies), which are evident among experts but are missing, inaccurate, or impoverished among novices (eg, Anderson, 1990; Chi, Feltovich and Glaser, 1981; Larkin, Simon, et al., 1980). To define competence in terms of the *shared work of people* in specific social settings, interactional studies of science and technology follow the practical activity of people who find and solve their own problems where they actually work. Learning is less at issue, since people appear as fully developed, competent members of these settings (eg, Knorr-Cetina, 1981; Lynch, 1990; Suchman and Trigg, 1993).

It should be no surprise that cognitive science is broadly accepted as a charter for reorganizing education (Breuer, 1993), even though research in this tradition selectively deletes (Star, 1983) phenomena that interactional studies tell us are central to competent scientific or technical activity: the historical durability of material in settings where people work (Fujimura, 1987; Star and Griesemer, 1989), the indexical nature of work as a shared activity (Coulter, 1991), and a broader view of learning as managing social trajectories across institutional settings (Traweek, 1988). Neither approach gives an adequate account of *both* competent activity in specific settings *and* how people learn to be competent as they move between settings of school and work. We need an approach that combines strengths from each line of research. Our continuing project is as follows: (1) to expand a comparative logic between individuals (ie, experts versus novices) into a comparison between settings where this competence is attributed, (2) to merge analyses of material and social interaction with specific attention to the disciplinary content of people's work, and (3) to focus on how people make the transition between school and work.

In the next two sections we explore the local, interactional work of being technically competent in school or in the workplace, and then attempt to show how this work is stretched in different ways over longer developmental trajectories and forms of social accountability.

Making space for a grade: middle school mathematics

As Scene 1 ends, four seventh grade students lean into a computer display and discuss ways to lower design costs when resiting a dormitory from Seattle to Duluth. They are table mates and, along with other groups of students, we have followed them for over a month as they designed a structure in which scientists could 'winter over' along the Antarctic coast. The dormitory design problem is their final activity in an applications-oriented mathematics curriculum (MMAP, 1992); it is also a working prototype for a 'performance-based assessment' in which competence is evaluated directly in activity rather through indirect indicators of individual capacity (Resnick and Resnick, 1991; Woolf, Bixby and Gardner, 1991). Each design team receives a brief asking for a dormitory unit that costs no more than $100,000 to build and heat over a twenty five year period. They are given 30 minutes to revise the existing dormitory floorplan and present their proposal to a 'client,' represented here by a member (Rob) of our curriculum development team.

As expected by this assessment, 'design' should appear when students become familiar with the Seattle floorplan, decide on a way to model annual temperature and heating costs, modify either the structure or materials of the dormitory to satisfy the design brief, and then present their proposal to a client. 'Mathematics' of a particular sort (NCTM, 1989) should appear when students estimate outside temperature at either site, reorganize floor area and/or material costs when modifying the dormitory, compare combined costs to build and heat the new structure with constraints given in the design brief, and explain their approach to the client's representative. What students actually do, of course, gets organized in different ways.

Achieving a view of designed space

Students look through different representational forms to 'see' a dormitory, its use, and its cost to heat in a colder climate. Some of these forms are 'imported'—i.e., they arrive with the curriculum environment[4]—while others are 'domestic' to the setting. As students select and assemble multiple forms, divisions of labour arise, creating opportunities for students to appear more or less competent at design and mathematics.

Figure 1 shows a CAD screen in which imported forms are layered over a scaled floorplan to represent a dormitory for student designers. The system (ArchiTech©) supports three modes of classroom activity: (a) a palette of design 'Tools' (not shown) lets students draw a three-story floorplan model with walls, windows, doors, and different types of furniture; (b) a column of 'Sliders' (top left) lets students manipulate global design parameters; and (c) an 'Analysis' window (below centre) lets students select and display the value of quantities. Updated values for different versions of a design can be saved in a table within the Analysis window and exported to a spreadsheet running as a background process. Students supplement these representations with a surprising variety of domestic forms: paper sketches, gestural manipulations of designed space, oral and hand-written calculation, calculation with hand-held calculators, and spontaneous narratives that create evaluative frameworks for design decisions—eg, dealing with university administrators who are 'cheapskates' or managing sleeping and bathing arrangements in a co-educational residence.

In slightly less than two minutes, students in Scene 1 explore how the dormitory unit will behave in a colder environment, then arrive at a collective strategy for satisfying the design brief that trades building against heating costs. Teri, Norm, and Susan start the scene in a 'Sliders' view of the floorplan, as Teri lowers the

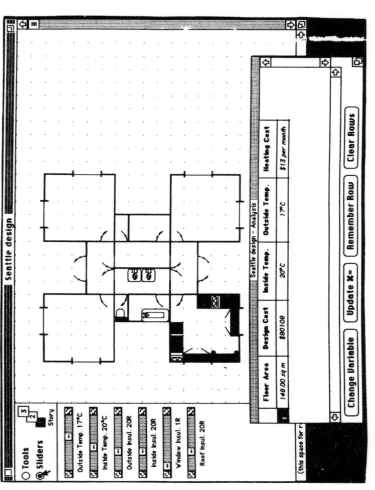

Figure 1 A screen image showing the dormitory unit floorplan provided to ParkPlace designers.

average inside temperature. The slider control for temperature is more than a dial on a black box—it sets a condition on living during a projected season (ie, Susan's 'hot enough . . . for when it's winter'), and that condition clearly can be violated as Teri scrolls through alternative values (ie, Norm's 'Not THAT cool!'). As these students work through the interface to create a colder environment, Ed starts a parallel series of hand calculations that follow directly from the client's restriction on total cost. Although precise, Ed's slow-moving calculations quickly diverge from the others' work, so that by the time he has a result in hand (ie, Ed says, 'If it's forty two dollars . . .'), his team mates are already working on a different 'dormitory'. They have changed the design (reset Inside Temperature), re-evaluated its behavior in Duluth (updated the display, obtaining a new Heating Cost), and produced a series of oral calculations that estimate the current combined costs.

Within this simple round of calculation, how should attributions of competence be distributed among these students? First, they do not use a spreadsheet available in the environment and so do not produce the kind of well-ordered, comparative investigation of how cost varies with outside temperature that would be easy to identify as mathematical reasoning. Focusing on the distribution of activity in what they actually do, we might evaluate Ed's relatively clumsy hand calculations as a lack of design or mathematical skill, by comparison with Norm and Teri's flexible oral arithmetic (Nunes, Schliemann, and Carraher, 1993) that keeps pace with the group's design activities. Alternately, it could be that the tools available push some people into less obviously fruitful activity, while giving others centre stage in displays of competence. Later in the team's work on this design problem, for example, Ed picks up the calculator and correctly finds a composite cost that satisfies the design brief, a critical contribution that brings great relief to his team mates. Rather than an exclusive attribute of individuals, we regard competence as a collective achievement in the setting, where both the performers and we, as curriculum designers or cultural observers, are implicated.

When is a design a problem?

Just as we stretch attributions of competence over multiple forms, actors, and observers in a collective activity, we also want to consider people's activity inside the longer temporal trajectories that give them meaning. The dormitory activity both has an internal structure and is an event inside broader trajectories in students' careers. The dense interaction and parallel streams of work inside Scene 1 are one among many 'design structures' (Schon, 1990) that students actively construct. In this case, several lines of calculation converge to reframe the design problem as a tradeoff between changing types of material (eg, Susan proposes, 'take away one window in each room') and increasing the insulating properties of existing materials. Students pursue both strategies and reach a 'solution' just as time expires.

Looking out onto school life, this activity is one element in several encompassing student trajectories: (1) Re-siting the dormitory finishes two months of student design work, and they clearly interpret the event as a performance of their joint capacity to develop a proposal under quantitative constraints; (2) moving into the eighth grade, some of these students will make a transition into 'algebra' coursework, where they will be expected to acquire a generalized perspective on quantity (eg, functions) and facility with symbolic and graphical forms (eg, variables, equations, and Cartesian graphs); and (3) approaching high school, the design team participates in an educational program for 'gifted and talented' students, and this affiliation may help them to enter highly competitive, private secondary schools. These embedded trajectories, from local interaction to matriculation across institutions, make up students' academic careers. As they move forward with an accumulated record of accomplishments, these trajectories may lead some students into distinguished work settings like OutBack (Scene 2). However, as their school counselor puts it to students, 'YOU make the record, I SEND it . . . you can't wake up one day and think . . . oh yeah, I wanna be an engineer . . .' [Fieldnote, 2/23/93].

What matters, and to whom?

Making it to the end of the period, a math project, the school year, or a junior high school career are not just temporal intervals. Along various trajectories that include the placement of a hypothetical dormitory, different relations of accountability appear for students concerning the quality and direction of their work.

For example, moving into algebra means passing through a standardized 'readiness' test that all students take. Ed, despite his capacity for assembling quantities under the right technical circumstances (eg, using a calculator), does not pass this barrier during our field trial. Instead, he continues with general math instruction while his team mates move into pre-algebra or algebra instruction in the eight grade. Ed also loses his position in the mathematical activities of a 'gifted and talented' cohort of students, further disrupting possible trajectories into technical subject matter or private school.

Members of this design team also have design-relevant capabilities that are not part of the official mathematics curriculum. For example, Norm is known as a skilled illustrator. He comes in during lunch to use graphics software and, surrounded by his delighted peers, draws hugely-muscled cartoon characters. Ed is likewise known for unusual skill in perspective drawing, and a line drawing that he made during an architectural field trip has been selected by a local church for inclusion in their public literature.

While these kinds of activities bring acknowledgment from peers and teachers, they are specific skills with little value in the more indirect, decontextualized assessment cycles of middle school mathematics. Deeply consequential judgments about individual competence are extracted from collective activity: they shape who Ed's peers and teachers are, what kind of mathematical work he is expected to do, and the character of his daily environment for doing that work. These institutionalized forms of accountability take students out of activity and pass them through a sorting device (Mehan, 1992) that simultaneously measures everything about the individual (from some curricular perspective) and nothing at all about whether or not they should become designers or mathematicians.

Making space for a living: civil engineering

Civil engineers also assemble heterogeneous representational forms to view designed space, manage overlapping temporal trajectories through the surrounding organization, and shape their work in relations of accountability that extend across these trajectories. Inside a large architectural engineering firm, Jake is a project manager with ten years of experience, and Evan is a staff engineer out of school for just over three years. Their work during our observations ranges from the layout of a parking lot to planning a 650 unit housing development (underway in Scene 2).

Our expectations about 'design' and 'mathematics' in OutBack are less certain than for school, drawing in part on studies that contrast design practice with professional or technical standards (Bucciarelli, 1988; Cuff, 1991; Henderson, 1991; Schon, 1990). Whether designers treat clients' interests as constraints, whether progress is linearly organized, whether or not mathematics is used to settle or justify design tradeoffs, and how technology supports this work are open empirical questions for us and for them.

Taking a look, making space

Imported and domestic representational forms are also mixed together when viewing projected[5] space at OutBack. The CAD environment imports a variety of forms that make up what Jake and Evan call 'model space'. While they say this roadway design project is 'ideal' for using CAD tools, they spend little of their time at the computer screen. Instead, they print and work with 'paper space' views of the design, a necessary arrangement they say blocked early adoption of CAD tools before the arrival of affordable, high-speed printers.

Paper space views (see Figure 2) include: (a) a 'profile' view of roadway elevation relative to the existing site surface, (b) 'plan' views of the roadway that 'snake' through this surface, and (c) 'section' views that 'slice through' a proposed roadway at fifty foot intervals to show areas where the client will need to 'cut' or 'fill' earth. Different paper views project the same space through a common set of conventions in which quantities label displacement from surveying 'stations' and measured elevation—eg, at 16 + 00 in both profile and section views, existing elevation at the centre line of the proposed roadway is 581 feet above sea level. The CAD system imports other forms that Jake and Evan seldom use, like a 3D wireframe view of the site and file versioning conventions to help keep track of design history. Instead they work around (Gasser, 1986) these features in other ways: Jake inspects the lay of the land and foliage by using a panoramic assembly of site photographs taken one sunny weekend with his personal camera; Jake and Evan rummage through boxes of rolled paper space views from ongoing projects to find current versions of their design.

The central work of Scene 2 is to explain why a proposed roadway is steeper than city code allows. Jake starts to 'look' in

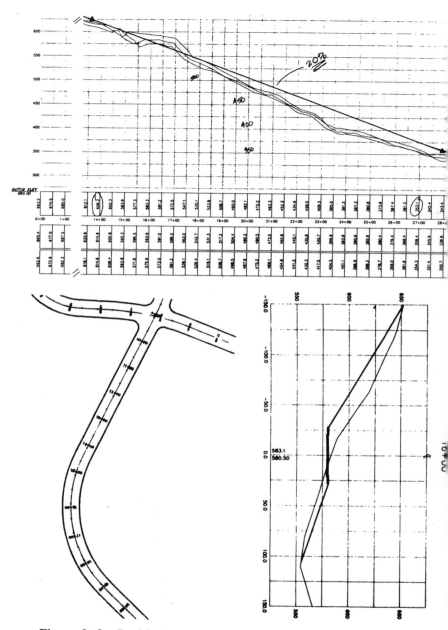

Figure 2 OutBack's 'paper space' views of a proposed roadway: (a) the 'profile view' of elevation, (b) a 'plan and station view' from above, and (c) a 'section' taken at regular offsets from a 'station'.

a profile view, pulling elevation quantities from the left margin into his calculator to compute the road's slope as rise over run (ie, twenty per cent). He then flips through a stack of paper views, indexed by a tiled arrangement of their bottom margins. By selecting regions from the site, rolling obscuring paper out of the way, and holding his fingers on linked views of projected space, Jake is able to narrate and manually illustrate an explanation. Designing a road that was less steep would force the developer to 'chase grade all the way up both sides' of a forested canyon. When Evan tentatively evaluates the resulting fill as 'brutal,' Jake makes free-hand drawings that compare a 'little bit less fill down here' and 'ripping down the whole side of the hillside' above.

Making space in time

Rather than stripping design activity out of the lived, temporal structures of practice (eg, Chan, 1990; Goel and Pirolli, 1992), we examine the meaning of Jake and Evan's reconstructed design rationale as one line of work inside enclosing trajectories of personal, organizational, and professional competence.

Noticing an anomalous road and reconstructing its rationale, Jake and Evan 'refresh' themselves on this project after a six month delay. During this period, the developer and the city have been negotiating who will complete an expensive environmental impact report that is necessary for moving the development along. Having decided to 'drop back' in the face of municipal opposition, the developer now wants changes in the design (eg, removing a road that cuts through unstable slopes) and asks for cost estimates in a phased plan of work. After months of inactivity on this project, an external deadline requires that Jake and Evan work through the coming weekend.

Scene 2 is one among many elements in organizational and professional trajectories of engineering work. Jake is about to 'hand off' the project to another manager (Ted), and so needs to provide a defensible account of its current state. Since the housing development will take another five years to complete, its accumulated historical commitments (ie, design decisions and technical documentation) will pull other engineers into scenes where they too must 'refesh (them)selves' by assembling views from the CAD system (Strauss, 1988). This requires technical skills that neither Jake nor Evan learned in school, and that many of their more senior coworkers do not have at all. Since their largest clients now require that design documents be prepared using CAD software, pressure to adopt these tools across the organization is growing. Jake recounts the company president announcing, 'five years from now, if you don't know CAD, there won't be a place for you here.' CAD technology has momentum at OutBack: engineers are joining a user support group (Gannt and Nardi, 1992), workspace is regularly cut apart to accommodate an evolving hardware infrastructure, and engineers talk about projects as they and their 'paper space' views queue up in the plotting room.

What matters, and to whom?

Along each of these trajectories engineers are accountable to shifting relations with clients, local governments, their employer, and coworkers. Being a competent designer in and out of Scene 2 involves keeping the interests of multiple actors present and accurately anticipating the reception of one's work in relation to these interests. To be accountable to a client and the city, code violations are traded against a greater evil of denuding entire hillsides in a forested region of the development site. Being accountable to a new project manager leads Jake to construct a decisively-illustrated account of the anomalous grade. If adopted, this justification will also need to convince others in the developer's organization and the city. Managing all these interests and their own standards of good engineering, Jake and Evan sacrifice 'balancing the site' (ie, optimizing the ratio of total cut and fill) to minimize environmental impact.

Because Jake and Even interact with people to whom they are accountable, their design practice does not sensibly reduce to a cognitive process of managing 'constraints' extracted from 'information' in the environment. What their work means, how it is structured in time, and whether or not it is carried out in a competent fashion depends on actively managing these shifting relations of accountability. The seemingly mundane activity of 'refreshing ourselves' turns out to be essential along multiple trajectories: Jake and Evan reconstruct the existing state of the project, Jake develops an explanation for possible trouble with municipal codes, and he tries to make sure that Even will carry this rationale forward when 'handing off' the project to another manager within the company.

Discussion

Our excursion into widely different scenes from design work creates more questions than it answers. Comparing seventh graders and civil engineers encourages us to look carefully at the progress of design, mathematics, and computing technology *in situ* before assigning competence (or incompetence) to anyone on the basis of (a) their institutional authority, (b) *a priori* commitments to 'right' problems and 'correct' solutions, or (c) decontextualized accounts of what individuals 'know' about design, mathematics, or CAD tools. But if we suspend fixed accounts of authority, problems solved, and the contents of individual minds (Bloor, 1991), how can we reassemble competent activity across these scenes?

Our approach is to reassemble competence out of local representational practices, trajectories of participation within and across institutional settings, and the means by which participants manage social relations of accountability. We hope to span micro and meso levels of analysis (Cicourel, 1981; Clarke and Gerson, 1990; Mehan, 1990) in understanding the development of competence in interactional terms. Although we are early in the project, several areas of contrast appear promising for further work.

Design as indexical work

Rather than defining a contrast in competence, interactional work across these scenes is comparable in being densely 'ordinary' (Sacks, 1984), necessarily 'indexical' in making up locally-relevant activity (Coulter, 1991), and collectively 'muscular' in its achievement (McDermott et al., 1978). These interactional features are missing or, at best, theoretically peripheral to stripped-down comparisons of 'experts' or 'novices' coming out of cognitive science (Suchman, 1987). These features of work in design or mathematics are important but they are uniformly present among both students (Amerine and Bolmes, 1990; Lynch, to appear) and adults. At the micro level, people appear to be working as hard as they can to be competent students, designers, employees, etc. We need these details to understand how competence develops, but we also need a great deal more.

Both students and engineers assemble representational forms to project views of space, but their work surfaces and projected activities are different. In ParkPlace, design activity and computing are relative newcomers, and the computer screen appears as a dominant surface for displaying design or mathematical competence (eg, Norm and Teri's rapid oral calculations track a fast-moving dormitory design). In this context, work on paper can actually lead people out of the activity (eg, Ed's hand calculations from a previous state of the computer display). In OutBack, integrated computing environments are a recent addition to entrenched design activity, and the computer screen sits further at the periphery. Support staff go to the computer to produce paper documents or implement changes in a design. But the actual work of design is carried out on paper surfaces that are more flexible (Henderson, 1991, this volume) in several senses: design alternatives can be rendered prior to making them public for coworkers or clients, workers can navigate rapidly through selected regions of 'model space', and gestures produced over the paper surface can hold multiple views stable while design alternatives are projected into spatial and narrative forms (eg, Jake's elaborate illustration of how an alternative design denudes a hillside). In both settings, the routine work of being competent is simultaneously *displaced* and *augmented* by the introduction of computing.

Representational practices for design and mathematics

Uptake and use of structuring resources (Lave, 1988:98–100) like talk, gesture, and paper or screen images are organized in different representational practices for managing space and quantity. In school,[6] talk and pointing at the screen support movement between relatively flat (ie, a floorplan) and personal (eg, gaining access to a bathroom) views of space. Quantities are changed in the interface to manipulate a design, then readout of the display and haltingly used in calculations to judge progress. At work, talk and activity with paper support views of space that are layered (ie, elevation, offset, and topological perspectives) and constructive (eg, 'snaking' a road through existing terrain). Quantities that appear in talk reflect this more complex geometry, and are used by engineers for many purposes: to index selected regions of the site, to move between perspectives, and to judge the consequences of design alternatives.

Representations are used to project design alternatives forward in both settings, but the complexity and relevance of these 'scenarios' for collective activity (Suchman and Trigg, 1993) are quite different. Understanding how these practices develop, how their appearance in school can be made relevant to participation in the workplace, and the role that emerging technologies can play in this transition are critical issues in the intersection between studies of practice, learning, and teaching (Lave and Wenger, 1991).

Organizational settings for competence

Our comparative analysis looks to activity in settings, rather than to individuals, for an account of what competence is and how it develops. In taking this approach, we are trying to embed specific representational practices in broader temporal trajectories of participation and then to consider how relations of accountability within these trajectories are managed. Two strong contrasts between settings for school and work appear relevant from this perspective: (1) institutional interpretations of different forms of competence and (2) the capacity of participants to shape the reception of their work by others.

In keeping with recent approaches to learning that draw from activity theory (Engestrom, 1989; Lave, 1988; Rogoff, 1990), both settings provide material and social support for the development of varied forms of competence. These appear when technical skills are distributed across coworkers, when domestic and imported forms are assembled by different people to 'black box' complex or tedious calculations (Latour, 1987), and when coworkers respond adaptively to situations where these forms break down in use. In school, these activities produce a range of opportunities for displaying competence (eg, drawing, calculating, or reframing design structures), but students' contributions to collective achievements are often overlooked in service of sorting individuals into standard curricular trajectories (eg, that Ed's just-in-time calculation completes the dormitory assessment or that his exceptional perspective drawings have a life outside of school). At work, varied forms of competence are more readily accepted (Becker, 1972), and differences or breakdowns sometimes become opportunities for learning in work shared between newcomers and old timers (eg, Jake reframes Evan's characterization of roadway fill from 'brutal' to 'no big deal').

A related organizational difference between school and work is the degree to which people can anticipate and actively shape the reception of their work prior to judgments about individual or collective competence. Recipient design of one's activity is possible in school through informal channels, which close during formal cycles of assessment for the purpose of evaluating individual achievements. At least in OutBack, shaping the reception of one's work appears to be a primary activity for engineers, extending out from relations with primary clients to municipal review boards and even construction workers at a development site.

While we are beginning to understand how people learn through participation in activity *within* particular settings (Hutchins, 1990; Jacoby and Gonzales, 1991; Lave and Wenger, 1991), we still know relatively little about how different forms of participation produce individual trajectories *across* settings. This is particularly true of transitions between school and work, where we have detailed accounts of how the construction of personal identity reproduces structures like social class (eg, Eckert, 1989) but nothing comparable on how students create and follow trajectories into specific, professional communities of practice. Reframing competence as a comparison across specific settings for school and work is a start in this direction.

Acknowledgements

We thank members of the Representational Practices group at Berkeley for help with analysis of these materials: Steve Adams, Robyn Battle, Rick Berg, Ming Chiu, Rodrigo Madanes, Susan Newman, and Bruce Sherin. We have also learned a great deal in conversations with Bev Bushey, Jim Greeno, Laura Kerr, Jeremy Roschelle, and Karen Wieckert. Finally, we thank Leigh Star for encouragement and editorial assistance throughout. This work has been supported by a National Science Foundation award to the Institute for Research on Learning and a Committee on Research award from the University of California at Berkeley. Opinions expressed are those of the authors and not necessarily those of the NSF or the University.

Notes

1 Study sites and participants are given pseudonyms throughout this report.
2 Turns at talk follow down the left column, and gesture/activity is described in

the right column. Co-occuring utterance and gestural stroke (McNeill, 1992; Schegloff, 1984) are in bold type. Transcript conventions: overlapping turns start with left brackets [; EMPHATIC talk is in upper-case; ellipses . . . show pauses of less than three seconds; and longer pauses or ambiguous utterances appear in parentheses.

3 We follow Star (to appear) in combining symbolic interactionism, ethnomethodology, anthropological studies of practice, distributed cognition, and activity theory within a broad approach to the study of human interaction.

4 Distinguishing between imported and domestic forms makes gaps between intended and realized use visible—eg, in computer-based social movements (Kling and Iaccono, 1988) like the 'paper-less office' or alignments between 'official' and 'lived' versions of school curricula (Lemke, 1990).

5 We use 'projected' in two senses: (1) selected features of the actual development site are projected onto screen and paper displays to give a nearly continuous three dimensional surface, and (2) proposed objects like 'collector roadways' or housing plots are projected into this model to assemble a development plan.

6 We use general terms for school and work only to propose that our analysis can be carried into other cases (Ragin, 1992) in an expanding program of research.

Contextualization, cognitive flexibility, and hypertext: the convergence of interpretive theory, cognitive psychology, and advanced information technologies

Robert Alun Jones and Rand J. Spiro

Abstract

Contextualization—particularly as exemplified in the history of social and political theory—has been the predominant theme in intellectual historiography for the last quarter of a century. In particular, pragmatists like Quentin Skinner and Richard Rorty have encouraged us to view the text as having as many meanings as there are contexts within which the text might be placed, and the contexts themselves as reflecting the special interests and purposes of the interpreter. Meanwhile, scholars in the humanities have been relatively slow to apply advanced information technologies to the problem of interpreting such texts; but the emergence of more powerful hypertext systems has led writers like George Landow and Jay Bolter to suggest a convergence between this technology and our understanding of the problems of interpretation. Still more recently, work based on cognitive flexibility theory suggests that there are good reasons to believe that people actually can learn and understand certain kinds of texts better through the use of these systems. In sum, there appears to be a convergence between cognitive psychology, interpretive theory, and advanced information technologies.

Texts, contexts, and the history of social and political thought

'Contextualization,' wrote Robert Darnton in 1980, 'is the strongest feature in the area of the history of ideas that has made the strongest progress during the last decade' (Darnton, 1980:339). The area to which Darnton referred was the history of social and political thought, and the major contributors to this progress were John Dunn, John Pocock, and especially Quentin

Skinner. In a series of programmatic articles followed by major books, these three writers shifted the emphasis from text to context, but in a way that resisted any mechanical or reductionist view of the history of ideas.

Skinner's approach—advanced in a famous essay titled 'Meaning and Understanding in the History of Ideas' (1969), exemplified in his two-volume *Foundations of Modern Political Thought* (1978), and refined and defended in *Meaning and Context* (Tully ed., 1988)—may be taken as paradigmatic. Relying on J.L. Austin's theory of speech-acts (1955), Skinner argued that to understand any serious utterance, we must grasp something above and beyond the mere sense and reference of the terms used to express it. Specifically, 'we need in addition to find a means of recovering what the agent may have been doing in saying what was said, and hence of understanding what the agent may have meant by issuing an utterance with just that sense and reference' (Murphey, 1973:45–50; Skinner, 1988:260). Words, in short, are also deeds, speech is also action, to say something is also to do something—and to grasp the meaning of a classic text is thus in some sense to recover the action performed by its author as well (see Wittgenstein, 1958:146). The very existence of the text (ie, the realization of an extended, voluntary communication), Skinner continued, embodies its author's intention to be understood; and to be understood, it follows that at least some of the actions performed by the author must have been conventional (ie, recognizable by his or her audience as actions of that kind). As the means to the recovery of such actions, therefore, Skinner encouraged historians to avoid anachronism by focusing on the linguistic contexts of past texts, to reconstruct the range of actions that might have been conventionally performed in that context, and to trace the relationships between the text itself and this wider form of intellectual life (Skinner, 1969:49). In the words of Richard Rorty—Skinner's critic, defender, and occasional collaborator—we need detailed reconstructions of the 'real and imagined conversations' past writers had (or might have had) with their contemporaries (Rorty, 1984:50–1).

Consider Durkheim's insistence in *Les Regles de la methode sociologique* (1895), that social facts be studied 'as things' (comme des choses). As every undergraduate knows, this injunction—the direct, linear consequence of Durkheim's Cartesian rationalism, Enlightenment skepticism, and 19th century positivism—marked a giant step forward in the inexorable progress of the scientific method applied to the study of social phenomenon. But if this injunction is placed firmly within the larger context of Durkheim's other writings and those of his contemporaries, an alternative reading is encouraged. In Durkheim's writings on education, for example, the insistence that social facts be studied 'as things' was frequently conjoined with some sharp criticism of the more traditional, Cartesian emphasis on 'clear and distinct ideas' deduced from axiomatic first principles. This 'older rationalism' of Descartes, Durkheim and his contemporaries insisted, was a philosophical language well-suited to the simple mathematical certainties of the 17th and 18th centuries, but one which had foundered on the social and political complexities facing the Third French Republic.

The particular social and political context to which Durkheim here referred was the sense of national humiliation that followed the Franco-Prussian War, and the growing sense that it was the superiority of German scientific and technical education—grounded in detailed induction, comparison, observation and experimentation—that had guaranteed the French defeat. In the years after the War, the brightest young French *agrégés* were thus sent to Germany to study; and it was as part of this more general practice that, in 1885–6, Durkheim studied in Berlin, Marburg and—most important—in Wilhelm Wundt's Leipzig laboratory. As Durkheim later indicated in several essays, it was in Leipzig that he learned to appreciate the value of empiricism and its language of concrete, complex things, in sharp contrast to the more abstract, clear and simple ideas of the Cartesian method. Education east of the Rhine—'à l'école des choses'—thus became Durkheim's model for the secularization of French secondary schools. By teaching students that things were complex and concrete rather than simple and abstract, he insisted, the French could create the 'new man' of the Republic, as well as a socio-political 'object' worthy of his veneration (Jones, 1993, 1994). In short, Durkheim's methodological injunction may also be read as a specific social and political action. The value of such historical reconstructions, Skinner and Rorty agree, lies in their contribution to our self-awareness—ie, they help us to recognize that there have been (and, by implication, will later be) forms of intellectual life quite different from our own, and thus that what seem to us to be necessary 'timeless' truths are but the contingent results of our own peculiar, and quite ephemeral, social and political arrangements. This kind of self-awareness, as Skinner has repeatedly observed, is an excellent foil against self-serving, ethnocentric and/or anachronistic readings of classic texts. By contrast with Skinner, however, Rorty has also insisted on the value of 'rational reconstructions'—ie, imaginary conversations between ourselves and classic writers, whose point is less self-awareness than that self-assurance which follows the recognition that we agree and disagree with our predecessors in ways of which, at least in principle, they might have approved. Such 'enterprises in commensuration,' *pace* Skinner, are naturally anachronistic; but they are also unobjectionable, in so far as they are conducted in full knowledge of their anachronism (Rorty, 1984:51–3).

Most important, if a difference thus exists between the historical and the rational reconstruction of such texts, it is not a difference between what the text really means and what significance it might later have acquired (see Hirsch, 1976:2 ff; Rorty, 1984:55n2). In fact, for Rorty, the question of what a text 'means' is never a question of the text's essential nature, or what it is Really About; rather, it is always a question of how the text fits into some larger context of thought and action. As a result the text will have as many meanings as there are contexts in which it might be placed, and the particular contexts we favour will always reflect our own interests and purposes (Stout, 1982:7–8). This means that our answer to the question 'What did Durkheim mean when he said, in the second chapter of *Les Regles*, that "the first and most basic rule is to consider social facts as things"?' will differ according to the range of discursive contexts, of real and imagined conversations in which we can imagine Durkheim participating. The more 'interesting' the text, the more contexts there will be—indeed, it is hard to imagine a more defensible distinction between 'classic' texts and their presumably 'non-classic' counterparts.

Hypertext and hermeneutics

What has any of this to do with computers? Even those scholars who have found positive uses for computers in the humanities— eg, word-processing, bibliographic databases, on-line catalogues, electronic mail, etc.—are sometimes hard-pressed to see how a machine might be helpful in the act of interpretation itself (see Mylonas and Bernstein, 1992). But if Skinner, Rorty, Stout, and other neo-pragmatists are right—ie, if meaning is a matter of use in context, of reconstructing real and imagined conversations in response to our own, myriad interests and purposes—then help may be on the way.

In July, 1945, Vannevar Bush published an article in the *Atlantic Monthly* entitled 'As We May Think'. As FDR's science advisor, Bush was concerned over the staggering and still rapidly increasing amount of information scientists were required to master, and his proposed solution was the Memex, 'a device in which an individual stores his books, records, and communications, and which is mechanized so that it may be consulted with exceeding speed and flexibility' (Bush, 1945). The medium was to have been microfilm, with several projection systems producing multiple 'windows' for the comparison and analysis of multiple files on the user's desktop. Data in these files were to have been linked together to form trails of associative, informational webs, built and browsed through by manipulating a system of pulleys and levers.

Bush of course had no conception of the microcomputer, and in fact the Memex was never built. But his vision inspired later pioneers like Douglas Engelbart, who developed Augment/NLS at the Stanford Research Institute in 1962, and Ted Nelson, who in 1965 coined the word 'hypertext' to refer to the kind of intuitive, non-linear reading and writing which the Memex would, in theory, have made possible. Experiments at Brown University produced the first working hypertext systems in the late 1960s, and twenty years later yielded *Intermedia*, a powerful prototype of the computerized information systems of the future. Commercially available hypertext systems now include *Guide* (Owl International), *ToolBook* (Asymmetrix), *StorySpace* (EastGate Systems) and, of course, Apple's *HyperCard* (Claris). *Mosaic*, a hypertext browser for navigating the Internet, can be downloaded free from the National Center for Supercomputing Applications. Other still more powerful systems are in development.

As these systems have emerged, writers like Jay David Bolter and George Landow have repeatedly and insistently pointed to a convergence between technology and our understanding of the problems of textual interpretation. In *Writing Space* (1991), for example, Bolter emphasizes that electronic texts are the first in which 'the elements of meaning, of structure, and of visual display are fundamentally unstable' (1991: 30–1). The aspirations of writers like Wittgenstein, Barthes, and Derrida—frustrated by conventional, hierarchical structures—are realized in the networked, hypertextual medium. The 'figurative text' emphasized by Stanley Fish—ie, the intertextual structure of sounds, images, and ideas formed in the mind of the reader—is actively constructed as the reader navigates among nodes, links, webs, and networks (1991:157–8). Similarly, in *Hypertext: The Convergence of Contemporary Critical Theory and Technology* (1992), Landow insists that 'we must abandon conceptual systems founded upon the ideas of center, margin, hierarchy, and linearity and replace them with ones of multilinearity, nodes, links, and networks' (Landow, 1992:2–3). Hypertext is the realization of Barthes, 'ideal text, [in which] the networks are many and interact, without any one of them being able to surpass the rest . . . a galaxy of signifiers [1967:5]', and of Derrida's focus on the intertextuality, multivocality, and de-centering of texts (Landow, 1992: 11–13). Rorty is the 'philosopher of hypertext,' Landow insists, because the hypertextual dissolution of centrality and authority is potentially democratic, a model of that 'society of conversations' in which no one voice dominates or pre-empts the others (1992:70; Rorty, 1979:377).

This convergence of interpretive theory and technology is both plausible and attractive to scholars in a post-modernist, neopragmatist world. But it is a veritable revelation within the traditional classroom. For (their technological, visual and auditory sophistication notwithstanding) our students arrive in our classrooms as confirmed interpretive essentialists—ie, they are convinced that there is something that these texts are Really About, 'timeless truths' inscribed in a cryptic code that only we can decipher. This in turn encourages our dangerously flattering self-image as academic 'priests' dispensing the intellectual 'sacraments,' as well as our students' view that education is a matter of passively receiving these sacraments in the traditional, ritual environment of the lecture hall. But as Rorty has observed, there simply isn't anything that the text is Really About, and thus there is no code to be broken in order to discover it. 'Reading texts,' he emphasizes, 'is a matter of reading them in the light of other texts, people, obsessions, bits of information, or what have you, and then seeing what happens' (1992: 103). What happens may be too weird and idiosyncratic to bother with, or it may be exciting and convincing; and it might even be so exciting and convincing that we have the illusion that we now see what a given text is 'really about.' But what excites and convinces, Rorty

151

insists, 'will always be a function of the needs and purposes of those who are being excited and convinced' (1992:105–6). In short, it will be a matter of the discursive contexts within which the text is placed, and of the imagined conversations—more or less useful to ourselves—that result.

Cognitive flexibility theory and hypertext

If Bolter, Landow, and Rorty are right, then one way to think about hypertext—ie, what hypertext 'means', if you like—is to think of it as a technology for generating and re-generating these edifying, imagined conversations, and thus subverting our students' tendencies to interpretive essentialism. However, implicit in the latter assertion is a distinction that we have not yet made. We have discussed the ways that the presentation medium of hypertext seems suitable to the goals of a neo-pragmatist contextualist and a poststructuralist understanding. What we have not discussed is the fact that this new medium of nonlinear and multidimensional presentation of texts will also require *new modes of thinking* if people are to make good use of the imagined conversations that are made available to them and if essentialistic biases are indeed to be subverted. That is, there is an important relationship between the hypertext *medium* and the cognitive *message* it both promotes and requires for appropriate use. If one can not think in this highly unfamiliar nonlinear, multidimensional, and contextual manner, the features of hypertext will not have their desired effect. In fact, there is an approach from cognitive psychology that has as much affinity to hypertext as context-oriented and poststructuralist philosophy do, and thus has the promise of being able to supply this missing cognitive link. That approach is *cognitive flexibility theory* (Spiro, Coulson, Feltovich, and Anderson, 1988; Spiro, Feltovich, Jacobson, and Coulson, 1991a,b; Spiro, Vispoel, Schmitz, Samarapungavan, and Boerger, 1987).

The development of cognitive flexibility theory was motivated by a concern that cognitive scientists had been developing their theories primarily in knowledge domains that were highly orderly (Spiro *et al.*, 1987). In such well-structured domains (eg, physics), essentialistic thinking makes much more sense than in domains of text interpretation like those under consideration in this paper. The originators of cognitive flexibility theory argued that hierarchical representations organized around central, superordinate concepts and highly generalized principles would not permit understandings to develop that would be sufficiently rich to support widespread application (Spiro *et al.*, 1988). This reduced applicability of knowledge within the older frameworks could be attributed to the mistaken assumption that the occasions for knowledge application would be much more regular and routinizable than would likely be the case given the ill-structuredness of most domains. These theory-based hypotheses of oversimplified understanding and limited transferability of knowledge were amply supported by empirical studies which found a great deal of evidence for a reductive world view, a pervasive bias towards oversimplified, essentialistic, decontextualized thinking in even highly advanced students (see, for example, Feltovich, Spiro, and Coulson, 1989; Spiro, Feltovich, and Coulson, 1989).

The basic tenets of cognitive flexibility theory are all intended to combat this proclivity for oversimplified and essentialistic modes of thought that are so inappropriate for complex and ill-structured knowledge domains (Spiro *et al.*, 1988). It will soon be evident to the reader, as it became clear to us, that the random access capabilities of computers are ideal for presenting information to learners so as to realize the principles of cognitive flexibility theory. Thus we began to develop hypertext systems systematically derived from those theoretical principles (Spiro *et al.*, 1988; Spiro and Jehng, 1990; Spiro *et al.*, 1991). These *cognitive flexibility hypertexts*, in areas such as clinical cardiovascular medicine, literary interpretation, history, military strategy, and biology, all embodied the principles of cognitive flexibility theory in a similar manner, attesting to the generality of the approach across diverse domains. Examples of some of the most important of these features of the theory and the hypertext systems derived from the theory include the following (see the cited papers for thorough treatments of these features and coverage of the features we are unable to discuss here).

Utilization of multiple representations

One of the most common problems we have identified in learners' inability to deal with complexity in ill-structured domains is their tendency to use a single dominant representation for some text or conceptual topic (Spiro *et al.*, 1988). The cognitive flexibility approach always incorporates multiple representations (multiple lines of argument, multiple organizational schemes, multiple analogies, multiple contextual settings, and so on). Knowledge that will have to be used in many ways must be learned and mentally represented in many ways. The employment of multiple representational logics is an antidote for complexity-reducing, essentialist thinking.

It should be noted that some of the representations that are employed will be foundation-like (ie, they would be some people's *preferred* foundational representation). However, in ill-structured domains are characterized by the *contestability* of foundational hypotheses, so the same text or case is likely to have multiple candidate foundations. Because each candidate 'foundation' for understanding will have considerable strengths (or it would not be a viable candidate), it is preferable to move toward 'multiple foundation-like representations' for the same entities (eg, texts), rather than moving in the opposite direction of removing foundation-like representations from interpretation altogether. As we said on another occasion:

> . . . Consider the necessity of combating the essentialist's regrettable tendency to think that a dominant, *foundational way of thinking* can be found for understanding a set of texts. Paradoxically, this is accomplished in hypertexts designed according to the principles of cognitive flexibility theory by allowing the learner to automatically re-edit text to see how the same material can be construed from *different* foundational perspectives. By allowing the reader to see how well (and, at the same time, how poorly) a variety of candidate foundations work for a text, it becomes clear that no single foundation can be preeminent for that text. By repeatedly demonstrating over a number of texts that multiple foundations are always applicable, it becomes possible to accomplish a more significant but difficult to attain goal: to convincingly undermine a student's *epistemic belief* that there *typically* is a single best foundation for an important text. Instead, 'foundations' come to be seen as alternative ways of thinking, each with strengths and weaknesses complemented by the others. Some combinations of these ways of thinking will be better suited to some situations, while other situations will be best approached with some other subset of the 'foundational construction space.' What seems certain is that students will be better prepared to deal with the ill-structured complexity of domains such as history to

the extent that they have mastered a greater variety of ways to criss-cross and contextually situate the multiply guised conceptual entities they are trying to understand. The greater the number of fundamental ways of thinking that are superimposed on texts, and interlocked with each other, the greater the fullness of coverage of material that inevitably is oversimplified in traditional approaches. [Jones & Spiro, 1992:147; italics in original]

Provision for massive interconnectedness of knowledge representations

In well-structured domains, it is often the case that assumptions of analytic independence are tenable. That is, the parts or components of the domain can be analysed independently and then additively assembled to form an accurate picture of the whole of the domain. In ill-structured domains this assumption does not hold. The parts of the domain have an interactive relationship with each other and so, in a sense, 'the whole is greater than the sum of the parts.' Discriminable parts of the domain form a context for the other parts. Thus, in cognitive flexibility hypertexts' tendencies towards the *compartmentalization* of information (into different 'chapters,' so to speak) are minimized by incorporating various means of connecting and reconnecting patterns of information, for different purposes, in different contexts. These hypertexts are inherently intertextual.

Emphasis on knowledge assembly rather than intact knowledge retrieval

All of the features of cognitive flexibility theory and the hypertexts derived from it are oriented towards developing the ability of readers to rely less on the use of prepackaged prescriptions from memory for how they should think, and to rely more on a flexible, situation-sensitive assembly of knowledge for the understanding, problem solving, or interpretive purposes at hand. In an ill-structured domain you can not, by definition, have a precompiled *schema* in your mind for every circumstance and context you may encounter. Alternatively, then, you must be able to flexibly select and arrange knowledge sources to most efficaciously pursue the needs of a given situation.

Robert Alun Jones and Rand J. Spiro

*Reliance on representational fragments as building blocks for
constructing understandings*

The goal of flexible, multi-source, situation-adaptive and context-sensitive knowledge assembly is facilitated to the extent that knowledge is not organized into large, monolithic blocks. Perhaps paradoxically, the potential for developing highly integrated representations of a particular given situation are increased to the extent that small and manageable building blocks are available for *tailored* construction to fit that situation.

It will not have escaped the reader's notice that these principles of cognitive flexibility theory (and the hypertexts based on that theory) are highly resonant to the themes of context-oriented and poststructuralist thinkers. (We have juxtaposed a contextualism influenced by neo-pragmatism and poststructuralism in several places in this paper. The two are clearly distinct; we have been using them together only with regard to certain of their points of overlap, as indicated by the contexts of their co-occurrence.) This should not be surprising, since the movement in each of these realms has been predicated on a concern for dealing with a complex and 'messy' world made up of rich and variously interpretable contexts (including the world of text understanding and interpretation). In the first two parts of the paper, we discussed the relationship between hypertext and context-oriented theory. In this section we addressed cognitive issues pertinent to the use of hypertext for neo-pragmatistic contextualist ends. A medium capable of conveying contextual complexity, like hypertext, will not do anyone much good if people are unable to think in the difficult and alien nonlinear ways those texts and complex topics require. Cognitive flexibility theory is a comprehensive psychological and educational approach to nonlinear learning in complex, context-rich domains. In fact, evidence has been accumulating that hypertexts based on cognitive flexibility theory can help readers to achieve more complex and transferable understandings; however, these positive effects have been tempered by the fact that some students with decidedly essentialist and anti-contextualist epistemic beliefs are not able to achieve those benefits (eg, Jacobson & Spiro, 1991).

Concluding remarks

Those who have been worried about the problem of complexity have at one time or another shared the frustration Wittgenstein expressed in the preface to his *Philosophical Investigations*:

> . . . I have written down all these thoughts as remarks, short paragraphs, of which there is sometimes a fairly long chain about the same subject, while I sometimes make a sudden change, jumping from one topic to another.—It was my intention at first to bring all this together in a book whose form I pictured differently at different times. But the essential thing was that the thoughts should proceed from one subject to another in a natural order and without breaks.
>
> After several unsuccessful attempts to weld my results together into such a whole, I realized that I should never succeed. The best that I could write would never be more than philosophical remarks; *my thoughts were soon crippled if I tried to force them on in any single direction against their natural inclination.—And this was, of course, connected with the very nature of the investigation. For this compels us to travel over a wide field of thought criss-cross in every direction.* [p. v; italics added]

The convergence of context-oriented pragmatist theory, cognitive flexibility theory, and hypertext technology that we have discussed in this paper illustrates a widespread disaffection with the tendency of traditional media and traditional modes of thought to cripple complex ideas and the contexts they are embedded in (and from which the ideas derive their alternative meanings). With hypertexts that are intended to serve the purposes of contextualization and promote nonlinear, multidimensional, cognitively flexible thinking, we may see a new generation of students who, as writers and readers, are able to travel productively over wide fields of thought criss-cross in every direction as Wittgenstein sought to do.

Constructing easiness—historical perspectives on work, computerization, and women

Randi Markussen

Abstract

The assertion that technologies have made life easier and consequently better, often lurks in how we evaluate technologies. It implies an idea of history linked to modernity with its idea of progress. With my point of departure in the concepts of space of experience and horizon of expectation, I try to develop another understanding of history and a reassessment of how we evaluate technologies. Horizons of expectation of information technologies and developmental work are described and examined in the light of its impact on women's work, and how we envision power and authority. Finally, possibilities and dilemmas in women's lives within this reconceptualization is stressed and the conditions under which women may change their lives.

Nothing says that the present reduces to presence. Why, in the transition from future to past, should the present not be the time of initiative—that is, the time when the weight of history that has already been made is deposited, suspended, and interrupted, and when the dream of history yet to be made is transposed into a responsible decision?

Therefore it is within the dimension of acting (and suffering, which is its corollary) that thought about history will bring together its perspectives, within the horizon of the idea of an imperfect mediation. (Ricoeur, 1988:208)

Introduction

A couple of years ago, a woman in Denmark reported her research on washing. She claimed that we spend just as much time on washing today as our mothers did earlier (Cronberg, 1987). The study gave rise to intense reactions in the papers from other women. Most of the participants argued that they definitely spent less time doing laundry today; the washing machine had freed them from a tiresome job and they lived happily without it. The debate however, never managed to question the discourse that the study presumably was intended to criticise: The idea of progress and the liberating role technology plays in reducing labour and transforming women's lives for the better.[1]

Ongoing change, often bound to the introduction of technology, is of course not a condition exclusively concerning women. Historicity, the temporality of history and the idea of progress often ascribed to this, expresses a fundamental figure in the attitude towards time and history linked to modernity. And ideas of human rights, equity and women's emancipation do share many of the same roots.

In this chapter, I'll discuss two conditions that have challenged our understanding of society and its boundaries. One is the growing integration of women in education, in life-long engagements in the labour-force and in occupations formerly occupied exclusively by men. Women's resurgent struggle in social, political and private domains has exposed mechanisms of signification, power and domination emerging from those processes. Crossing the boundaries of traditional divides in society—public and private, impersonal and personal, masculine and feminine—may have intensified conflicts and dilemmas in women's lives. At the same time, it challenges dominant hierarchies and is a source of insights and basic experiences.

The second condition is the appearance of new technologies that question our understanding of well-known boundaries between what is conceived as natural and as cultural, between what is physical and social in terms of distinctions between artefacts that are designed, built and used, and human communication and interaction. Technologies of different kinds have played an important role in transforming not only work and labour processes but all of everyday life. We live our lives in a more and more created environment, global in scope. Technologies take on new forms and raise new issues in our understanding of our relation to nature, the social world, ourselves and consequently ideas of progress.

When we consider the influence of information technologies in women's lives, we have to reconsider the concepts that embody our understanding of history and the traditions we set into play in our understanding of both women and technology. What I

159

find interesting in the debate on washing is how it repeats what it sets about to discuss. It repeats a significant 'figure' in making the equation of technology and progress, centred around the idea of easiness. It implies an understanding of time, implicitly at stake in the way we tend to accept *easier* as the same as better. Technology is not only equated with labour-saving; it also means time-saving. Time saved is not regarded as a useless emptying of time. This saved is time that opens up for new options and possibilities. The ability to organize time and space is an important aspect of power in both its enabling and restraining capabilities. What does it imply if this is primarily understood and legitimated by linking easier with better? Is power really the same as leisure, ease, free time—all for discretionary use? How is it we construct easiness in our understanding of technology, and how can we apply a historical perspective that goes beyond easiness?

History

The past is a foreign country. (Hartley, 1966)

In his analysis of a hermeneutics of historical consciousness, Paul Ricoeur takes as a point of departure the concepts of space of experience and horizon of expectation. The concepts and the analysis of their polarity were originally introduced by Koselleck, who devoted them to the specific interpretation of history that took shape with the Enlightenment. Space of experience indicates that the past is not just 'something assembled as a simple chronology'. It implies that something foreign has been overcome, and the word space 'evokes the idea of different traversals following a multitude of itineraries.'

Horizon of expectation not only stands in opposition to space of experience, they mutually condition each other. Expectation 'is broad enough to include hope and fear, what is wished for and what is chosen, rational calculation, curiosity—in short every private and public manifestation aimed at the future. As with experience in relation to the present, expectation relative to the future is inscribed in the present.' And horizon in opposition to space indicates 'the power of unfolding as much as of surpassing that is attached to expectation.' The point is that the previously existing space of experience is not enough for the determination of the space of horizon of expectation. Together

160

they describe the temporal structure of experience (Ricoeur, 1988:208 ff).

Ricoeur points to three themes in this new understanding of history, which Koselleck calls the temporalization of history. One is the belief that the present age has a new perspective on the future. 'Time is no longer just a neutral form of history, but its force as well. . . . The present, henceforth, will be perceived as a time of transition between the shadows of the past and the light of the future.' Another is the belief that changes for the better are accelerating, thus defining progress, and the third is the idea of history as something to be made and which is submitted to human action (Ricoeur, 1988:210f). Ricoeur thoroughly discusses how those ideas today have lost their meaning. The double edged character of modernity is becoming more and more evident. Today we are in the words of Ricoeur more inclined to speak of an acceleration in historical mutations than in an acceleration in the march of progress. And we realize that the idea of mastering history fails to recognize that we are affected by history and that we affect ourselves by the history we make. What happens is always something other than we expected. Even our expectations change in largely unforeseeable ways.' (Ricoeur, 1988:213).

However, when it comes to technology, rhetorics of progress still surround the way we tend to think about the changes it implies. The obsession with formalisms and abstractions often implies discourses of equating 'automated with better' without further reflections on the social and historical circumstances of technological changes. I'm not so much criticising the risks and inventions at stake, as the lack of consideration of *cui bono*?

When we consider how women may have benefited from technologies, questions of progress become even more delicate. In a study of the microwave oven Cynthia Cockburn shows how a sense of the commonplace and the banal still clings to work and activities done by women, wage labour or not (1993). Women's skills are easily perceived as a natural displaying of femininity. The polarization of nature and culture, so fundamental in establishing modernity with the linking of women with nature and masculinity with culture, constitutes a symbolic order, the scope of which we are only beginning to grasp (Ortner, 1974; Griffin, 1978; Latour, 1993; Star, 1994). That we are affected by history, as much as we ourselves affect it, is not just a theoretical insight, proposed by philosophers, however, but an everyday experience shared by most women. The intensity in the debate about washing thus reveals the many dimensions of ambiguity we face in understanding technology and women's conditions.

In her remarkable study '*The Creation of Patriarchy*', Gerda Lerner makes an important distinction. On the one hand she stresses that women are and have always been actors and agents in history, central in the creation of society and in making history. On the other hand, 'women have been systematically excluded from the enterprise of creating symbol systems, philosophies, science, and law. Women have not only been educationally deprived throughout historical time in every known society, they have been excluded from theory-formation.' (Lerner, 1986:5). Her analysis genuinely shows, how a space of experience and a horizon of expectation mutually condition each other. 'The approach we use in interpretation—our conceptual framework—determines the outcome. Such a framework is never value free. We ask the questions to the past, we want answered in the present.' (1986: 15). Lerner examines how patriarchy became institutionalized from Mesopotamia in the fourth millennium BC. Contrary to her initial assumptions, she finds that it was not a single event with a distinctive origin, but is better understood as processes of exploitation and experiences taking place over several thousand years. She reveals a space of experience that convincingly shows how deep-rooted patriarchy has been in the creation of western civilization. The horizon of expectation here, is however one of hope and confidence in the possibility of women's emancipation, but also an understanding of the wild patience needed for this to happen (Rich, 1981).

The statement that we spend just as much time on washing today as women did earlier on, may provoke us to reflect on our assumptions about the role of technology in our lives and the significance we ascribe to it. As an analysis, however, it mirrors the logic it criticizes. In '*Technics and Civilization*' Lewis Mumford speaks ironically of the doctrine of progress and the historical consciousness it implies. 'Assuming that progress was a reality, if the cities of the nineteenth century were dirty, the cities of the thirteenth century must have been six centuries dirtier: For had not the world become constantly cleaner?' (1963:183). Optimism and pessimism about technology often share the same basic assumptions, but we tend to evaluate them differently. The assertion that the labour-saving properties of the washing machine and other household technologies have made it more possible for women to enter the labour market and education, is perhaps more in line with the general view. The coming of the so-called affluent society in the sixties, the profound spread of mass production and mass consumption, and in a Scandinavian context the welfare state formed a material base for women's emancipation.

Usually this is understood in a purely functional manner. But it goes without saying that younger generations of women were on the run from the dominant images of femininity in society, eager to take part in the real life outside the family (Markussen, 1984).

But housework did not disappear, even if agencies outside the home and technology 'took over' the labour, as the functionalist perspective wants us to believe. In *'Washing, seems it's all we do': Washing technology and women's communication'* Victoria Leto (1988) shows that technologies have isolated women in the home. We no longer work around technologies within women's communities, but work with technologies, isolated from other people. Technologies have been assimilated in ways that have isolated women in performing work that previously had a social and communicative significance. Consequently, she suggests that laundromats should be developed as more inviting places for women to meet, and that new household technologies should be invented, which truly liberate women from repetitious, time-consuming, isolated work (Leto, 1988:176).[2] Leto touches on an important theme, the social conditions under which work is carried out, and stresses the isolation and loneliness of women in domestic work. But following Lerner, women are not just victims of history and patriarchy, but in our work and self-understanding help social conditions. Not only women, but families, tend to exploit technologies in this fashion. Why? It is true that technologies may suggest certain usages, but this cannot explain the isolation of women in household work.

Those different assertions speak about the ambiguities we face in understanding interplays between women, work and technology. The different evaluations tend to centre around either a pessimistic or an optimistic utilitarian horizon of expectation. They may be said to invest hopes and ascribe values to technology too unreflexively, giving the critique a moral edge, but little analytical depth. They reproduce a certain way of conceiving history, centred around progress. As long as we argue with the past in terms of more or less of the same old thing, be it time, cleanliness,

163

easiness, communication, we limit ourselves to a discourse bereft of qualitative dimensions of the past. We are in a static, predictive, cumulative mode, one which closes out new ways of perceiving.

Ricoeur asserts that we today are more inclined to speak of an acceleration in historical mutations than an acceleration in the march of progress. In turn, this entails a reconceptualization of technology in order to understand these mutations. Even though the categories of 'space of experience' and 'horizon of expectation' were originally devoted to the specific interpretation of history in modernity, Ricoeur suggests they make up metahistorical categories with ethical and political implications. Together they thematize historical time. There will always be a tension between the past and the future, if we are to speak of history at all. But the topos of progress is only one variation of the relationship. Ricoeur sees the task as preventing the tension between experience/expectation from becoming a schism. 'We have to keep our horizon of expectation from running away from us. We have to connect it to the present by means of a series of intermediary projects . . . Every expectation must be a hope for humanity as a whole.' (1988:214f).

Ricoeur's analysis touches on themes that have been at the heart of feminist critique of modernity (Harding, 1986; Lytje & Markussen, 1989; Braidotti, 1991; Star, 1991). Feminists have argued that this view of 'the subjugated' is in fact a privileged point of departure, whose implications have been intensely scrutinized and reinterpreted. Donna Haraway suggests that: 'Feminist objectivity is about limited location and situated knowledge, not about transcendence and splitting of subject and object . . . The knowing self is partial in all its guises, never finished, whole, simply there and original; it is always constructed and stitched together imperfectly, and therefore able to join with another, to see together without claiming to be another. Here is the promise of objectivity: a scientific knower seeks the subject position, not of identity, but of objectivity, that is, partial connection.' (1991:583ff).

Consequently, the vision of power in this perspective is not a question of gaining majority power, as Isabelle Stengers puts it. 'I dream about multiple connections among minorities, so that each of them will be able to work out its own singularity through the creation of alliances, not in isolation, and so that each individual would be simultaneously part of many minorities' (1994:41).

How can technology be thus reconceptualised within other understandings of history, and how can we account for its impact on work? Which horizons of expectation may arise from this and how is it important to women?

Work and information technologies

Even though we might spend the same amount of time on washing today as earlier on, it is in some respects different. We no longer rub and scrub with our hands deeply buried in water and soap. We no longer rinse the clothes, heavy with water. Part of the physical labour has been automated. Instead, we choose a programme on the washing machine, and perhaps the tumble drier, and bring the clothes back and forth from one machine to the other. We do not talk about a washing day whose rhythm is set by the task, we talk about washing hours. Washing is integrated in the structure of everyday life as a background task. Waiting for the washing machine to finish, while we are busy elsewhere, adjusting to timetables set by other everyday agendas, making different ends meet, tailoring different needs is part of the web of the everyday (Howe, 1977; Kling & Scacchi, 1982; Markussen and Foged, 1984).

We may have lost the feeling for the materials: how to judge quality of soap water by hand; how to sense the age of a garment and its weak points; which things to pull through the wringer and which to dry gently. The idea of doing without 'high' technology may seem frightening, as it confronts us with how heavily we rely on it, how we trust it, and how helpless we seem without it. We easily project our fear of being without it backwards in history, creating a space of experience around the idea of a burdensome, and uncivilized form of everyday life.[3]

The machine certainly has taken over part of the labour; on the one hand this is deskilling. On the other, we must now read the programme instructions, often as highly sophisticated interfaces, and trust the machine's execution.

This elementary transformation of washing labour is in many ways similar to complex industrial changes. The transformation of mechanical machines into cybernetic machines also represents a profound change in work (Beniger, 1986; Boland, 1989). Instead of working directly on materials, using a machine, cybernetic machinery creates an indirect second order relation. Work takes on new meaning, when automation implies increasingly self regulating machinery: 'Steady state functions—the control of expected errors—are turned over to the feedback-based controls; but discontinuities, whether based in failure, in the introduction of new materials, or in the redesign of the machine system itself, draw on worker knowledge, attention and watchfulness. Thus in cybernetic systems machines and workers complement each other with respect to a typology of errors: machines control expected or "first-order" errors, while workers control unanticipated or "second-order" errors.' (Hirschhorn, 1984:72)

The accident at the Three Mile Island nuclear power plant is significant in trying to understand the changes in our relation to nature and work (Perrow, 1984). Operators in the control room do not handle objects and materials; they live in a world of signals and signs to be interpreted, a hermeneutic one.

Embodiment relations imply a partially transformed experience of the world through technology. In use, the experience is transformed, and the resulting transparency has an enigmatic quality (Ihde, 1979). Ihde describes it in terms of sensory-extension-reduction relations. When we are on the phone, our hearing is extended to the distant other, but the other is only partially present. We cannot see, touch or smell each other, and thus experience is also reduced.

The hermeneutic relation, however, is not so much this experience via machine as of the machine, as in the control room. In hermeneutic relations, there is a partial opacity between the machine and the World, and the machine is a text. It has one property of a sign—it can be used to tell lies. How can you make sure that the signs in the control room are telling you the right things? Kafkaesque possibilities may arise. In this case, we not only experience the machine in a 'thematized form', the machine also becomes 'other'. Ihde illustrates this by describing a computer application for an experimental program in mathematics. The computer is programmed to simulate a conversation. And even though the machine has no intentionality, '(I)n the relations in which machines are focal "others" all the ambiguity of other relations becomes a possibility. The machine is capable of anthropomorphization in terms of its "otherness".' (Ihde, 1979:13).

Here the world takes on machine-like characteristics. Lucy Suchman suggests something similar in her analysis of human-machine communication (1987:7). She argues that the description

166   © The Editorial Board of The Sociological Review 1995

of computational artifacts as interactive is supported by their reactive, linguistic, and internally opaque properties. Computers challenge the dominant understanding of machines. That the smooth functioning black box should also have a deep interpretive side comes as something of a shock.

A horizon of technological expectation focused on automation and easiness, barely touches on embodiment relations, and fails to articulate the hermeneutic aspects. Shoshana Zuboff analyzes the technology in terms of both its automating and informating capacities: 'The distinction between automate and informate provides one way to understand how this technology represents both continuities and discontinuities with the tradition of industrial history. As long as the technology is treated narrowly in its automation functions, it perpetuates the logic of the industrial machine that, over the course of the century, has made it possible to rationalize work while decreasing the dependence on human skills. However, when the technology also informates the processes to which it is applied, it increases the explicit information content of tasks and sets into motion a series of dynamics that will ultimate reconfigure the nature of work and the social relationships that organize productive activity.' (1984:10)

The informating function translates activities, events and objects into visible information, highlighting the hermeneutic aspects of the technological representations.

Zuboff's perspective both stresses a continuity with mechanical technologies and points to a familiarity with technologies of representation. It widens our understanding of the powers at stake in modernity and the industrial revolution. As Mumford made clear, the clock, not the steam-engine, is the key machine of the modern industrial age (1963:14). Both the clock and the printing press helped transform time and space, the form of life. The written word was key: 'Compared with oral communication any sort of writing is a great labor saving device, since it frees communication from the restrictions of time and space and makes discourse wait on the convenience of the reader—who can interrupt the flow of thought or repeat it or concentrate on isolated parts of it. The printed page increased the safety and permanence of the written record by manifolding it, extended the range of communication, and economized on time and effort . . . Custom and memory now played second fiddle to the written word: Reality meant "established on paper." Was it written in the bond? If so, it must be fulfilled. If not, it could be flouted. Capitalism, by

committing its transactions to paper, could at last make and preserve a strict accountancy of time and money' (Mumford,
1963:136f).

These technologies have contributed to the dynamism and the
historicity of modernity (Eisenstein, 1979; Latour, 1986).
Anthony Giddens suggests that order is a question of how social
systems 'bind' time and space, how they are organized to connect
presence and absence. The time/space separation is brought
about by disembedding mechanisms, the 'lifting out' of social
relations from local contexts, and their restructuring across indef-
inite spans, which requires re-embedding as well. Globalisation
implies increasingly complex relations between local involvements
and interaction across distance. Symbolic tokens and expert systems are central means of disembedding and bracketing of time-
space. Expert systems rely on reflexivity, ordering and reordering
of social practices in the light of continual inputs of knowledge.
Contrary to the early modern belief, this does not equal greater
control, but contributes to a manufactured uncertainty. 'The
point is not that there is no stable world to know, but that
knowledge of that world contributes to its unstable or mutable
character.' (Giddens, 1990:45).

Striking another chord, Haraway and Leigh Star stress that the
power in stabilized networks is rarely total. Even though the
powerful may create order and homogeneity from their own perspective, and chaos and inconvenience for those excluded, this
does not explain the perspective of the 'as yet unlabelled,' that
which is permanently escaping, subverting, but still in relationship with the standardized. Haraway calls this the cyborg, coy-
ote. Both suggest multiple membership and multiple marginalities
as an alternative to the power-powerless dichotomy (Star, 1991).

All these arguments show an interest in surpassing old
nature/culture and technical/social dichotomies. They capture the
interwovenness of technology and the social, and the dynamics in
historical development. Different horizons of expectation may be
said to arise from them. Other arguments explicitly suggest a
horizon of expectation of work and technology embodying specific political and ethical implications. These are visions of
utopian realism: realistic in the sense that the expectations build
on a transformation of important institutions backgrounding the
problems they face, utopian in the sense that they envision 'a
hope for humanity as a whole' in Ricoeur's words.

Horizons of expectation of information technologies and developmental work

> It is paradoxical, but true that even as we are developing the most advanced, mathematical and abstract technologies, we must depend increasingly on informal modes of learning, design, and communication. (Hirschhorn, 1984:169)

In the Tavistock tradition, Hirschhorn has pointed to the paradoxes and challenges that computerized technologies raise for work organization and technological design. Our relationship with nature and the environment is so complex that it cannot be grasped, planned or controlled in advance or from a centre. The dream of control embodied in mechanical machinery at first seemed to be fulfilled with cybernetic machines. But as nuclear accidents and experiences with computing implementation show, questions of who controls the controls have not become obsolete. The traditional chain of command, authority, and responsibility somehow implodes if you literally or metaphorically are managing a bomb, eg contingencies, risks, unintended consequences, failures come to the fore. The Taylorite ideas of explicitly and purely codifying all knowledge, of separating doing and knowing, limiting the competence of shop floor workers, are inadequate for these new complexities.

In their empirical studies of the introduction and usage of information technologies in plants and firms in the US, Hirschhorn and Zuboff locate new problems and conflicts between employers and employees. They vividly show the difficulties inherent in anticipating the nature of information technologies, and how they affect work. Design and development of flexible automation systems and information systems differ from traditional machine design; they require a much more detailed knowledge of the specifics of work practices.

There is a critical gap between the tacit, experiential knowledge of the shop floor, and the theories of system developers and managers. The conflicts arising from this gap put into question well established divides between formal and empirical, manual and intellectual, doing and knowing. These new dilemmas of control and learning call for a reinterpretation of the employer-employee contract that may be systematically explored in sociotechnical job design, based on teams and a conscious integration of work and learning. Their analyses emphasize the significance of hermeneutic aspects of technology, and its importance for a growing reflexivity.

Reflexivity, communication and cooperation

Work is redefined in encounters with 'the electronic text,' as Zuboff calls computing. Hirschhorn describes these changes as a need for diagnostic skills that integrate dense perception, heuristic knowledge and a theoretical understanding of work. The action-oriented skills of manual work, and the relational skills of office and managerial work, are different from the intellective skills of textualized work. Tacit knowledge is inherent in action-oriented skills, while intellective skills put on new demands on verbalising abilities. Mastery in the symbolic medium depends on explicitly constructed meaning (Zuboff, 1984:192).

People must interpret the text, articulate their own meaning and communicate it to others. 'Pooling intellective know-how depends in large measure upon language—not as a minimalist vehicle in the consolidation of face-to-face interaction, but as a precise vehicle for conveying explicit reasoning, often in the absence of action. (Zuboff, 1984:196). In other words, managing the symbolic environment tends to intensify the reflexivity that Mumford underscored in written records, and transform the division of labour.

The electronic text makes work visible in new ways, as information is gathered and codified in one system. It renders public what used to be discretionary, with panopticon power. It may be difficult to trace the authorship of a certain text, due to both design and communication at a distance. Hirschhorn describes the new hermeneutic competences as boundary work, and underscores how the flexible capacities of the technology may be exploited. For example, the transformation of work in an information services company means selling bibliographies to business research librarians. Computerization made it easier to develop highly specialized bibliographies, and these became new competitive products. 'The salespeople had to cooperate with the customers to produce this specialized product, and worked intensely with their specialists: The old sales call was transformed into a riskier design-and-negotiation process. By entering more deeply into the customer's world, the salesperson integrated producer and consumer by knowing much more about each . . . Standing at a more complicated boundary between producer and customer, the salesperson could no longer simply follow proven practices for selling the company's product but had to appreciate the unique features of each new sales encounter.' (Hirschhorn, 1988:6f). Here, work becomes more situational, and people must integrate diverse sets of facts, interests and claims.

The text may in principle be simultaneously constituted and accessible at any place and time and thus enable a decentralization along with the panopticon. Put differently, the dichotomy between centralization/decentralization 'implodes', and reveals some paradoxes. The informating capacities demand both flexible and reflexive organization, an exploitation of technology, and an empowerment of the workers: 'For the first time, technology returns to the workers what it once took away—but with a crucial difference. The workers' knowledge had been implicitly in action. The informating process makes the knowledge explicit: it holds a mirror up to the worker, reflecting what was known but now in a precise and detailed form. In order to re-appropriate that reflection, the worker must be able to grapple with a kind of knowledge that now stands outside the self, externalized and public. Intellective skill becomes the means to interact competently with this now objectified text, to re-appropriate it as one's own, and to engage in that kind of learning process that can transform data into meaningful information and, finally, into insight.' (Zuboff, 1984:304).

Zuboff suggests that early computerization was primarily seen in terms of automation; informating capacities have as yet been poorly understood. To what extent managers may find it relevant, depends in large measure on the organization and its flexibility and reflexivity. From the perspective of the employees, however, the more the technologies become inextricably interwoven in the work, the more important are the informating capacities. Hales (this volume) discusses a similar challenge and paradoxes in information work in a multinational corporation.

Inscriptions, visibility and women's work

Ina Wagner's study of the cultural transformation of nursing is especially important here (1994). The hierarchy in hospitals is based on the status ascribed to science and the ability of the physicians to create 'objective' representations. The cure

171

perspective dominates, while the care perspective, assigned to nurses, is defined as a residual category, without clear-cut systematized knowledge. The actual reality in hospitals, however, is characterized by a much more catholic distribution of knowledge. Informal networks play an important part in the complex and distributed problem-solving that a hospital depends on. Nurses are the 'glue' that holds it together, balancing contradictory demands, the visible and the invisible. Boundary work has been at the core of many women's jobs. 'Typical of many women's lives has been and still is an organization of space and time which grants their limitless availability. This compliance with flexible, not always status-adequate work schemes is typical of the work situation of many women. The ideology and practice of nursing fits this image. Nurses on principle should be limitlessly available to their patients and to doctors. Their work is governed by rigid but not necessarily timed schedules and doctor's orders, restricted to small, well-defined space-time corridors.' (Wagner, 1994)

The computer systems so far introduced tend to affect this, both by demanding that nurses account for their work in categories of working time, and in the sense that they decrease the need for interpersonal task synchronization. Nurses become less dependent on the cooperation of others in order to get information. Nursing managers directly involved in systems development argue that the computer-based documentation of nursing activities—'panopticon power'—might help to make the nurses' work more visible, support demands for better staffing, pay, etc.

Wagner stresses, however, the ambiguity and the contradictory demands that nurses face in these processes. The transformation of work puts new demands on nurses in terms of relating the formalized electronic depiction of work to caregiving activities, which may still be considered residual and subordinate. 'With the transition to explicitness and to working with models and codes, old definitions and meanings of caregiving are not necessarily replaced. The layering of the new upon the old, the explicit upon the implicit, the self-evident upon the problematic, creates ambiguity and pressure.' (in press) And even if nurses themselves seek to combine this with a profession-enhancing strategy, it might not be recognized within the organization, thus leaving nurses with traditional double messages.

The overall rationale in introducing information systems in American and French hospitals has been an automation perspec-

172

tive, with information technology as the best answer to exploding costs. In the US, the hospital administration has held the initiative, and the development has been part of increasing management power *vis-a-vis* physicians. In France, the development was shaped by an effort to balance administrative demands and the staff's professional interests, often by nurses in management positions.

In order to develop information systems that support the nurses' work, not just management, nurses go beyond the image of 'scientific care,' and enhance their control of context and working standards. Wagner offers a couple of examples of how this has been attempted, but by and large the development has been shaped by the managerial perspective.

Gender is embedded here in the shaping of work practices, and work practices also shape gender. The habits of limitless availability and inability to structure time and space reflects a less powerful position; the lack of inscriptions of their own voices in the written and coded materials, renders the nurses' work invisible. The introduction of the electronic text may open a space for renegotiating the meaning of work, but there are dilemmas inherent in this from the perspective of women. Given voice to the traditionally invisible requires a purposeful effort to understand work practices, currently not articulated within the dominant understanding. It implies other, complex images of authority and power.

Power, authority and politics of an informated work environment

We can know more about the complexity and morality of authority in private that our institutions allow us to know in public. Why should we be prisoners of simplicity in public affairs? Only the interest of our masters are served if we do not seek to make the complexities of our consciousness standard for collective experience. (Sennett, 1972:164).

The analyses that I have drawn upon reveal many mechanisms of power in traditional bureaucracies and the dynamics of processes of change. What strikes me is the exposure of paternalistic traits, and how they build on imaginary dichotomies of having or lacking: power, influence, responsibility, knowledge.

173

Managing responsibility and its attendant anxiety is woven into patterns of guilt, reproach and punishment in our culture, one that neither supports learning and cooperation nor democratic recognition.

When people must articulate and communicate the meaning of work, they bring their personal feelings and private senses of self to bear on the situation. This makes it difficult to preserve a split between what management demands and one's own feelings about the situation and sense of self, a split that models the paternalistic structure of bureaucracies, with management as the adults and employees as irresponsible, ignorant children (Sennett, 1981). The split between power and love is part of this patriarchal heritage. Thinking of power in unloving terms and of love as powerless has shaped our understanding of authority, power, and work (Hartsock, 1985).

Sennett distinguishes between two different voices of authority in this century (1972). One is traditional, authoritarian, exemplified in management terms by Fordism: 'I know what is best for you, so I will decide.' The other is much more ambiguous, with a certain autonomy, embedded in system thinking (eg Herbert Simon's work): 'I know you need me, but I do not need you.' This technocratic voice from nowhere dominates modern management. Both discourses present themselves as static, denying their relational, and dynamic positions—what Haraway calls the god-trick. The masculine basis of the legitimacy and authority of these voices is usually unquestioned.

Conflicts, tensions, and dissonance will intensify, as more people are asked to commit themselves and become emotionally involved in their jobs. An informated work environment is both more demanding and less forgiving: 'The new technologies of automation, communication, and information, integrate interdependent units and divisions so that it becomes more difficult for people in one unit to deny the claims, experiences, and requirements of another. People inhabit a more multidimensional terrain, where stereotyping and scapegoating become less viable defences. Just as men and women may experience greater anxiety when losing the protection provided by their stereotyped roles, so can the postindustrial milieu create greater anxiety by complicating and intensifying relationships across role and organizational boundaries. People work in an increasingly imploded organizational environment.' (Hirschhorn, 1988:144).

Within the psychoanalytical framework, bureaucracies are

social defences to contain the anxiety inherent in work and management. An informated environment increases anxiety and challenges, where people must manage increasingly sophisticated boundaries. The informating processes erode the pragmatic claims that have lent force and credibility to the traditional managerial role (Zuboff, 1984:309). Organizational restructuring to support people in taking responsibility and managing conflicts and flexible boundaries is a key challenge.

Philip Agre notes how a discourse of empowerment finds its way into not only sociological studies but also management rhetorics: 'The rhetoric of liberation that surrounds the empowered worker has led to widespread hopes for democracy . . . but . . . the empowered worker shares one thing with the rationalized worker: the ubiquity of measurement. Indeed, the measurement of work activities, in both manufacturing and services, has grown tremendously in the last decade. When work processes were designed once and for all, it was only necessary to record single measurements for each of those processes' atomic components. Measurements of empowered work, though, focuses on outcomes as well as components, and empowered workers are supposed to innovate in the service of these outcomes. Measurements are no longer administered from the outside by time-and-motion specialists; rather it is continuous, built into the processes of work by their very design. Management employs these measurements in comparing work performance, identifying 'problems', evaluating innovations, and in an unbounded variety of other ways. Empowered work then is just as heavily monitored as rationalized work. But it does not afford the intellectual detachment that Lukacs could ascribe to the factory work . . . it seeks the total involvement of each individual's self. Empowerment and measurement, in short, together form a single disciplinary regime.' (Agre 1993).

Agre eloquently describes the emergent reality of an informated work environment. At the heart of the horizon of expectation here described is not the question of whether to measure, but rather what to measure, how to measure and who will measure. Measurement and surveillance are ambiguous and ambivalent phenomena, as Hall and Stevens' paper (this volume) also illustrates. They are inherent in modern reflexivity, inextricably bound up with growing social interdependencies and globalization, in which technologies are *sine qua non*.

Therefore, this horizon of expectation is not about the

empowerment of a grandiose self, abstract and beyond social obligations. Neither the psychoanalytic perspective in the writings of Hirschhorn, nor the Foucault inspired analysis of Zuboff suggest this. Within their theoretical and analytical frameworks neither technology nor the person is abstract, but culturally, socially and politically situated. The person is not something just to be disciplined or liberated (Stengers, 1994:49). To me the power in their approaches are their genuine understanding of the dualities of the technology, as a non-neutral but also ambiguous phenomenon. The electronic text, with its panopticon possibilities and both local and global reflective monitoring and surveillance, challenges our understanding of what is private and what is public.

Hence, the genuine message in their analyses is that the personal is political, and increasingly so. The utopian element in their horizons of expectation is their vision of power, authority and responsibility with its ear for 'that which is permanently escaping, subverting, but in a relationship with the standardized' (Star, 1991). Power is only a static phenomenon in our imagination, and however important, that does not account for all realities. We may take the initiative and at responsibly.

Dilemmas in women's working lives

> It was secretaries who were expected to look out for the personal things, to see to the comfort and welfare of guests, to show them around and make sure that they had what they needed. And it was around secretaries that people at higher levels in the corporation could stop to remember the personal things about themselves and each other (appearance, dress, daily mood), could trade the small compliments and acknowledgements that differentiated them from the mass of others and from their formal role. In many ways—visually, socially, and organizationally—the presence of secretaries represented a reserve of the human inside the bureaucratic. (Moss Kanter, 1977:69f)

Kanter's description of the office is still a pervasive reality. The naturalization of women's work (Cockburn), the tradition for limitless availability (Wagner) all echo Simone de Beauvoir's famous statement that women are the second sex. The mark of sexual difference has fallen upon women, the structural other, leaving it to men to carry the norm of the universal human being. And yet as we become more visible in Western societies, we may raise new questions of the past (Lerner). The domestication of women in this century with the construction of men as the real wage earners sexualized women's relation to the labour market: young women have been welcomed; single women tolerated. The problematic has been the combination of work and marriage, the public and the private, power and love, and the idea that women could not have both (Markussen, 1984).

There has hardly been a linear progression towards equity. Mechanisms of domination may have become more subtle, but violence against women instead of violence among men about women, has grown. The persistance of job gender segregation, with a systematic devalorizing of the female, shows how we are still both inside and outside of a man's world, working at the boundaries of the visible and the invisible (Star, 1991).

Why do gender relations change so little through successive waves of technological innovations? What is the connection between organization and gender identity? (Cockburn, 1992:44). Kanter explained women's position in terms of structural mechanisms of power. Since then, many studies have focused on the discursive and material practices in constructing and negotiating gender in the micro politics of everyday life. But in the background lurks an uneasiness in knowing that sex dominance antedated and in many ways shaped class dominance and the idea of the structural other (Lerner, 1986:209). Cockburn concludes that if issues of gender is not openly addressed in technological and organizational developments, little will change.

Wagner demonstrates this impasse. On the one hand, the inscriptions of women's voices make women's work visible within the organization. On the other hand, nurses themselves inscribe the care perspective into the electronic texts. Our images of caring may thus develop beyond the stereotypes of limitless availability, the image of women as the structural other. Women's voices here are important in developing alternative images of authority and management.

Hirschhorn makes a similar point about a management development programme for executive nursing (1988:119ff). It was the first all-female programme at the institution, but issues of gender were not even addressed. The programme was designed to give the participants status and a new vocational identity, more than to educate them. The teachers were men, who were unaware of the significance of gender relations. The women were treated as girls while the programme pretended to make them into men, reflecting the homosocial culture of senior management. In order to cooperate and control their competitiveness, they degrade women, treating them either as sex objects or patronizing them as girls (Kanter, 1977:63). Why can't they be women, that is sexual adults who are subjects, not objects? In the psychoanalytical framework power and sexuality is intertwined: 'The gain, of course, is that people can feel like adults rather than like children. Work can be truly sexualized as people draw on their sense of adulthood to work together.' (Hirschhorn, 1988:139)

Gender is inextricably interwoven into our images of authority. When interaction and communication across traditional lines of commands are intensified, and when women enter formerly male-dominated work communities, awareness of gender must be involved, if authority relations are to change. Developing women's voices, even how we conceive of the masculine, and developing our images of the caring and relatedness in authority, not just the rules and rights, is a challenge to the work organizations, on which so much of our lives now depend. How empowerment and measurement may interact is indeed an important question.

The time of initiative

> Revolution is turning to your point of departure—wiser. (Inger Christensen)[4]

The moment of initiative is a time where the weight of history is deposited, and when the dream of history yet to be made becomes a responsible decision. As Ricoeur says, this may take on many directions and imply different horizons of expectation, different spaces of experiences. The arguments put forward here do reflect a certain place, a certain time and a certain space of experience. And yet in many of the voices speaking of women's experiences, I find a common idea, the idea of patience. The 'wild patience' of Rich, the insights of Lerner', the feeling for the 'as yet unlabelled', that which is permanently escaping, subverting, but related to the standardized, as Star suggests, Braidotti's tightrope-walker, the revolutionary patience of Fink, form an important point of departure. Patience involves both an awareness of the body as situated at the intersection of the biological and the symbolic, and an awareness of that the inclusion of women in theory formation historically is still very new. Women are still both inside and outside.

We need a revolutionary patience to grow new selves, as we cannot change what we are not at peace with (Fink, 1991). Fink suggests that women learn to appreciate and develop sensitivity to 'express what they perceive and believe, but cannot yet tell that they know, and to express it with self respect and without defiance' (1991:14). I have pointed to some of the dilemmas women face in doing this, but also the need to stand by the paradoxes of being both inside and outside: Not to identify with dominant institutions, not the least science as an institution, in order to shape our own lives and horizons of expectation.

Among other things, we need patience in coming to terms with the cultural construction of 'easiness,' in the middle of the challenges and paradoxes of informating.

Acknowledgements

I would like to thank Susan Leigh Star for her inspiration, helpful comments and translation. Childhood memories of washing days have been with me during writing, and I'd like to thank my mother, Henny Samson for her ease with housework and what I learnt from that.

Notes

1 There exists an extensive literature on women's work in the home and the appropriation of technologies, the most famous and influential no doubt being Ruth Schwartz Cowan's 'More work for mother: The ironies of Household technology from the Open Hearth to the Microwave.' (1983) For an overview see Wajcman, 1991. I'm not doing justice to the insights in these studies. My focus is on the positions in the debate because they reflect perspectives that I know only too well from my own experience.

2 Most of the time, I do not find housework that bad: Cooking, cleaning, hoovering, washing, ironing may have meditative qualities, and I enjoy the results of the work. It is of course a choice to invest these kind of feelings in the work, others may experience it differently.

3 Ethnographic accounts, literature and film are an enormous source in exploring the seamless web of work, technology and people. I have particularly in mind the French study by Yvonne Verdier: *Facons de dire, facons de faire: La*

laveuse, la couturiere, la cuisiniere; and the Swedish author Kerstin Ekman's novel *Springkallan* (the Spring). The film *Clotheslines* talks about the long hours of doing laundry in the old days, but also about the 'art' of hanging up clothes, matching colors, getting the feel of the cloth, making a neat clothesline, and how that made a strong moral statement about you as a tidy housewife that the neighbours and your mother would remark on.

4 The Danish poet Inger Christensen is quoted from a radio programme, referred to in the newspaper *Information* from the 18th of August, 1978:6.

'Pulling down' books vs. 'pulling up' files: textual databanks and the changing culture of classical scholarship

Karen Ruhleder

Abstract

The culture of classical scholarship is changing as traditional paper-based materials are being repackaged in electronic form. This paper investigates the changes effected by a Greek textual databank, the Thesaurus Linguae Graecae (TLG). The TLG changes the textual landscape, making available to scholars texts previously accessible with difficulty—or not at all. At the same time, it changes the traditional relationship between scholar and text. 'Knowing' a text is replaced by knowing how to construct search algorithms. Critical notes, repositories of centuries of expertise, are decoupled from the source materials. And new forms of technical expertise are becoming necessary in order to exploit domain expertise. The questions raised by classicists' use of textual databanks concern all communities which move from 'pulling down' books to 'pulling up' files.

A technology gives threefold shape to work; it gives form to the everyday experience of work; it defines the concepts with which we think about experience; and it imposes control upon the social relations of work. (Lyman, 1984).

Introduction: artifacts and work cultures

This chapter was written at a time when personal computers and electronic mail were just beginning to proliferate on campuses and in offices. They were originally cast as calculating machines for large organizations and scientific projects. Recent advances, however, have led to a diverse set of computer-based artifacts, ranging from personal finance packages to architectures supporting distributed, collaborative work. There is a complex relationship between these artifacts and the *cultures* which both shape them and absorb them. 'Culture' encompasses that which is learned and transmitted within a community or population; it includes its patterns of behaviour, institutions, customs and conventions. Traditionally associated with 'exotic tribes,' this notion applies equally well to the behaviours, conventions, institutions and experiences of professions or disciplines (Gregory, 1983). The artifacts used by the members of a profession reflect this culture, and become an integral part of cultural transmission.

Artifacts themselves represent complex 'packages' embodying expectations about work process, expertise, users' values, and the infrastructure necessary to create and maintain them.[1] The combination of skills required to produce and use particular artifacts help to shape and define their cultural integration (Clanchy, 1979; McLuhan, 1964; Ong, 1979). And when artifacts serve as abstract representations of data, characteristics such as reproducibility and transportability affect the nature and extent of this integration (Eisenstein, 1979; Ivins, 1953; Latour, 1986). New representations change old work practices and require new cognitive skills or classification techniques (Eisenstein, 1979, 1983).

The culture of classical scholarship is undergoing such a change as more materials are becoming available in electronic form. Over the past two decades, there has been a slow but steady shift from paper, in which textual editions, concordances, and indexes in book form provide a central focus for work, to an electronic medium, where new computer-based tools redefine the information available to the scholar. These computer-based texts and search tools are changing the textual landscape of classicists' work. They alter the delicate linkages between past and present members of the professional community, and between scholar and text. And they raise questions about new forms of expertise and their transmission.

This chapter on the integration of textual databanks into classics is drawn from a broader empirical investigation of a variety of information technologies including word processors and electronic mail (Ruhleder, 1991). I conducted 60 unstructured interviews over five months with faculty in Classics Studies departments, tool developers, and editors of traditional journals and electronic mailing lists. These were supplemented by participant observation and the use of secondary sources, including journals, newsletters, and conference proceedings. Data were also gathered via telephone and electronic mail.

Classical scholarship: work and values

Classical scholarship traces its roots back to the 8th century BC. It aims to bring to life 'Graeco-Roman civilization in its essence and in every facet of its existence (von Wilamowitz-Möllendorff, 1982). In order to reconstruct this ancient world, classicists piece together both literal and figurative fragments of information, including scraps of papyrus, shards of pottery, and margin notes in early manuscripts referring to works now lost. These multiple sources help establish various aspects of ancient Greek life. Scholars apply *analytical techniques* in weighing and interpreting evidence, and they use *tools* to locate particular pieces of textual evidence.

Classicists see themselves both as preservers of a link to the past and as explicators of current aspects of American and European culture. They view classical literacy and scholarship as culturally essential to intellectual development (Reedy, 1988), and consider the literature of classical antiquity to be for the Western world 'its source and its point of reference' (Kresik, 1981). How each epoch borrowed, adapted, modified, and interpreted Greek culture serves as a window into that epoch (Bolgar, 1981); 'the problems of humankind' (Latinist) lie within these ancient texts, and studying how these cultures constructed themselves, '[helps] you understand how to place yourself within your own culture' (Hellenist). Occasionally, findings have direct contemporary ramifications; one study, for instance, overturned conventional wisdom about the meaning of word 'disciple' in early Christian writings, thus potentially changing doctrine within some churches (Wilkes, 1988).

The text is a key resource for literary critics, and for all subareas within classics, including archaeology, art history, and philosophy. It is an artifact with emotional meaning for classicists; they speak easily of a love for books. Textual evidence provides an important source of discovery about Greek and Roman civilization, and an equally important source of support for evidence gathered by other means, such as archaeological digs or works of art. But to talk about 'the text' is deceptive; any scholar working with ancient Greek and Roman writings knows there is no such thing as a definitive text. One relies on fragments of a questionable nature. Often only copies of copies exist, some dating back no further than the Middle Ages and subject to scribal error and emendation.[2] The reconstruction of the original, or Urtext, is thus a primary activity.

By the time a particular text appears in book form, the editor of the edition has made a series of decisions about variant readings and about the inclusion or exclusion of questionable passages. Sometimes, the original authors might have even produced multiple versions of a text over time and the editor must decide when distinct versions can be identified. These problems and considerations affect anyone working with similarly fragmentary or questionable textual data, such as medieval scholars or archaeologists. One of the differences between various presentations of the text lies in how implicitly or explicitly these editorial decisions are represented in the text 'package' and how critical materials are physically coupled to the text.

Traditional tools: textual editions, concordances and indexes

A classicist working on the use of allusion in Euripides' *Alcestes* explains the tangled, hermeneutical quality of the work:

> [You find a word or phrase that looks like an allusion and ask,] where else might that word or words be? And there comes the rub. That would then entail [for each] author, say Homer, taking the index or concordance to Homer, and checking how many occurrences of that word or phrase there are. . . . But then you need to check other places, so then you check, is it a rare word? You start out with a dictionary. Sometimes that will indicate it to you, but then, basically, you have to go to individual indexes and concordances for each author, and just see where all it's used, how it's used, if it's used very often. It's a laborious process, you can only play out a certain number of your hunches, go with the best ones.

Various formats capture the fragmentary, disputable nature of classical texts. Methods for marking missing, questionable, or spurious sections of text had already been standardized by the third century BC (Reynolds and Wilson, 1974; Youtie, 1974). These markings, as well as other forms of commentary or critical notes, form a part of the printed books most scholars rely on for a given text. The introduction to a new edition typically explains the editorial methods or criteria, and places the new edition within the established literary tradition. One special form of critical note is the *apparatus criticus*. This set of textual notes lists variant readings in all or at least the major alternate manuscripts or editions, thereby tracing the history and logic of editorial decisions—vital in a field where the family tree or 'textual tradition' of an author forms a major component of information about that work.

To use these texts effectively for literary criticism, scholars must locate words, phrases, and grammatical or metrical forms to support or dispute particular points. Several basic tools have traditionally allowed a scholar to search for words and phrases. These include indexes, concordances, and dictionaries. Concordances differ from indexes in that they not only indicate the location of a word, but include some context for the word, perhaps even a definition or translation. The words chosen for a concordance are up to the editor; their comprehensiveness and accuracy varies. As with textual editions, search tools are generally created for one work or one author's canon, such as Rengstorf's concordance to Flavius Josephus (Rengstorf, 1983). Dictionaries or lexicons, on the other hand, span numerous texts and authors, and both define a word and give information about its history and usage.

The *Thesaurus Linguae Graecae*: repository and search tool

The same classicist explained how his work changed once computerized textual databanks became readily available in the late 1980s:

> Now once the Ibycus [TLG] came along, . . . [I could] put up an all-Greek search on the screen, type in that word, tell the machine to search through, and then just turn my back and go about my work and 40 minutes later I'd look, the machine has a match for me. It will have that match from the Odyssey and if there are any others, they'll be there. And if there are no others, it will tell me there are no others. And, with only the amount of time it took me to type in the word and set the machine going, I'll have the answer.

The earliest electronic versions of Homeric texts were created in the 1960s using mainframe computers. Scholars continued to encode individual texts for themselves or a limited number of colleagues. None of these early on-line, individually-constructed text versions impacted the discipline as much as the Thesaurus Linguae Graecae (TLG). This Greek textual data bank was begun in the early 1970s at the University of California, Irvine by classicists Theodore Brunner and David Packard. Brunner was a faculty member in the Department of Classics; Packard was the son of a founder of the Hewlett-Packard Corporation (a large engineering firm and computer manufacturer). The TLG currently contains electronic versions 'of all of ancient Greek literature surviving from the classical and post-classical periods' (Brunner, 1987), and has begun incorporating medieval Greek texts. The TLG is the only widely-used, comprehensive textual databank for ancient Greek texts (Brunner, 1987, 1988, 1991). It is well-respected in the classics community, and has developed a strong infrastructure for acquiring, encoding, and disseminating texts. Originally conceived as a databank for Greek literary texts, other materials (such as Latin texts and other Greek materials) are becoming available through the TLG infrastructure. The TLG texts are accessible on CD ROM, or by using the Ibycus, a dedicated minicomputer which incorporates the TLG texts, a set of search programs, and a word processor for Greek texts. Several search packages, developed independently of the TLG project, are available for use with CD ROM versions of the TLG accessible via IBM-based or Macintosh microcomputers. Search results can then be transferred into several popular word processing programs.

The TLG allows scholars selectively to access Greek texts easily and quickly through a series of on-line search programs. The texts themselves are represented using a special encoding scheme for representing Greek characters and diacritical marks, but none of the critical notes from the textual editions are included. They can search through all TLG texts, or they can narrow a search *via* a list of specific texts, such as all lyric authors or all Greek tragedians. Once the range is set, the word or phrase is entered and the TLG searches for a match. If one is found, it is displayed in boldface, printed, or saved to a file. Three lines of context are included: the line on which it occurs, the line just before, and the following line. An 'index' into the original text is also provided so that the user can locate the phrase within the text itself. Search results can be printed and/or saved to a file.

Computerization and changes in the scholar/text relationship

Changes in technology affect the resources and infrastructures for particular work tasks (Ruhleder, 1994, 1995). They also effect more subtle changes in how individuals perceive their work, the tacit knowledge embedded in the artifacts they use, and their self-perception as members of a discipline. Below I examine several ways in which the move from paper-based to computer-based textual materials affects the *culture* of classical scholarship, including classicists' overview of their materials, their relationship to the text itself and to (literally) generations of scholars before them.

Reshaping the textual landscape: the Canon concretized

The 'computerization' of texts and their incorporation into textual databanks has changed the way that classicists think about the materials they use. The textual landscape has become broader, but it has also become 'flatter'; words or texts which the creators of indexes and concordances imbued with qualitative nuances are weighted equally with all others in a computer search.

With the TLG, scholars conveniently access textual materials unavailable at their own institutions, as the range of encoded texts is broader than any single library's holdings. This is crucial in a field where many texts are out of print or exist only in manuscript form. In fact, one of the TLG's greatest contributions is its role as a *repository*.[3] Collecting and centralizing access to *all* Greek texts is a milestone in classical scholarship. The TLG staff, which maintains originals or facsimiles of all texts included in the databank, located many through hearsay and obscure citation; one was hand-carried from what was then communist Czechoslovakia, another sent from a private library in Crete. These efforts culminated not only in the TLG itself, but in its accompanying reference work, the *Thesaurus Linguae Graecae Canon of Greek Authors and Works* (Berkowitz and Squitier, 1990).

In a discipline plagued with fragmentary and incomplete data, the *Canon* and the TLG serve as concrete embodiments of the very idea of a single corpus of ancient Greek authors. This provides graduate students and faculty with a richer sense of the breadth of texts:

. . . the range of texts that are out there, and sources, that's almost an education in and of itself. . . . I think it really does give people a sense of a broader horizon. . . . They see all these medical writers coming up [in a search]; they wouldn't have thought about medical writers. Or late grammatical writers (Classicist).

Interlibrary loan services and travel grants have existed for a long time to help scholars overcome physical barriers (one classicist cites the former as 'the single most valuable computerized resource outside my office'). With the TLG and other databanks, however, texts that once lay at a scholar's *mental* periphery are pushed centre stage on to the computer screen.

Restructuring the relationship between scholar and text

Computer-based searches lead individuals beyond traditional genre boundaries, as they easily cover a wide range of texts, even all of Greek literature. They are more accurate than the human eye or incomplete or poorly-constructed concordances, indexes and dictionaries. They compensate for the lack of indexes and concordances for some authors or works. Computer-based searches allow scholars to ask questions that formerly could only be answered by extensive reading and experience in the field. It is unclear, however, whether one can *legitimately* make definitive statements about a series of texts without personal familiarity, without starting 'where a scholar has to start—with the text, the manuscripts, the textual tradition' (Hellenist).

Expanded accessibility changes individuals' need or willingness to read and assimilate as much as possible of the extant corpus. Reading and *knowing* a text has always been a highly valued activity. One papyrologist explains, 'It gives you a real sense of what X was like to have read it yourself,' and a Greek historian concludes, 'I find it quite salutary, as a matter of fact, not to have [access to the TLG] because I sit down and read the stuff.' Another classicist finds that using the computer for searching 'detaches you from your work. . . . Sometimes you want to completely digest, master, live with the text. I'd like to just take two books and read and re-read them for a month like in grad school.' All three are senior faculty members. Compare their comments with those of a graduate student using the TLG in order to use materials he has never read: '[Without the TLG], I would have to read . . . through the orators, which is a pretty large corpus, and the philosophers, which is huge.' The graduate student writing about discipleship (cited above) used a similar process to incorporate more materials than he could have read in his short career.

On-line searches not only disturb this scholar-text relationship, but they change the nature of serendipitous finds that occur when reading. A Latinist explains, 'When you read, you learn things that you aren't even searching for. The human brain may be searching for X, but will be confronted with other things.' Schmitt (1990) cites a similar phenomenon with respect to on-line library information services. They do, however, support a different aspect of academic life, the 'publish or perish' imperative: 'The computer helps you cope with professional pressure [to produce papers in quantity]' (Classicist). If individuals cease to read and understand in-depth the texts on which they comment, what happens to their ability to contribute to the larger community of scholarship, and to understand their findings in context?

Decoupling critical notes: losing the voice of the community

One element of the traditional textual edition is the *apparatus criticus*, a set of textual footnotes which form a pointer to previous scholarship. Physically coupled to the text in the traditional edition, the apparatus forms a vivid reminder that the text is one person's 'best guess' at one point in time, an approximation of an unrecoverable Urtext.

'Creating an apparatus is a very labour-intensive and intelligence-intensive process if you want to do a good job at it. Because of the way the apparatus is written in relation to the text that's above it, it takes some intelligence to decide what to put in your version. . . . And for some authors there's so much controversy over the text that whole phrases are in question. You have to make a decision; . . . Are you just reporting a single word? In some cases, that single word will be incorporated into a larger word in a conjecture.' (Classicist)

The TLG includes no critical notes or materials, and only a single edition of each text. These limitations have led to serious criticism of the tool, particularly where there is dispute over the version of choice. One classicist explains,

189

'You might do a search on the Ibycus and find something interesting, and then open up your newer edition and see that it was just [so-and-so's] choice, and [so-and-so] was wrong.'

'Wrong' may simply mean that the newer and preferred edition contains a different editorial decision with respect to a word or passage.

The lack of critical materials deprives the scholar of an important set of links to other scholars both present and past. Editions not only serve as representations of the text itself, but include information about the text, its history, and its reliability as a witness to the archetype. These linkages provide a connection in a field where 'collaboration' doesn't necessarily involve two living individuals. One classical philosopher describes his work on epicureanism as a 'cumulative, collaborative effort,' explaining, 'by collaborative, I mean by other scholars over the generations.' Interpretations of texts can be seen as examples of their local instantiations, and their interpretation over time as their 're-representation path' (Star, 1989). While this kind of information about the text is still available, it must now be recovered by the individual in another form and from another repository altogether. The TLG may provide a broader view, but the view also becomes shallower as critical information and a sense of social and cultural location is decoupled from the artifact at hand.

Ambiguity and forms of expertise

Critical notes, addenda, and choices about the presentation of materials represent elements of a collective expertise developed over centuries. This expertise is not embedded within computer-based tools such as the TLG. For example, if one turns to the TLG in place of a traditional concordance to locate a word or phrase, the user must be aware that spelling might vary over time, by place, from scribe to scribe, or even within a text created by a single author (Reynolds and Wilson, 1974).

One of the things I'm working with is the corpus of fifth century decrees . . . on the Ibycus. It's a little bit tricky to use because the orthography is in flux at this point. (Graduate Student).

The editor of a concordance, an expert on a particular text and era, might indicate orthographical fluctuations. Even if this were not the case, similarly spelled words will still be located near one another, increasing the likelihood that the scholar will discover a close variant. A search through the TLG, however, would locate only the *precise* pattern the user had specified. Again, computer-based texts and search programs might provide more extensive search coverage, but they also increase the amount of critical knowledge and expertise required of the user/scholar even as they discourage personal familiarity with a text. What was once the responsibility of the editor to know and compensate for is now the responsibility of each individual database user—a complex mix of deskilling and demanding additional skills.

To make effective use of one's domain expertise, one must develop the technical expertise to correctly construct search lists of authors and patterns of characters. This expertise is often acquired sporadically, relying on local knowledge of colleagues or graduate students, or haphazard support by the campus computing center. Its acquisition may become easier as tools spread throughout the community; at the same time, however, it is considered by classicists to be peripheral to their 'real' work. Classicists are introduced into the discipline as apprentices; as a 'younger' generation of classicists enters with greater technical expertise, the traditional patterns of knowledge transmission and understanding are turned upside-down.

Even classicists who develop the various forms of expertise needed to use the TLG and other textual databases effectively may not understand the limitations inherent in their creation. For instance, classicists attribute great objectivity to the TLG in terms of its search results *because it is a computer*, hence, 'objective.' Yet the texts included are still constructed by 'subjective' humans, and their selection is accomplished by a panel of 'experts' as selected by the American Philological Association with whom not everyone may agree. They are entered and verified according to a set of programs and algorithms developed by the TLG staff. When included in the TLG's *Canon of Authors*, they are 'tagged' or labelled according to various characteristics, such as genre, using a schema developed over time by scholars in the field and augmented by the TLG staff. These designations may sometimes be open to dispute, yet their use to construct search lists determines the texts included (Bowker and Star, 1991). There is nothing magical or 'objective' about any of this. However, in direct contrast to a textual edition with explanatory notes, these complex decisions are hidden from view. Furthermore, it is not clear that this technical material could be presented in a way which would be useful to the scholar/user community. The construction of a concordance or dictionary is easy to understand; not so a set of computer-based verification and correction programs for encoded data. An increasing amount of technical expertise is necessary not only to use tools, but to understand their creation and their limitations, opening up a layer of uncertainty and ambiguity that cannot be addressed by domain expertise.

Summary: moving towards a techno-culture?

Just as the printing press secured the future of classical texts (Reynolds and Wilson, 1974:187), the TLG serves both to disseminate textual materials and to preserve them through profusion. It allows greater access to the text through its search capabilities, overcoming (some of) the limitations of incomplete, poorly constructed, or simply nonexistent indexes and concordances. We can visualize the shift from one type of artifact to the other in Figures 1 and 2.

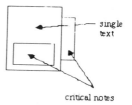

single
text

critical notes

Figure 1 Textual edition: single text with coupled with critical materials

Both the TLG texts and search programs serve as 'reproducible, transportable inscriptions' (Latour, 1986) ready for uniform local instantiation in multiple work settings. Encoding techniques and search algorithms can be transported across technological, institutional, and cultural boundaries, permitting a faithful reproducibility previously impossible. These features support certain forms of inquiry, such as matching papyrus frag-

Figure 2 TLG: many texts decoupled from (paper-based) critical materials

ments with established texts or basing arguments on the frequency or co-location of words or phrases.

Yet even as the TLG facilitates a critical set of activities, it is also beset by limitations. These should concern not only classicists, but all critics of technology. The electronic medium has 'flattened out' the corpus; it has reduced it to a collection of bits and bytes. So far, classicists have demonstrated a willingness to manipulate bits and bytes as though they were the texts themselves; to 'pull up' a search in the same way that one might 'pull down' a volume from a shelf. And so far the culture supports a kind of scholarship that is deeply vested in reading and the original texts. But is this because the traditional tools support this culture? What will happen as computer-based tools become more prevalent, and paper editions with supplementary materials become either less available or less ready-to-hand?

Scholars already accept others' readings of the text, and take secondary evidence for granted without returning to the original sources (Youtie, 1974). So, this aspect did not come with computing. For instance, the *editio princeps* produced by the early printers was very likely based on a questionable original manuscript, yet it became the established vulgate text through 'the forces of inertia and conservatism [which] made it difficult to discard it in favour of a radically new text.' The very act of printing a text 'tended to give that form of the text an authority and a permanence which in fact it rarely deserved' (Reynolds and Wilson, 1974:187).

Similarly, materials presented in electronic form are often granted an undeserved authority because of the 'scientific' objectivity attributed to the medium. The pre-inscribed 'correctness' of computer-based information presents a particularly great danger when the mechanisms of its manipulation and retrieval are invisible to the user.[4] Criteria for data inclusion and manipulation are based on underlying assumptions that may be technical in nature, but may also be motivated by intellectual or other biases (ie, scribes were sometimes told to include or exclude sections of text for political reasons). As they incorporate more computer-based tools, classicists increasingly use artifacts whose development and construction they may not understand, and which remove them yet another step from the original source text.

Computing technologies are malleable in terms of the configuration of hardware, software, infrastructural components which define them. However, beyond a certain point, these configurations lose their malleability (Law and Whittaker, 1988). As design decisions are made, information and the means for retrieval and manipulation becomes concretized. The TLG strips the text of its attendant commentary and critical notes, thus removing a robust encapsulation of cumulative and collaborative effort. It could be reconstructed or expanded to capture materials or linkages now excluded, perhaps building on recent advances in hypertext or multimedia.[5] However, both its architecture and infrastructure have now become so firmly established that it is unlikely that any great changes will soon take place in the construction of this tool.

The 'computerization' of classics is still in its early stages, and some consider the TLG to be a catalyst whose impact is just beginning. One prediction follows:

> All these various computerized versions that work from the TLG are going to be spread around in our highly computerized American universities. American research is going to be quite dominant and the character of American research is going to be technological. (Classicist).

Will this 'technological' character translate into the growth of statistically-based research? Will analytical approaches and questions that cannot be easily pursued using computer-based tools be thrust aside? Will we witness the demise of the intense and individualistic relationship between scholar and text, even as we see a new relationship emerge between scholar/programmer and computer?

Whatever direction future research may take, the TLG and similar computer-based artifacts used by scholars have already changed the questions classicists address and the means by which they address them. They have redefined scholarly expertise. And they have profoundly affected the information readily available to the scholar, even as they embody a new set of assumptions about text and about scholarship. The larger questions raised by these shifts concern all of academic culture, as we shift from 'pulling down' books to 'pulling up' files.

Acknowledgements

Many people contribute to the development of a paper, but I especially wish to thank John Leslie King, Susan Leigh Star, Samuel L. Gilmore, and Jeanne Pickering for their comments on earlier versions of this paper. I wish to thank Carolyn Green, Dennis Adams, and Rudy Hirschheim for their suggestions and comments on this version.

Notes

1 The 'package' metaphor was first articulated in Kling and Scacchi [24] with respect to *computing packages*. They define these as consisting of hardware and software, skill sets, data, beliefs about computing and organizational support infrastructures. Ruhleder (1995) more fully explores applicability of this metaphor to the domain of classical scholarship.

2 Corruptions can be attributed to carelessness, handwriting variations, or a tired scribe. Sometimes, however, sections were omitted or modified for religious or political reasons.

3 See Star (1987) for a discussion of repositories as boundary objects.

4 Even experts in a given domain will not necessarily question incorrect results when using an expert system developed for that domain (Will, 1991)!

5 Since 1987, the now-Tufts-based *Perseus* Project has been constructing a hyper-text/multimedia tool for teaching and research across many sub-disciplines of classics. It draws its textual materials from the TLG; other materials, such as maps and photographs, are quite incomplete. *Perseus* requires special, expensive hardware, and is not widely used. Dr. Gregory Crane is the director.

The visual culture of engineers

Kathryn Henderson

Abstract

This chapter defines and illustrates the visual culture of engineers as situated in practice, delineating the components of engineers' visual culture and its relationship to tacit knowledge. A historical account traces the development of drafting conventions in the West, discussing how engineering designers' daily practices have constructed a visual culture not necessarily compatible with the assumptions built into computer-graphics design. The visual literacy which engineers develop in practice is described along with levels of encoding in engineering drawings. Parallels are drawn between these encoding structures and those found in language and artworks in order to explain how visual representations function as boundary objects and conscription devices and why visual representations are such a powerful tool.

Introduction

A design instructor at a major engineering school stops abruptly as he checks a student drawing. A form that should read as a cylinder has been represented as a flat surface. The encoding reads like a glaring grammatical error to the experienced designer. The same error shows up on several other student drawings. These students learned drafting using CAD (computer assisted drafting) software. The conventions of drafting are historically based on paper-world practices; the students' different renderings are not silly mistakes or lack of intelligence. They are the result of differences in the practice that produced them. The everyday practices involved in constructing representations of the world are so powerful that they become interlocked with a particular way of seeing. This is a visual culture, a way of seeing that reflects and contributes to the specific manner in which one renders the world.

The visual culture of engineering is a world in which people turn to drawings when asked a design question, such as a member of a NASA Research and Design team who was told, 'better go get the drawings' when he tried to describe a part using gestures and an adding-machine tape. It is more than the collaborative visual thinking, exemplified by two engineers, deep in discussion of modifications to their surgical instrument design, who sketch, using one pad of paper and one writing implement, unconsciously passing the pencil back and forth with a co-ordination suggesting one mind instead of two. The visual culture of engineering is more than the sum of its parts: the practices of sketching and drawing constitute communication in the design world. Other forms of knowledge and communication (verbal, mathematical, tacit) are built around these representations. Visual representations are so central to engineering design that meetings wait while individuals fetch drawings from their offices, or sketch facsimiles on white boards. A shared visual literacy and ability to read encoded meanings facilitates co-ordination or can be a medium for conflict in collective projects. They not only shape the final products of design engineering, but also influence the structure of the work and who may participate in it. These situated, collective practices create a visual culture that, in turn, constricts and constructs the literal ability to see or imagine.

This chapter defines and illustrates the visual culture of engineers as situated in practice, delineating the components of engineers' visual culture and its relationship to tacit knowledge. A historical account traces the development of drafting conventions in the West, discussing how engineering designers' daily practices have constructed a visual culture not necessarily compatible with the assumptions built into computer-graphics design. The visual literacy which engineers develop in practice is described along with levels of encoding in engineering drawings. Parallels are drawn between these encoding structures and those found in language and artworks in order to explain how visual representations function as boundary objects and conscription devices and why visual representations are such a powerful tool.

Practical epistemologies and visual culture

A *visual culture* is a particular way of seeing the world linked to explicit material experience. That engineers think visually is well documented.[1] That their cumulative social environment influences their visual thought, has been given less attention. In art history visual culture has been presented as the link between 'art' and daily visual skills, tied to the material conditions of rendering the world using brush, pen, stylus, or whatever. Citing Alper's analysis of Dutch paint, Latour (1986) points out that visual culture is not a metaphorical but a literal, material 'world view': 'how a culture sees the world, and makes it visible' (Latour, 1986 p. 9). Thus 'A new visual culture redefines both *what it is to see* and *what there is to see* (p. 10). For those engaged with drawing, painting or mechanical drafting, how they see their world is strongly tied to the learned conventions of rendering it. Engineers who generate and manipulate visual renditions of objects do so using the conventions of drafting. But daily work is not school; work habits also play a major part in the construction of engineers' visual culture.

Sketches are the real heart of visual communication. They serve both as an individual thinking tool and as an interactive one. A senior drafter, promoted to engineer, fought with management for the return of her drawing board, stating 'I can't think without my drawing board.' It is the place she solves problems. Sketches facilitate both individual thinking and interactive communication; they allow these processes to occur simultaneously so that sketches become group thinking tools. Thorough designers continually use sketches, from early drafts talked over with designers and fabricators, to rough drawings in margins to clarify an idea (Henderson, 1991).

Sketching is essential to getting ideas across. One designer stated that you never 'get two designers who just sit down and just talk,' adding, 'Everybody draws sketches to each other.' Another pointed out that a meeting where the product is actually built 'works wrong if you can't communicate.' He takes his drawings to 'sit and talk' so others understand him. Likewise he sketches for workers so they can understand how to create what he has in mind, clarifying more formal layout drawings. This interactive use of sketches and drawings knits together people with shop expertise, such as welders, with various designers, tapping individual expertise in piping, electrical circuitry, lubrication systems, etc. to think through a machine. But cognition must be situated in practice.

Lave (1988) stresses the link between everyday material experience and thought, visual or otherwise. Her work challenges functionalist, conventional views that formal school-based knowledge makes cognitive skills available for generalization and everyday use. Observing the expertise of grocery shoppers, she argues that knowledge-in-practice is the locus of our most powerful knowledgeability. Lave's practice theory denotes no division between domestic life and work, domestic and public domains, routine maintenance and productive activity, or manual routines and creative mental work. Similarly, it is not school-learned drafting conventions which make up the visual culture of engineers but rather the everyday practices of sketching, drawing, and drafting which construct their visual culture—a visual culture which in turn constructs *what* and *how* design engineers see.

Alpers (1983) documents the seventeenth century Dutch visual culture, illustrating that artists' attention to surface detail reveals how their culture saw the world. Unlike the Italian Renaissance painters who gave us grandiose historical scenes rendered as if viewed from a carefully placed window, using perspective to create the illusion of deep space, seventeenth-century Dutch painters rendered their world viewed as a close-up mirror, reflecting real details of daily life. This included rich domestic fabrics, reflective vessels, the forms and textures of tools and utensils, fruits and flowers, ornaments and mirrors themselves. This cultural space was constructed by contemporary preoccupations with the camera obscura, which transformed large three-dimensional objects into small two-dimensional surfaces around which onlookers could turn at will. Also influential was the notion of artifice in Kepler's account of the retinal image; rather than Alberti's windows through which one observes, retinal images are passively observed, like the mirror surface which reflects what is already there.

The Dutch were primary contributors to the development of technologies involving mirrors and lenses, including the camera obscura, telescopes and microscopes. They were also significantly advanced in cartography. Their descriptive way of seeing is analogous to the way one views a map—an image without a viewer. To see a map is not to look from some imagined window but to see the world in a descriptive format. This is not relations to 'social interests' or 'economic infrastructure' but rather 'the new precise scenography that results in a world view which defines at once what is science, what is art and what it is to have a world economy' (Latour, 1986:10).

Similarly, Baxandall (1972) points out the relationship between the proliferation of cones, cylinders, and geometric spaces in fifteenth-century Italian paintings and the obsessive pleasure merchant art patrons took in demonstrating their mathematical skills by applying them to the volumes illustrated in paintings. The visual culture here was such that it was as if painters and their patrons saw the world as compositions of perfect geometric components.[2]

Anyone who has undertaken drawing seriously knows that learning to put what the eye beholds on to paper, in detail, influences the level of detail one literally sees. The art student is trying to recreate something; she or he sees shape, framing, point of view, shade, texture, and detail in more levels of nuance than the casual observer. This affects mental representations too, but is easier to trace in actual renditions. Drafters, illustrators and shop workers are used to a 'way of seeing' rooted in practice. If the format is changed the work becomes foreign, difficult to understand, eg, Westerners tend to think of pictorial renditions within a rectangular frame which recedes according to the rules of perspective. Why? Despite the available variety of shapes, reproductions we see most often are captured in rectangular shapes, using a lens that creates an illusion of depth. Photographers 'frame' their shots in rectangular lenses, and we in turn see our world recreated in such frames in magazines, on cereal boxes, and in posters. The unnaturalness of the world seen through a 'fish eye' lens seems distorted because both the perspective and frame are round.[3]

Visual thought, spatial intelligence and kinesthetic intelligence

Engineering documents are intrinsically linked to visual thinking, from earliest conceptual stages to final production. The mind's eye can range from a fully developed realistic representation to a more general sketch or a simple schematic. The image is not static. Its formal aspects (such as size, shape, texture) can be adjusted at will.

Psychologist Howard Gardner (1984) argues that visual image processing is not mere intuition but is indeed distinct intelligence. According to Gardner the characteristics of spatial intelligence include:

- the ability to recognize instances of the same elements
- the ability to transform or recognize the transformation of one element into another
- the capacity to conjure up mental imagery and then transform it
- the capacity to produce a graphic likeness of spatial information.[4]

While Gardner's multi-intelligence model remains controversial, other researchers do confirm the presence of visually-oriented thought processes (Smith, 1964; Shepard and Cermak, 1973; Neisser and Kerr, 1973). My focus here is how to link the self-evident skill in visual cognition with engineering culture.

We find links between thought and practice in the visual documents so crucial to engineering. As we move into the world of practice another, often overlooked, 'way of knowing' becomes apparent—what Gardner terms 'kinesthetic' intelligence, otherwise known as fingertip or craft knowledge.[5] Both spatial and kinesthetic knowledge combine, of course, with practical experience which uses and enhances them. Together these *other ways of knowing* are *practical epistemologies*. Developed in situated practice, they shape the visual culture of engineers. Logico-mathematical and verbal skills are not primarily responsible for good engineering design, but rather these practical epistimologies.

Eugene Ferguson (1977, 1985, 1992) points out that the objects of our daily life (carving knives, comfortable chairs, lighting fixtures, and motorcycles) were determined by technologists— craftsmen, designers, inventors, and engineers—using nonscientific, nonverbal modes of thought. Scientificity is overemphasized, even mythologized. Practical visual thinking in design means that the qualities of the objects in the mind of the technologist are not formal verbal (I would add, or mathematical) descriptions. If we are to understand the development of Western technology, we must appreciate visual thought, the determinant of our physical world. Pyramids, cathedrals, and rockets exist not because of geometry, theory of structures, or thermodynamics, but because they were first a visual image for those who designed them (Pye, 1964). Turnbull (1993) documents how cathedrals like Chartres were built using local knowledge, templates and string. Another way of talking about such non-verbal and non-mathematical ways of knowing is through the concept of 'tacit knowledge.'

Tacit knowledge

Not all non-verbal knowledge is visual. What Michael Polanyi (1958, 1967) calls 'tacit knowledge' or a personal way of knowing, informs the explicit knowledge characteristic of science. It is present in the creativity of laboratory practice and the passion of discovery. Knowing is action that requires skill such as the carpenter who knows just how a type of wood must be handled, or what type of joint will best serve. To say that the carpenter 'knows' these things is not to claim that the individual could put the knowledge into words (Harper, 1987). All elements and uses of scientific knowledge are thus vital—not only the formal and the informal but the political and persuasive, the emotive and intangible, and *the unspeakable* (emphasis mine).

The role of tacit knowledge has become a growing concern in practice-oriented studies of science and technology.[6] I am using the term here in the broadest sense, that is to signify knowledge which is not verbalized—in some cases because it cannot be but in other cases because it may simply be taken for granted or regarded as too trivial to warrant verbalization. The generation and/or elicitation of all types of tacit knowledge is intrinsically linked to practice. H.M. Collins states that 'all types of knowledge, however pure consist in part of tacit rules which may be impossible to formulate in principle' (1972:46). His study of newcomers' attempts to build lasers using documentary information reveal that even with access to accurate diagrams and blueprints they could not build lasers without having participated in real laser building. Those whose lasers worked made personal visits and telephone calls. Even then some failures occurred due to lack of understanding of all the relevant parameters.

Hindle (1981) remarks on how 'fingertip knowledge' from Europe informed the growth of so-called 'American ingenuity.' Throughout the colonial period technology was transferred by bringing in a group of skilled operatives familiar with its mechanisms. In the sixteenth and seventeenth centuries German miners, Flemish weavers, French glassworkers and clock makers transferred technologies from the continent to England. Realizing the source of technological knowledge, in turn, the English sent Italian silk reelers, Dutch and Polish glassworkers and German sawyers to their new colony in Jamestown.

Tacit knowledge, like intuition, is a residual category which encompasses many dimensions of non-verbal knowledge; I focus here on visual or spatial knowledge. Ivins (1953) has pointed out that technological innovation was blocked for the ancient Greeks because they lacked a reproductive capacity for pictorial information. Given the Platonic mind/body split, only slaves worked with their hands. However, hands-on knowledge is intrinsic to visual knowledge and thus technological know-how. Because slaves were the power source in ancient times there was no impetus to invent technology to conserve human energy.

Practical epistemologies versus perspective—constructing optical consistency

Inscriptions are images which have been extracted from the laboratory to appear later cleaned, redrawn, and displayed as figures in support of a text (Latour and Woolgar, 1986; Latour, 1986, 1987). Inscriptions are mobile, presentable, combinable with one another and are immutable. This immutable quality derives from its translation into optical consistency with the original source; internal properties of the subject represented are not modified (1988:7) In visual modes this is accomplished through some device such as the conventions of map-making or drafting.

Based on Edgerton (1976), Latour includes perspective as contributing to optical consistency (1986). But this has only limited validity for engineering practice. Renderings in perspective played a historical role and continue to be used to generate financial and organizational support for design and commercial promotion. But these are not design functions; they utilize a different kind of representation. They are drawn by illustrators, not engineers— who have been known to refer to them scornfully as 'pretty pictures.' The early drawings for transfer of technological knowledge across time and space were illustrations, not plans. Architectural layout drawings of this early period were actually more similar to the layout drawings which carry engineering information today. Perspectival illustrations play only a supporting role in design, not the optical consistency crucial to creating an object from a drawing.

Designers place representation devices at 'centres of calculation' (Latour, 1987) where they are collected together so as to hold pieces of information in the absence of the thing itself (such as a sketch of an existing machine to be modified). The cascade of sketches ultimately made concrete in the final design representations depends on the mobility, stability, and combinability of the representations for extension of the network of participants and information.

Scientists distrust the use of 'mere' metaphor, similarity, or surface resemblance in representations as inadequate, to be abandoned in favor of 'deep', 'genetic', or 'mathematical' reconstructions of a phenomenon's organization which 'penetrate' the depth of the phenomenon, its unraveling, its dissection (Lynch and Woolgar, 1988: 105). Visual representations in engineering must capture the process of building up an artifact, requiring visual articulation of a minutely detailed nature to reveal the object's inner structure and workings.

How do the practical, situated epistemologies of design engineers work with drafting conventions to facilitate optical consistency from large machine to flat representation and back again? Baynes and Pugh (1981) show that up to the late eighteenth century no standards of engineering drawing existed. They note that while it is tempting to include certain medieval manuscripts, publications by Renaissance military engineers, and Leonardo da Vinci's notebooks in the 'prehistory' of engineering drawing, these are not design and production drawings, but illustrations. The rationalization of sight during the Renaissance enabled quantification of visual information for accurate transfer of visual information. But it was not until the middle of the eighteenth century that official French patronage, spurred by war and trade, brought official backing for applied drawing. It was the French military engineer. Gaspard Monge, who developed and codified the conventions of descriptive geometry on which the theoretical aspects of modern engineering drawing are based, and a Napoleonic officer brought the concepts to America, via the military academy (Booker, 1963). Sponsorship of perspective renderings of architecture and technology proliferated, certainly serving to create a 'centre of calculation,' with networks of patrons to support them. While expensive books with beautiful drawings in perspective proliferated for gentlemanly clientele during this period, what did *real* production drawings look life? Barnes and Pugh note that the document collections of the Royal

Navy, 'that very commercially minded and middle class organization, since the early years of the century had required that a
model and plan for each of its ships should be prepared for the
Navy Board' (p. 32). The standardized layout and simple conventions of these ships draughts remained unaltered until the advent
of steam in the 1830s. These drawings, as well as other commercial plans from the period, were rendered, not in perspective but
in profile, section, and plan views as are production drawings
today. A profile view, as the name implies, is straight on at 90-
degrees from the side. A plan view is top-down or bird's eye. A
section view shows a slice to reveal an interior; like the profile
view it is represented from a straight view perpendicular to its
center. These are rendered in two dimensions without the distortion of perspective's illusion of three dimensions.

The model thus became available for the total three-dimensional representation. The elegant perspective renderings in
expensive books of the period were for gentlemen, not working
designers or builders. Although the first practical application of
steam power was made by Thomas Newcomen in 1712, no engineering drawings exist from the period (Baynes and Pugh, 1981).
Rather, the depictions of Newcomen engines from the period
were drawn by artists, not engineers. While the Newcomen
engine appeared in a variety of technical illustrations, several are
inaccurate. None of these renditions was in any way connected
with production work. Engravers, too, faced problems in depicting machinery, noted in this remark by Newcomen's biographer:

> It must be emphasized that early pictures of Newcomen
> engines are not an infallible guide to chronological develop-
> ment. Artists either failed to understand the principles of the
> valve gear and drew it indistinctly or inaccurately, or else they
> copied their predecessors' work. Thus the Sutton Nicholls
> engraving [which Barnes and Pugh illustrate] of what purports
> to be the York Buildings engine shows the buly gear only,
> which is certainly incorrect. (L.T.C. Rolt, *Crown Copyright,
> Science Museum, London.*)

Edgerton (1980), arguing for the deterministic quality of perspective in the development of Western technology, similarly
observes inaccuracies in Chinese copies of Western technical
drawings in the sixteenth and seventeenth centuries. He maintains
that the decorative conventions of Chinese art did not support
the depiction of technology, while in the West perspective and

the exploded view had a direct effect on technological development. I disagree.

The missing ingredient in both the Sutton-Nicholls engraving and the erroneous Chinese woodcut prints of Ramelli's Windlass Pump is tacit knowledge. Actual hands-on understanding of how the machine works is not captured by perspective or any other drawing technique. It is the tacit knowledge of the craftsperson— the practical epistemologies of eye, hand, and situated practice that gets the job done. Any drawing only captures a small piece of tacit knowledge even if experts are consulted. Drafting conventions were designed to elucidate more unspoken knowledge through standardization, but those conventions do not arise until the late nineteenth century. Renaissance perspective drawings were also illustrations, rather than production-oriented draughts, made for gentlemen not engineers or workers.

Newcomen, who made the first viable steam pumping engine in the world, did so without drawings, using techniques that were well-established to the point of being almost medieval in their rugged durability. (Baynes and Pugh, 1981). The after-the-fact drawings of Newcomen's engine, many inaccurate, represent the absorption of his innovation into the scholarship of his day by the use of drawing conventions similar to those of Diderot's *Encyclopedie*. Practical engineers of this period did not use perspective drawing as an everyday part of their work.

When the ability to transfer tacit technological knowledge was lost, explicit drawings became necessary (Hindle, 1981). At the end of the nineteenth century, technology became more complicated, and innovation expanded beyond small workshops in which the innovator had direct control. The appearance of engineering drawings as a mature medium in their own right coincided 'almost too neatly' with the establishment of the first factory for the construction of stationary steam engines (Baynes and Pugh, 1981). In 1773, Matthew Boulton and James Watt founded their Soho Manufactory in Birmingham to produce modified Newcomen engines. Watt, able to codify drawing practice, is credited with developing the conventions of drafting. In their scope, style, and direct application to design and manufacture, these divided engineering drawing from technical illustration. Watt's unusual background combined his practical apprenticeship training in instrument making with his membership in the circle of natural philosophers at Glasgow University. Watt drew together the threads of architectural, technical, scientific, and military draughtsmanship and formed them into a practical means for design, development and production control (Baynes and Pugh, 1981).

In contemporary engineering design, Barnes and Pugh note the emergence of a typology of drawings, including:

Designer's drawings—early sketches and notebooks

Project drawings—formalized early sketches which show proposals in a broad outline, produced according to rules and conventions, often produced by the drawing office rather than the engineer

Production drawings—drawings which lay out all aspects of design for use in actual production

Presentation and Maintenance Drawings—drawings made after the product is finished for use by the customer

Technical Illustrations—illustration for popularizing books that use the conventions of engineering drawing.

Historically and in contemporary engineering, perspective may be used in all of these formats except production drawings. However, production drawings are central in the implementation of a design into an actual product. Perspective is used where engineers must interact with others, often in non-engineering networks: project drawings for funding and organizational support; presentation and maintenance drawings for direct consumers; and technical illustrations for public relations. Although Edgerton focuses on these, they are not the drawings that get the design to production work done. Those that facilitate fabrication are two-dimensional plan, profile, and section drawings, using drafting conventions and the clear practical epistemology of everyday design work. For engineers, designers, and drafters, perspective drawings have a particular space and function as illustrations. Orthogonal or two-dimensional plan, profile, and section drawings are the acknowledged carriers of engineering production information.

Design engineers and drafters, though they may see their design object in many views in their head, eventually reduce them to two dimensions on paper. That is the conventional way such thoughts are rendered. They do not put down the design from just any angle. The plan or layout is an orthogonal view, seen straight down at 90 degrees, viewed from the top. Orthogonal means mutually perpendicular. Such views, which are sometimes simply called 'two-D' represent the object from a 90-degree or profile view. By contrast, an isometric view, used conventionally for illustrations, shows two sides at once, one at 30 degrees and the other at 60 degrees. This is less clear—perspective distorts sizes and shapes when showing them at an angle. Computer graphics were formatted at one of my field sites so that the drafter had to draw the package in an isometric style but in 'true' perspective. This was less familiar to the drafter's eye than conventional isometric, but did represent the object from a corner viewpoint. Neither true perspective nor isometric are used by designers to convey official design specifications. Plan and profile are the most widely used. Section views are rarer. Isometric views are used in illustrations—'pretty pictures' for manuals and operations.

These conventions become entrenched in practice. A shop mechanic who was responsible for putting together 'build books' for product construction gave me a good example. Drawings for build books are generated from the actual process of building the first production model. The drawings may be computer-generated or hand-drafted by professional drafters, some in-house and others from vendors. Problems have arisen with some drawings generated on the graphics system. Carol, one of the mechanical engineers whose responsibility is to assemble the build book, mentioned a particular problem with some illustrations which came through the computer graphics system:

> When I can, I use theirs [CAD/CAM drawings]. But a lot of times the angles and things they use are not sufficient for us. For instance, I've got a seal oil system I was working on for about a year and I did use a lot of CADS drawings but they were confusing to the people on the floor. See, like I ended up drawing this [points to drawing illustrated in Figure 2] to tell them the location of where these switches were going to go. Whereas originally I had something like this [Figure 1]. And they felt that angle was too, too drastic and they couldn't read [it] that well. They wanted to look at something and see it. So they threw out my CADS drawing and I redrew it. And that happens a lot. . . . Its nice to make pretty pictures but the main, important thing is to make it as simple as you can for these guys 'cause they're the ones we're doing it for so they can do it right.

The hand-drawing of the mechanical engineer was simple, without dimensions or drafting skills, no more polished than the

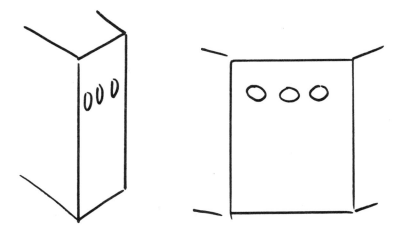

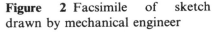

Figure 1 Facsimile of isometric view as represented
in computer graphics ren-
dition rejected by shop
workers

Figure 2 Facsimile of sketch
drawn by mechanical engineer

crudely drawn facsimile the author has provided (Figure 2). Yet
it got the point across when the cleaner, computer-generated
drawing failed because the crude drawing followed the norms of
the visual culture. The mechanical engineer's drawing became
part of the build book. Similarly, the packaging design manager
reported his troubles in getting designers to accept computerized
representations because they insisted on orthogonal or two-
dimensional views and the CAD/CAM system produced a different view:

> Designers and draftsmen always have very very rigorous rules.
> I'm in real trouble here with the CAD/CAM system because
> mostly the guys that design are used to producing designs in
> orthographic representation and-ah to them they don't con-
> sider a design until that's done. Whereas the CADs system
> really is designed around producing isometric, three-dimen-
> sional representations and then, from that the CAD system
> produces plainer drawings that are essentially orthogonal
> representations. I myself am not a design engineer. . . . You've
> got a problem here in that the engineer perceives that every-
> body needs orthogonal drawings to build this thing. I don't

think you do—but you try and tell that to some of the engineers. one of them particularly . . . He gets very, very upset with the whole CADS system because he says, 'Its easy enough for you to work in these stupid isometric pictures but in the end you've gotta have a, an ortho— a, you know, a 'proper drawing', as he calls it.

At my second site, an experienced designer said, 'If you were going to make a dress, would you want the pattern to be in perspective?' Actually to design and produce something, be it a turbine engine, a medical instrument, a nuclear power plant or a garment, plans with only one relationship to shape and dimension are needed. This is most clearly and simply accomplished in two-dimensional representations, by convention. Illustrations using perspective create illusion, not exactness. Dimensions are distorted to give the appearance of recession in space. The glass box approach in engineering design sets a model in which each side of the object would be hypothetically traced on to the box face against it and then the box opened flat so that each face is rendered in two planes only. Each side is clear, illustrated both in visual terms that make visual sense with the measurements. Perspective would present a shorter and longer line both with the same measurement, a confusing state of affairs. Hence at the transfer of information for fabrication, two-dimensional drawings became conventional since they allow the immutable transfer of the information.

Some formal drafting conventions are:

• Standardization of line thickness for specific design designations, eg thickest line for major components;
• Template use for standard curves and shapes
• Specific manners in designating dimensions on a drawing, keeping the zero origin point consistent throughout the drawing
• Keeping specifications to a minimum
• Use of a standard lexicon of symbols

While some conventions remain standard in all drafting, others are company specific, such as symbol system sets and lettering. Military drawings have their own standards and conventions. The learning and constant use of such conventions leads to the acquisition of a type of practice-oriented visual literacy—a situated practice. The actual process of drawing is not a school-learned activity that carries across to practice. Engineering designers do not follow text-book protocols. They structure their work in an apparently random fashion, moving from one part of the design to another as the ideas flow (Ullman et al., 1987). The two engineers mentioned earlier, sketching with one tablet and pencil, unconsciously sharing the writing implement as part of their conversation concerning a particular design problem, were not exhibiting formal drafting behavior. But they were certainly highly accomplished visual practitioners.

Visual literacy

Patricia Greenfield (1984) has documented children's acquisition of a visual literacy for editing techniques, acquired through television watching. She notes cross-cultural research on the comparative success in teaching ability of Sesame Street for young audiences (Solomon, 1975, 1979). This shows differences in visual abilities in children who grow up watching television and those who do not. Television watchers recognize that different views or cropped views of a room are indeed the same setting; non-television watchers see each view as a different site. Similarly, non-television watchers are more likely to identify a long shot and a close-up of the same person as two different people. Constant exposure and interaction with a 'way of seeing' develops skills in visual reading analogous to verbal reading and writing literacy. Language is tied to culture; the way we speak both reflects and reinforces our cultural outlook and values. Similarly the visual literacy of engineering designers reflects and informs their visual culture. As with language, not all visual literacies are the same. They may be embedded within one another or read on different levels by different users.

Universal and restricted codes

The acquisition of a literacy necessitates the learning of symbol systems or codes. Basil Bernstein (1971) initiated the concept of restricted and elaborated codes. Restricted codes, such as the syntax and jargon used within social classes or work groups, are generated by social structures and serve to transmit culture. Restricted codes are predictable, simplified and narrow, impersonal, concrete, condensed, neither analytical nor abstract. While restricted codes limit vocabulary and flexibility, they also designate group solidarity. Elaborated codes include: unpredictable form, a high level of grammatical organization, and verbal selection, relatively explicit meaning and elaboration of unique experiences, allowing for modifications to suit the listener. Mary Douglas (1970) and Belinda Loftus (1988) have applied the concept of elaborated and restricted codes to visual phenomenon. However, Bernstein, Douglas, and Loftus maintain the division between restricted and elaborated codes, missing the point that codes may be embedded within one another and that speakers and lookers may be multi-lingual or multi-sighted.

Embedded codes

Bernstein's codes are somewhat reified, dichotomized. Codes in fact are *embedded* in a visual representation and can be read on different levels by different viewers. Some of these decodings will adhere to the artist's and/or patron's intent while others may not. Recognizability of code systems for a broad audience occurs in degrees, not as elaborated or restricted. For example, thirteenth-century artists and patrons would be able to decode the most restricted code of meanings in an annunciation scene such as the *Merode Altarpiece* [The Master of Flaemalle (Roger Campin) circa 1425–28), (see Figure 3). Culture member viewers would recognize the lilies as signifying the chastity of the Virgin, the roses as standing for her charity, the violets for her humility and the shiny water basin and towel as tribute to Mary as the 'vessel most clean' (Janson, 1977). At an intermediate level, contemporary art viewers, familiar with the Christian tradition, might not decode the work on such a specific level, but would still understand the narrative content of the scene as depicting the angel Gabriel announcing to Mary that she is pregnant with the son of God while remaining a virgin. However, those unfamiliar with Western Christian culture would merely see long-haired figure with wings facing a preoccupied woman in a richly furnished interior. The ability of the painting to create fully shared cultural meaning depends on more than mere realism. It includes the larger visual culture. The depiction functions on multiple levels: some audience members read all of the coding, some are able to read less. Realism is not the whole criteria, as Douglas (1970) suggests.

This is what I mean by an *embedded* code. For those who

Figure 3 *Triptych of the Annunciation,* Robert Campin. The Metropolitan Museum of Art, The Cloisters Collection 1956. (56.70)

understand the code, it is there for deciphering, but the work may be read on other levels as well. I have similarly argued elsewhere that a diverse community of individuals which support a folk art museum appreciate the same objects through diverse levels of interpretation and understanding. It is the 'embeddedness' of codes, their ability to be read on many levels simultaneously coupled with the various visual literacies of engineering specialists that contributes to the flexibility of engineering drawings enabling them to serve as boundary objects and conscription devices.[7]

Boundary objects and conscription devices

Objects which allow members of different groups, stratified or non-stratified, to come together for some common endeavour, though their understandings of the object of their mutual attention may be quite different, have been labelled by Leigh Star (1989) as *boundary objects*. Successful boundary objects exhibit some flexibility, allowing for more specific, or restricted readings of codes embedded within a more universal one. I first realized this in coming to understand the different appreciation levels for folk art works in a museum's community of supporters. (Star's initial example is that of a gopher in a natural history museum and its community of supporters.) In both cases one object is understood on multiple levels by diverse groups and/or individuals.

However, in engineering design, multiple readings do not always result in coordination. Contested readings can also occur. In one such case the manufacturing team at a medical optics firm read drawings for a new product as inadequate. Their perceptions were colored by erroneous rumors from field tests and aggravation over a previous project. In such cases the question of power to define who has the right to participate in constructing and interpreting the boundary object becomes an issue.

I have developed the term *conscription device* to accentuate the role of engineering drawings as network-organizing devices and to draw attention to the *process* of their creation that includes power issues. Conscription devices, a subgroup of inscription devices, enlist group participation and are receptacles of knowledge created and adjusted through group interaction with a common goal. To participate at all in the engineering design process actors must engage one another through the visual representation of the conscription device. Participants focus their communications in reference to the visual device. Moreover, during early design decisions, drawings are guarded from exposure to unwanted input, including that of management, which may otherwise be difficult to ignore.

The focus of conscription devices is process and the focus of boundary objects is a product. During the design process conscription devices exert a powerful influence. Participants find it difficult to communicate about the design without them. In the absence of visual representations at a meeting, someone will sketch a facsimile on a whiteboard (present in all engineering conference rooms), when communication begins to falter, or leave to fetch crucial drawings.[8]

As a *product* bearing knowledge which means one thing to some group members who use them and something else to other members, these conscription devices serve as boundary objects. Star (1989) describes boundary objects as 'objects which are both plastic enough to adapt to local needs and constraints of the several parties employing them, yet robust enough to maintain a common identity across sites.' Detail renderings in engineering drawings are one of the 'tightly focused' portions that make up the more flexible whole of a drawing set. For example, the depiction of a welded joint may stand for part of the support structure to the designer; and for labour expended to those in the shop. If workers suggest a formation to save welds and designers incorporate the advice, collective knowledge is captured in the design. One small part of the welders' tacit knowledge becomes visually represented in the drawing. Hence the sketch or drawing as a boundary object facilitates in enlisting additional work and knowledge.

It is the practical epistemologies of drafting conventions which ensure optical consistency during the process of knowledge accumulation, from large scale machine to flat rendition and back to machine again. Representational conventions in contemporary engineering incorporate many different techniques to embed information into flat renditions. One such is an entire lexicon of schematic symbols which designate types and specific functions of component parts of the machine being designed. In this pictographic lexicon an abstract symbol represents a functional component and additional visual codes elaborate the basic shape to add specific information. For instance, if two triangles designate a basic valve, the addition of a third triangle can indicate a three-way valve. The lexicon allows the schematic drawings in which it is employed to remain sufficiently flexible so that engineers can read the coded functions in the layout and understand the interrelations of the various functional components of the whole project. The main concern of an individual engineer may be more tightly focused on design aspects in her/his own area of expertise, for example, the electrical components and functions embedded in the drawing for an electrical engineer. Schematic layout drawings utilize this pictographic lexicon to depict the entire relationship of functional components and give detailed information for those working on a specific aspect of the design. This illustrates Star's definition of boundary objects as 'weakly structured in common use,' and 'strongly structured in individual-site use.'

I have discussed visual literacy as analogous to reading literacy in terms of the ability to read symbolic codes. To be literate, one must not only be able to decipher a given code, but also be able to manipulate its components in order to communicate. Moreover, this is constrained by cultural conventions. The violation of such conventions was the problem raised in the above example of the students' erroneously coded cylinder. The mistake is interesting because it reveals conflicts in the visual cultures of paper-trained and electronic-trained designers, exemplifying the link between practice and a way of seeing.

The visually literate design instructor reads drawings as one might read a text. He is brought up short by an anomalous figure which only makes sense in its context as a cylinder, but several students have represented it as a flat plane. The error glares; it affronts rationality as well as breaks drafting conventions. Materially, it is only the omission of a single line, running across the top opening of the cylinder. But it designates the difference between a cylinder and a flat plane. For those long initiated in the visual literacy of drafting, the omission of the line is analogous to a glaring spelling or grammatical error in a text.

When we look at the difference in paper-world and computer-world practices in generating the drawing, it becomes obvious why many design students trained using computer-graphics systems would leave out the line. In paper-world practice, in order to draw the cylinder, first one would pencil in very light guide lines using a hard pencil. These guide lines would have been used to block out the piece in the correct dimensions. The cylinder would then be sketched in within the guide lines using a darker pencil. Afterward, the final version of the cylinder would be inked in over the pencil drawing. The line across the opening of the cylinder would already be in place from the guide lines and would not be likely to be forgotten since it is essential to the process.

In electronic-world practice no guide lines are needed. One types in coordinates to compose only one side of the cylinder, creating either a set of rectangles or an 'L' shape. In electronic drafting a symmetrical shape can be produced using the mirror function to simply copy one side in reverse, as one might cut a paper folded along its center axis to produce a symmetrical shape. Having completed the half-profile of the cylinder, the drafter would tell the computer to use the 'mirror' function to create the other side of the figure. To the computer-trained drafter, the job is now done. The figure looks like a cylinder. There is nothing in the practice of creating it that suggests it should have a line across the opening. There is only the memorized drafting convention, unrelated to the process of creating the figure, to remind the student of the need for the crucial line. The meaning of the line is part of the process, the visual culture, and the visual literacy of the paper-trained designers. But not for computer-trained designers and drafters, for whom it is an arcane memorized detail, easily forgotten. Young designers trained on graphics software are developing a new visual culture tied to computer-graphics practice. It will influence the way they see and it will be different from the visual culture of the paper world.

Visual culture is not static, it can change just like other aspects of culture. But as it changes it becomes a different kind of knowledge, hopefully just as rich as the knowledge it replaces. Zuboff (1984) maintains that paper plant workers develop 'intellective' knowledge as they develop literacy in reading the computerized monitoring of paper pulp and this replaces former tacit knowledge for gauging the correct pulp viscosity by touch. Modern homemakers use sophisticated washers and microwave ovens for convenience. However, knowledge of special fabrics may demand hand washing and special occasion meals may be produced 'the way Mom made it.' Like embedded codes that may be read on multiple levels by various multi-visual readers, choices need to remain flexible in the computerization of design information so that users may choose the best use for each application: automation for routine, repetitive tasks, with the option of paper-world practice for visually thinking, analysing, and solving more complex design problems.

Notes

1 Arnheim (1969) discussed visual thought as a cognitive activity over twenty years ago. Gardner (1984), uses studies with child prodigies and idiot savants to explain the specificity of types of intelligences, of which 'spatial' or 'visual' is one of seven. Ferguson (1977, 1992) points out the importance of visual thought throughout engineering history to the present. He notes that Francesco di Georgio Martini's *Architecttura* (1475) has no meaning without its abundant drawings and at least one technical codex had no text, words being thought unnecessary to elucidate the drawings. Recent studies have brought attention to the importance of visual knowledge in science as well as engineering: Latour and Woolgar, 1979; Latour, 1986; Knorr Cetina and Amann, 1988, Lynch and Woolgar, 1988, to name a few.

2 See Martin Jay (1998a, 1988b) for a discussion of the ocularcentrism of Western culture which embodies its own ideologies.

3 Ivins (1953) makes the point that at the advent of photography, the depiction of the world as a photograph appeared strange to those used to the conventions of painting.

4 I take exception to Gardner's strong emphasis on biology, though he does acknowledge that child prodigies do not develop without the appropriate environment.

5 Zuboff (1988) in her study of automation in industry notes that in various factories 'action-centered skill, like all purposeful human activity, requires the intelligent participation of the human brain, but it is an intelligence that tends to be blended with the body's responsiveness and capacity to act' hence the development of such skills along with their execution and memory remain confined in the sphere of tacit knowledge. She cites earlier studies which illustrate that few machine operators used fully rational or conceptual approaches and that better operators made decisions based on intuitive understanding based on experience alone. Hindle (1981) documents the necessity of both visual and 'fingertip' or kinesthetic knowledge in the transfer of technologies from Europe to colonial America. David Sudnow (1981) points out the physical 'fingertip' memory of accomplished pianists.

6 See Cambrosio and Keating (1988) for an excellent overview of current definitions and discussions of 'tacit knowledge.'

7 'The Folk Art Museum: An exercise in Defining' presented at the 12the Annual Conference, Social Theory, Politics and the Arts, October, 1986.

8 Suchman (1988) has discussed the whiteboard in other design contexts as a locus of cognitive science practice in that the board both supports and is organized by the structure of face-to-face interaction. Her on-going research aims to identify systematic practices of the whiteboard in use in order to understand how those practices and the inscriptions they produce constitute resources for particular occasions of technical work.

Cross-classroom collaboration in global Learning Circles

Margaret Riel

Computer-mediated-communication makes it possible for teachers and students to work cooperatively with their peers around the world. This process helps students realize the diversity of world views and the role of language in organizing experience. It provides for teachers an extensive educational resource. This chapter describes one form of network learning—cross-classroom collaboration and a specific model for accomplishing this activity—Learning Circles.[1]

In current social-constructivist conceptions, learning occurs in social contexts where students use propositional knowledge to construct shared meaning or solve real world problems. These ideas are rooted in the educational philosophy of Dewey, Piaget, and Bruner but they are also stem from recent systematic analysis of needed workforce skills (SCANS, 1991), of the work of science communities (Latour and Woolgar, 1986; Roupe, Gal, Drayton and Pfister, 1993) and learning in informal settings (Lave and Wegner, 1991). Memorizing concepts and definitions is increasingly being replaced by understanding actions, reactions and interpretations and explaining them to others. Teaching is shifting from controlling the transmission of information to providing intellectual leadership in challenging conversations among a community of learners (Sizer, 1992).

In these current formulations, education is creating a shared way of thinking about one's self, the community, and the world. It is not only preparation for life, it is a way of life. Technology extends the range and diversity of available experiences in this social-constructivist framework. Network learning provides a forum for intellectual development of both students and teachers. Philip Noel, a teacher and principal (Clarenville, Newfoundland, Canada) describes this effect:

For me telecommunications was not simply the medium by
which I received professional in-service. Telecommunications
itself, was the in-service. My being involved with telecommunications has been the greatest in-service of my life.
Telecommunication's very nature of involving me with others
was a powerful force that took hold and changed me forever.
   Two years ago I was merrily working away, very content as
classroom teacher for grade eight, and my duties as the vice-
principal. I loved my work and I was doing OK, or so I thought!
Then along came an ad for telecommunications through
Learning Circles and my life, both as a teacher and person
changed forever—and for better! That simple process of learning
about telecommunication caused me to learn so much more than
I had expected or could have foreseen. It forced me to see that
through technology there was a gold mine of learning opportunity for my students, one that I could not ignore. (Noel, 1993)

This 'gold mine' enabled groups, separated by time and space,
to engage one another in meaning making activities. Until very
recently, communication over distances involved either one-to-
one communication through voice, print and images, or one-to-
many 'broadcast' communication. Computer networks facilitates
both of these forms, but also made possible new forms of *group*
communication with a high degree of interactivity.

This group interaction can be distributed through electronic
mail to closed groups or posted on public computer conference
spaces. It can also involve simultaneous interactions with others
who travel via computer to a common electronic city or space
(Kort, 1991). These 'virtual communities' are not bound by geography or characterized by cultural homogeneity (Rheinhold,
1993). The wide ranging diversity makes them excellent settings
for community development.

A community, either virtual or face-to-face, involves more than
technology. Communities develop when people with shared interests work together developing a personal connection defined by a
shared task. Electronic links to millions of unknown people will
not create new educational communities. Schools are busy places;
neither students nor teachers have time for extended network
exploration. However, participation in collaborative teams
extends the range of understandings. Noel (1993) continues:

Experiencing the power and the freedom and the learning with
other teachers and students on-line from around the world was

almost totally overwhelming. The change in my students was easily measurable. Their motivation to become actively involved in the learning going on across the network was more than evident. Students who were no more than 'place holders' in the classroom became 'real numbers' and wanted to participate . . . and to participate was to learn. We became a real learning team. The environment of the whole class changed.

As students became more actively involved in projects with others far away, their sense of self changed. Noel suggests this identify shift defines classroom behavior. Group membership powerfully forms self-definition.

Learning Circles as community

Learning Circles, organized around the concept of an electronic school rather than the more common conferencing model, encourage a cross-classroom team approach (Riel, 1989, Riel and Harasim, 1994). Instead of linking one class to another or to all participating classes, Learning Circle classes are grouped into small geographically diverse clusters with specific curricular themes. They are virtual communities with no fixed locations or time zones. Joined for the length of a session, they accomplish projects defined by their chosen curricular theme. The network interaction can be thought of an extended virtual class.

But what happens online is only half the story. The other half is the real-time classroom discussions and the research in the local community as teachers and students become experts on their school and community. Virtual and real classrooms become inseparable. The class becomes a community of learners.

In Learning Circle interaction, each class works as part of a larger team to complete projects drawn from each other's classrooms. A timeline, the interdependence of the Circle members, and regular messages from the AT&T Learning Network team, are designed to create team spirit and group responsibility. Teachers use this virtual space to collaborate with other educators. Learning Circles provide a channel for the diffusion of creative ideas, support and advice, and cooperative planning. Global community encourages students to locate ideas in a wider system of meaning than is available in a contained classroom. It promotes a view of education as a process of cultural definition rather than cultural transmission. As students compare and contrast meanings they create a sense of the shared world.

The following description of cross-classroom collaboration in Learning Circles is illustrated by teacher messages and student work that I obtained through personal observations and interactions with Learning Circles for over five years. It is followed by a report of research finding and observations of effects on student achievement.

Learning Circles: cross-classroom collaboration

Cross-classroom collaboration, like classroom learning, needs careful planning and structure. Models of network learning in this area are evolving specific 'telecomputing activity structures' (Harris, 1995) or 'participant structures' (Phillips, 1982, Riel, 1989) to accomplish this objective. In Learning Circles, teachers and students are grouped into teams based on grade level, and curriculum. Their interaction is structured by six phases with goals and tasks encouraging cooperative planning within a specific timeline.

1. Phase one: forming the Learning Circle

Approximately eight geographically diverse classrooms with a common focus are joined to form a Learning Circle with a curricular theme.

The network matches teachers and students in small clusters to accomplish shared goals. Teachers select a particular type of Learning Circle (*Computer Chronicles, Mind Works, Places and Perspectives, Society's Problems, Global Issues* or *Energy & the Environment*) at either the elementary, middle or high school level. During the introductory phase students provide a profile of themselves, their school and their community for their partners.

> Sheldon Point School (Alaska) has 5 classrooms, with a total of 45 students in grades 1–12, most of who are Yupik Eskimos. We live in a small village of less than 300 people on an area of about one square mile isolated from other locations by the rugged terrain. We drive snowmobiles to school. The school is the chief source of jobs in the community and families hunt, trap, and fish.

The students also send 'Welcome Packs' through postal mail. This encourages students to creatively illustrate who they are, and how their social and physical worlds are similar and different. Students send photos, maps, train schedules, candy wrappers, music, postcards, coins, homework examples, sport cards, taped messages and many unusual items (shark teeth, shells, rocks, maple syrup, pressed flowers) from their community. Bill Burrall (Moundsville, WV) reports on his students plans for their Welcome Pack.

> The kids are brainstorming to come up with items that will tell 'who we are' and show 'where we are found!' One boy is bringing in small pieces of 'authentic West Virginia coal.' Not quite the beach sand that we received from Bermuda one year, but genuinely a piece of our culture here in coal country. (Burrall, 1993).

Lois Kaczor (Syracuse, NY) describes her students working with Welcome Park materials.

> From: !jamesvny002 (Lois Kaczor)
> To: !ppe1:cir
> Subject: Classroom update
> Dear Circle Mates,
> . . . Picture, please, a group of ten fourth graders spread about the Library floor with bits and pieces of the Welcome Pack from British Columbia. Each is deeply engrossed in reading the brochures, maps, clippings, etc. There is considerable verbal exchange as they call out pieces of information they find interesting. Two other youngsters get out an atlas, check a map, put the atlas away and get a 'better' one. A girl carries a clipboard and is writing down questions to be used in the next message. Teachers move in and about this scene answering questions, or making suggestions. This goes on for thirty minutes and must end only because another group wishes to use the floor space. Grudgingly, things are put away, but the conversation continues.
> . . .
> These deeply involved, actively engaged, turned on, task-oriented learners are a group of 'reluctant readers' who normally have far more interesting things to do with their time than to attend to their studies. But on the network, they are the best workers and thinkers I've seen in a long time. They

Margaret Riel

are writing, they are reading, they are asking questions, they are learning and they are enjoying it!

That's it for today—

Lois in overcast Syracuse.

Sharon Kubenka, Ingram School, Texas shows how the introductory activities can inform classroom lessons.

As the surveys arrived, we learned how to make charts and graphs, discuss difference of opinion and manipulate data mathematically with 'what if . . .' statements. With the Welcome Packs from Canada and Saudi Arabia, we learned metric conversions and money exchange rates. Looking at the location of all our partners, we had a meaningful lesson on time zones. (Kubenka, 1992)

Learning Circles joins students from different cultures, regions, religions, ages, perspectives, and with a range of physical and mental strengths in a medium that treats diversity as a resource.

Difficulties sometimes arise during this phase because teachers and students tend to think of message writing as a personal rather than group form of communication. If the several hundred participants in an average Learning Circle were in the same physical space, it would be clear that group size and time constraints would make long personal introductions inappropriate. But in virtual group space, some participants take the time to write at length. Writing and reading personal messages can be time consuming. These messages also invite personal (one-to-one) communication that runs counter to the group communication encouraged in Learning Circles. Circle teachers vary in terms of their reactions; some find personal communication critical for student motivation, while others find it distracts from the collaborative work. Circle Coordinators often discuss strategies for balancing individual needs in group settings. The balance seems more difficult in the high school level Learning Circles where collaboration and group work are less common in the classroom environment.

2 Planning Learning Circle projects

Each class sponsors one activity in the Learning Circle that can be drawn from the classroom curriculum and integrated with ongoing activities.

224

Teaching someone else is an effective learning strategy because it requires advance organization and understanding. Learning Circle projects involve reciprocal teaching and learning. Each class has the opportunity to sponsor one Circle project. This cooperative definition assures relevance and can create a strong sense of group ownership. But for some this creative participation represents a high level of risk-taking. Detailed suggestions in a curriculum guide, an online newsletter, online help from a circle coordinator, and partner teachers all provide support for development of a 'sponsored' project. But the success of this model depends on students and teachers taking responsibility to define and organize learning activities for distant partners.

Learning Circle projects often encourage the integration of school subjects within community contexts. Students are asked to use community resources and experts to complete their responses. Here are some examples of Learning Circles projects:

Elementary students in a Places & Perspectives Circle from Saudi Arabia sponsored a project on solutions to the Gulf crises. Together with their partners in different countries they discussed the world dependence on oil, kingdoms, democracies, and conflicts between political and religious beliefs.

The project of junior high students in West Virginia in a Society's Problems Circle linked their partners' classes anonymously with felon inmates in a maximum security prison. The inmates answered student questions on a range of social problems from their personal life experiences. The inmates' reflections on their life decisions have had a very strong effect on students.

Students in British Columbia sponsored the 'Environmental Investigator' as their section of their collective newspaper in a Computer Chronicles Learning Circle. Among other things, they invited Circle students to send environmental questions to a column called 'Ask Dr. Enviro.' To find answers, the elementary students took a trip to their nearby middle school science department.

Students in a Places and Perspective Learning Circle from Belgium sponsored a research project on waste caused by excessive packaging of goods. Students collected and compared the packaging of many different types of products, and assessed the best and worst examples in different counties and countries.

From elementary class in Massachusetts, the project asked for community histories. Students from New York described how the early trading centre at the junction of two railroad lines developed into a thriving business centre and finally into a suburb of a larger city. Australian students described how the discovery of opal mines led to the settling of Coober Pedy where people live underground to escape the severe weather of the desert. Native people trading furs with the British, as well as stories about Loyalists fleeing from the New America came from Quebec.

A project comparing weather effects on decomposition came from elementary students in Ohio in an energy and Environment Learning Circle. They sent partner classes materials which students were to measure, weigh and describe and predict changes that would occur if the items were buried underground for two weeks. The students charted local weather for two weeks and then dug up the materials and measured and described the changes.

These are the sets of sponsored projects for three Learning Circles:

Elementary School Level 'Places and Perspectives'	Middle School Level 'Society's Problems'	High School Level 'Global Issues'
Price Comparisons	Pollution Experiment	Democracy and
City Guides—Historical	Gangs—Survey &	Education
Sites	Opinions	The Global Economy
Local history timeline	Homeless Children	& Recession
World War II	AIDS	Ozone and the
interviews	Teenage Pregnancy	Environment
Weather Reporting	Drunk Driving	Solar Power
Local endangered		Racial Hatred
species		Health Problems

This multi-project team approach to exploring and solving real problems provides a strategy for integrating projects with class-room activities and situating knowledge and skills in a commu-nity of learners. The open structure of Learning Circles encourages teachers to share their best teaching activities with their peers. However a structure that encourages creativity is likely to have projects of uneven quality. While many teachers demonstrate unusual skill, talent and creativity in the design of network learning from the beginning, other teachers find it takes time and experimentation to design effective cross-classroom collaborative projects. One or more projects may seem superficial to other teachers who are experienced. Sometimes a specific simulation may interest a majority of the Circle, and yet be of little interest to a specific teacher or class. Each Learning Circle is a unique set of people who create a specific learning context that will never be exactly replicated again. Teachers who have participated in dozens of Learning Circles view them in much the way they do different years of teaching—different groups of students lead to very different teaching and learning experiences.

3 Exchanging work on the projects

Students work closely with those in their own classroom as well as in distant locations to complete the projects.

The project information requests from distant classes are usually assigned to different groups of students who collect the information and send it over the network. Working across classrooms helps students appreciate the difference in perspective from adaptations to different conditions. Cross-classroom collaboration provides a range of diversity of perspectives not often found within a single classroom. Participating with learners in different places can significantly change the dimensions of the dialogue. Marilyn Wall, an elementary teacher (Bridgewater, VIA), provides a glimpse of this as she describes what is taking place in her classroom in response to Circle projects:

Date: Thu Nov 19 22:19.00 EST 1992
From: !johnwinva001 (Marilyn Wall at John Wayland)
Subject: Great responses
To: !ppe3:cir

WOW! WHAT WONDERFUL RESPONSES EVERYONE IS SENDING! We sure have one fantastic circle! I can't believe that I made it. It is 8:30 Thursday night. I can actually just sit here in front of my computer and just 'talk!' I am so proud of my class. Fourth grade is such a neat grade. Learning is so exciting to them. They have heart!!!! How lucky I am to work with kids like this!

Barbara [NJ] . . . my kids have had fun with the cost of living. Their little eyes popped open when they saw the cost of housing Candy's class [CA] sent in. They also noticed that the general cost of living in Dodie's class [MI] was generally much higher. A big thanks to your response to our artifact project.

Rhoda [NY], we hope your class will enjoy our Indian history. When the class first began their Indian project, they thought all Indians lived in teepees. They have come a long way.

Dodie [MI], your assembly sounded so great! I think we might steal your idea and do something similar. The kids are keying in their response to your recycling project. It might be interesting to compare the response from a rural school as opposed to an urban school in NJ or Mich.

Candy [CA], my kids really have enjoyed interviewing new arrivals to this country. I used two great books to introduce your project. One is a book put out by Scholastic called Immigrants. The other is a new magazine called 'Faces,' published by the same people who put out Cobblestone. It deals with other people's culture and the APRIL 92 issue dealt with your topic. I hope my kids finish typing their essays tomorrow.

Let me know how (and when) you are planning to publish your section. I will try to keep us on schedule so we get the publication out in time for Christmas break.

Burning the midnight oil . . .
Marilyn Wall, Circle Coordinator
JWE, Bridgewater, VIA

The most critical aspect of project exchange is to help teachers and students understand the importance of reciprocity in team work. Each class needs to understand that while they depend on others for information, they are also important information suppliers. Often the students who complain that other schools have not completed their survey are the same students who have *not* responded to other information requests. Learning Circle coordinators chart team progress in weekly updates to the Circle. While complete reciprocity characterizes only a subset of the Learning Circles, most projects receive response from 4–6 classes. Students are encouraged to experiment with strategies to motivate distant students to complete the project requests. Knowing how to motivate others to meet deadlines is an important workforce skill.

4 Creating the publication

The task of each Learning Circle is to summarize the collective work in a final publication.

The project sponsors are responsible for evaluating, editing, summarizing, formatting their project. Teachers often report on the writing interest and skill shown by students during this phase. The most common observation is the change in the teacher's role. The students ask each other and the teacher for help, rather than the teacher telling students to review or revise their work. Ron Oastler (Ontario, Canada), describes student work on the Circle publication:

> The project also provided a vehicle for practicing thinking skills. Students compared the characteristics of the different schools and communities within their group by looking for similarities and differences and analyzed their findings. This resulted in a great deal of research as well as discussion.
> Through the messages the students learned to distinguish facts from opinions and become alert for signs of bias and prejudice in their work and the writing of others.

Denese Wierzbicki (Gillette, Wyoming) finds this process works well with students with a range of skills:

> I work with high risk students and high school dropouts. For the first time in five years I actually had students doing reports without complaints. They took a lot of care with their grammar and tried very hard to make the content look like a real report. They said things like 'students in other schools will be reading or using this information so we need to get it right.'

The Learning Circles coordinator sends the title page, an opening letter and the table of contents listing participating schools and projects. The sections are sent directly by the schools and the publication is assembled.

Sometimes students will have to face the situation where one or more classes fail to complete their work by the deadline. Some classes decide to publish the book without the section, others contact the school to find out how late the section will be and push back the publishing date, and others do the missing work themselves. In any team, there will be variation in the level of commitment and accomplishments of the participants. Learning how to work successfully in teams is a critical part of education.

5 Evaluating the process and closing the circle

Learning Circles encourage students to take responsibility for their learning. During the last phase students and teachers review what they have accomplished. Over time they develop a world-wide network of friends and colleagues.

Many educators see Network Learning as a tool to use with 'gifted' students who can work independently. However, research with high school students suggested that the most positive effects of this model may be with students who struggle in traditional writing classes (Spaulding and Lake, 1991). Two teachers of 'at risk' students describe the success of this collaborative model with their special students.

> . . . I expected it would improve their geography and writing skills as well as their awareness of the similarities of people all over our planet and it did. What never entered my mind was the change in my student's behavior when communicating with their Learning Circle. My kids didn't want the other students to know they lived in Juvenile Hall! They wanted to be normal. Usually these kids have a false bravado and brag about their criminal aspirations. It was so unusual for them to deny this. I was fascinated. The attitude prevailed all year with few exceptions and they actually presented real goals to the students from other classes. (Ruth Mikkelsen, Principal, H.P. B. Carden Court School, Marysville, CA.)

> Hi Circle Teachers,
> . . . So far all the discussion has been in the intellectual area of learning. Another benefit is in interpersonal skills and emotional support. On of the biggest problems we have in our district is the inability of students to get along with teachers, hence a 25% drop-out rate. As I talk with students at the Alternative Transition Center their most frequent complaint is not that the teacher isn't knowledgeable, but rather that they feel isolated, see no relevance between subjects or between a subject and real life. I see being in contact with other students through telecommunications as offering one way to reach some of these students. They are working on problems that are (or at least appear to be) real to their peers that validates the problem for them. They learn to communicate with people in their school and community as they look for information and answers. My students have made a real effort to use correct

grammar etc. so as not to appear 'dummies' to the other schools in the circle. Right now and probably for some time yet telecommunications is so rare in our district that it gives these kids something they are 'better at than anyone else,' which at this time in their lives they really need. (Denese Wierzbicki, High School Teacher, Alternative Transitional Center, Gillette, Wy.)

In these examples, students used the invisibility of the network to help them 'pass' as regular students. Network interactions are often characterized as more democratic, as markers of status are not as immediately apparent to participants (Spoull and Kiesler, 1986). The asynchronous communication extends work over time so that a response carries only minimum clues about the amount of social support required to compose a message. Thus, students of different abilities can work side-by-side without the negative effects of stereotypes or prejudice. Below, another teacher describes the effect of Circle collaboration on a troubled student.

. . . Let me tell you about one student in particular. He is a kind of a street-wise kid who comes from a broken home. His father is an alcoholic who does not have any control over his problem. Basically he's a bum. Well, this boy got excited about the network last spring when we did the Computer Chronicles Learning Circle. He ended up being the student editor and artist. The experience turned him around. He stays after school just to do good things. His teachers this year are all pleasantly surprised as they had expected a terror. He is getting good grades, hanging out with a good group of kids, and generally being a young gentleman. He now helps me do our school paper as he has become quite proficient with PageMaker, MacPaint, and Microsoft Works. (So long . . . [names withheld to protect the student] New York.)

In these examples, like those described by Noel at the beginning of this paper, learning is identity. Network Learning for these students involved a process of self-reflection and redefinition. Telecommunication is clearly not the answer to all educational problems. But it does provide a powerful technology for changing the existing social setting and encouraging students to work within a wider range of opportunities and constraints.

In a society undergoing rapid change, there can be no blueprint for building the effective schools. School reform must be seen as process rather than product with active learners as the model teachers.

Learning lessons across distances

Do students who work across classrooms learn any more or any better than students within an enclosed classroom? This is an important question with only partial answers (Riel and Harasim, 1994). Network learning is a new field and cross-classroom collaboration is best studied collaboratively.

The Learning Circle concept evolved from research that suggested that writing for a distant peer audience improved language skills (Cohen and Riel, 1989; Riel, 1990b; Spaulding and Lake, 1991; Gallini and Helman, 1993). The use of standardized and controlled tests in the area of writing and language mechanics make it easier to assess these benefits.

However, there are other benefits. For example, many teachers report that students spontaneously brought in stories or information about places to which they were connected and were more interested in events and people in other regions. Changes include deeper understandings of issues from multiple perspectives, increased sensitivity to multicultural differences, systemic awareness of social/global issues and cooperative team skills. The degree and intensity of these changes vary and it is often difficult to predict the type of change. These areas need systematic exploration.

Language skills and audience effects

Audience considerations are vital for experienced writers, but are often non-existent in classroom writing. When students were involved with peers in cross-classroom collaboration, they showed a marked increase in writing motivation and performance.

Elementary school students from California, Alaska and Hawaii participated in a prototype Learning Circle 'news wire.' The teacher taught grammar through the use of peer editing groups and teacher reviews of writing rather then through writing exercises used in past years. All written work in the classrooms was graded by the teacher and holistically scored by the research team. Over the course of the school year the students published three class newspapers with articles from their partner schools. The written work showed a steady increase in writing skill over the school year. In addition to these research scores, the California Test of Basic Skills (CTBS) administrated by the state was used to examine the effects on the language skills of fourth graders (Mehan, 1989; Riel, 1990b). At the beginning of the project the class average on the CTBS was slightly below grade level in language and math. The CTBS class average on the language subsection indicated gains of two years, while the math subsection remained close to grade level. This suggests that teaching writing skills in the context of writing for an audience was an effective strategy for all of the students.

Students who served as editors for the first edition of the class newspaper scored two to three grades above their current grade in the language mechanics subtest, or a gain of four years. While it is difficult to match classrooms as controls, students scores in another class, similar in most respects but without a network link, showed the expected growth of one year on the CTBS.

In Alaska, the teacher involved in the news wire exchange also charted student achievement by standardized test scores administered by their state. She used two controls groups, the student scores of a sixth grade class she taught the previous year and a sixth grade taught by a different teacher the same year. She found significant gains in the reading skills of those who participated in network learning (Riel, 1990b). These findings suggest that reading, writing and editing to create a publication is a more effective way of learning language arts than the worksheet lessons common in classrooms. The distant audience may play a crucial role in student motivation.

Cohen and Riel (1989) examined students' writing in two audience conditions: to their teacher for a term assessment, and to a distant peer audience to share ideas. Seventh grade students wrote two compositions on the same topic a week apart. One was addressed to peers through computer networking, and the other was written for their semester grade. In a second classroom, students followed the same procedure but in reverse order. The papers were evaluated anonymously. Again, papers written to communicate with peers were ranked significantly higher than those written to demonstrate writing skill. The essays written for a distant audience were more fluent and better organized than in those written for a grade. These findings were recently replicated in a similar study of student writing skills in a Learning Circle by

Gallini and Helman (1993). They found significant differences after only six weeks of interaction in Learning Circles.

Computer networking may be of most benefit for students who traditionally do not perform well in schools. Spaulding and Lake (1991) studied 28 first-year high school students who did not pass district-level competencies in writing. Some of the students took part of a Learning Circle interacting with students from six classes in three countries. They worked on sponsored classroom projects and published their work cooperatively. A control group did similar work but used encyclopedias and resource books to create their publication. The same 'writing process' approach was used in both classrooms.

Linguistic and computer self-efficacy were assessed by pencil and paper self-report. Students low on linguistic self-efficacy scores who participated in Learning Circles showed the most dramatic gains. Students who rated themselves low in writing skill in the control class did not improve significantly. Thus, collaborative network learning can be an effective teaching tool for students who have not been successful in traditional classrooms. The use of intrinsic motivation in real communication exchanges may increase interest and competence.

Seeing the world from the perspective of others

Definitions of self come from understanding one's self in relationship to others. The Learning Network challenges students to define themselves for distant others. Students are asked to reflect on similarities and differences. These activities help students think about symbolic representations. Statues, flags, music, natural formations, clothing styles, foods, preferences, and images represent what the group hold as important. These comparisons expose students to variable patterns of everyday life resulting from different cultural adaptations to geographic and climatic conditions. Both similarities and differences encourage students to be more conscious of their own identity and life patterns. For example:

> Students discovered that their peers in the desert terrain of Coober Pedy, Australia live in underground homes to escape the heat of the sun. These dugout homes are neither heated nor cooled because the earth provides a constant pleasant

living temperature. Living underground rather than on top of it creates different types of harmony with the environment. For example, other underground creatures, like snakes sometimes block air passageways.

As students consider these differences they gained a richer understanding:

Alaskan students described the 'setting' of the sun in the fall and attending school in the 'everyday' of night.

Students in the southern hemisphere sent revisions of Christmas carols that describe holidays in the bright summer season sun.

Messages arrive from Japan written on a day that has not yet arrived.

Thus students locate themselves in a global environment and reflect on how their unique location forms their experiences of day, night, seasons and time.

Learning Circle interaction also helps students who need more time to express ideas or have language problems to interact in a way that does not emphasize their difficulties. The presentation of self can be very strong in this alternate format. Here, a deaf student and a student from a juvenile court school challenge their circle partners stereotypes.

To my circle friends.

MY FEELINGS ABOUT BEING DEAF
IN THE HEARING WORLD

It's not easy being deaf in the hearing world because there are many problems that you may confront. For example, some deaf people are treated as if they were different or not normal. Sometimes a hearing person who doesn't know about deafness acts as if we, as deaf people, are not very intelligent. . . . I sometimes am confronted by others who never saw a deaf person speaking. I've been asked if I knew how to swim or ride a bicycle! It is kind of weird when I am asked if I do things that most kids do. Especially if I think of myself as a normal, ordinary kid who does everything but hear.

. . . We don't need pity if we are normal. It won't work if you try to pretend to like a deaf person out of pity because they soon won't want to be friends with you. We are

somebody! A lot of deaf people have gone on to become teachers, lawyers, actors, actresses, authors, professors and so forth. We are human just like hearing people because we make mistakes and learn from them. . . . I am a hearing person who cannot hear. I don't think of myself as a deaf person.
In fact I never did.

April

DESPERATE
Willy Ridgley
Thomas E. Mathews Community School
Marysville, CA

Starved for destination.
A beggar man by trade.
A desperate man needs more
Than someone else to blame.
Friendless.
It appears he hides behind his
     tears.
The things he's lost.
The things he will never have
     at all.
The forgotten man wanders
Misplaced in the world.

Obscurity is all that he sees
     and can recall.
He's all alone.
The destitute find meaning
In a different way of life.
The doorways that they dwell
     in are shelter
For in the night
The shining crystal possessions
Are set out for his display.
His only purpose is to find
     food
To get him through the day.

Contrasts such as these challenge student assumptions about their world. Writing becomes the vehicle for sharing ideas and 'taking the role of the other.'

Increased multi-cultural understanding

Students without exposure to others develop ethnocentric positions. They assume that others *should* be like them. Cross-cultural awareness involves learning how people who look very similar are different and how people who look different are similar. Local communities and neighbourhoods offer a limited range of variability. Network learning can extend the range of interactions:

> When students in Louisiana received the class photo from their partners in New York, the students turned to the computer and wrote, 'Great to see the pictures of you all, but where are the brothers?????'

These students were very surprised to discover that their network friends were all white. People interacting by computers often assume the others to be similar until presented with contrary evidence. Network learning makes it easier for groups that are commonly segregated to learn from one another. Problem solving creativity can arise when students compare local solutions to cultural clash:

> The students from a west German classroom described an increasing number of students from different ethnic backgrounds that were entering their schools and resulting in cultural conflicts. The relationships among students were becoming a serious problem in their schools. These German students, relying on American television as their source of knowledge, asked their Circle partners to tell them how schools in the US managed to achieve such a high degree of successful integration of minorities.

US schools responded in different ways perhaps reflecting the degree of racial conflict in their community. Some student groups accepted the characterization of successful integration and explained how this achievement resulted from valuing cultural diversity. Other schools worried that television provides an unreal picture of everyday life. Most schools responded that racial conflicts were far from solved but offered some advice on how to work together.

Sometimes the requests from network partners resulted in a students searching for the best ways to describe themselves:

> Students in Alaska were surprised by the active interest that members of their Learning Circle expressed about all aspects of their lives. They had initially felt isolated and timid about participating, but their teacher reported that with each question they answered, the students developed a stronger identity and pride in their cultural background.

The students invited The Elders to come to their class and help them answer questions about their Eskimo way of life and thus about themselves.

The absence of visual markers of race, ethnicity, gender, age or physical appearance, not initially available in computer messages, reduces the tendency to form stereotypes. Instead, the 'voice' created in the text creates the impression of the writer. Well-dressed students in a suburban neighbourhood school and students with purple spiked hair, tattooes or torn clothes are unlikely to be able to work comfortably together. However, the collaborative setting of network learning makes it possible to share ideas across cultural boundaries while physically remaining distant and comfortable and may increase student sensitivity to common human conditions.

Some of the different perspectives which arise from working across cultures have to do with highly charged areas like perceptions of teenage sexuality, or discussion of topics like rape or AIDS. High School students in Canada reacted to an essay by a German student on teenage sexuality by calling it 'The most disgusting piece of writing I have ever seen.' What followed was a highly charged discussion of the politics of representation and the way in which gender and culture affect the language use in these cross-cultural exchanges in Learning Circle (Lichte, 1994). These discussions can be highly controversial which raises the issue of censorship and control. While teachers are responsible for the conduct of their students, regional and cultural values can lead to very different judgements of what is appropriate for students.

Systemic awareness in the international arena

Gaining an understanding about the systemic relationships in our world is a challenge we all face. Dramatic events such as the invasion of the Persian Gulf, or riots in South Central Los Angeles, create world-wide focus on actions within larger systems of meaning. What is the meaning of these events for people in different locations? Are shared meanings constructed? Distant and international links do not, in and of themselves, create deeper or more insightful understanding. But contact with people there can provide valuable clues as we piece together an understanding. This awareness is more likely to develop among high school students who are being encouraged to see past scud missiles, gas masks or beatings, as the following example during the fall of the Berlin Wall illustrates:

> In 1989 when East Germans began to flee their country through Poland to relocate in West Germany, students in the United States were sending surveys to their German peers in their Learning Circle to better understand their views of this new development. These students were exchanging information on the problem when the course of history began moving so fast that it was difficult to follow. The students in West Berlin sent daily messages to their Circle trying to make sense of each new development and the consequence it would have for world democracy. In this circle, the work on projects was suspended as the participants in all classes tried to deal with events that were taking place and what the fall of the Berlin Wall would mean for a new world order.

The complexity of social problems becomes an object for study as students try to understand each other. Consider this example from Japan.

> Students in Japan wanted to know more about parent-child relationships in different locations. They constructed a parent-child survey with many questions about activities in the family and attitudes of children and parents.

This project led to discussions of the meaning 'dependent' and 'independent' have in different cultural systems. Japanese students described themselves as highly 'dependent' on their mothers for their daily needs making it possible for them to devote maximum time to their studies. 'Independence' in this frame was to lack this support, and traditionally had negative connotations. Dependency was a positive feature of group consciousness and family life. For students in the US to be too 'dependent' on parents was a sign of immaturity. Independence, or self-reliance, was highly valued as it led to individuality and self-sufficiency. However institutions are changing in both countries and the students in this Circle struggled to understand the relationship of these concepts to changes in their social, political and economic institutions.

Systemic change also can be the result of new technology and social organizations.

> A school in West Germany located in a farming district sponsored a project on the plight of small farmers. They were surprised to find that students who lived on small farms in

Illinois were facing many of the same extreme conditions that faced German farmers.

By comparing the state of the small farms in both countries they were able to understand the economic and political forces involved in the change of farming practices. Network Learning extends student understanding beyond their own circumstances and encourages thinking within complex economic, political, environmental, cultural and social systems.

Cross-classroom collaboration provides rich learning opportunities for exploring and understanding systemic relationships, but the use of these opportunities depends on the skill of the teacher who directs the learning. It is unlikely that these openings will lead to systemic understandings without the skill of an experienced teacher using these openers to encourage further research on these topics.

Cooperative patterns for tackling problems and issues

Schools are in a sensitive position with respect to political activism. Teachers must educate not indoctrinate. They must present students with strategies for participating in local, national and international settings without promoting particular political positions.

The purpose of global education is to promote certain attitudes in students—an awareness of the world, an openness to alternative perspectives, and a self concept that isn't dependent or belittling others. When students face real problems, they get a sense of their own agency as an actor in a larger social frame. Many issues discussed in school are political yet plans for social action are influenced by community values. For example, a logging community may be intolerant of a school-sponsored writing campaign to save the spotted owl, while for another community, this is a valuable learning experience. Students have begun school-based recycling programs, joined environmental programs for cleaning up oceans, lakes and parks, and promoted issues of health and safety. In this example students discuss problems surrounding alcohol use:

> Students in a New York school chose to explore drug abuse by teenagers. Student opinion in this New York school was against serving alcohol at parties. Their Australian peers wanted to know 'How do you have fun at a party without

alcohol?' The New York students responded by citing the high risks associated with alcohol, particularly the number of accidents that involved drinking teenagers. Their survey reports that 80% to 100% of the students at all schools in the Learning Circle have driven or ridden in cars with drivers under the influence of alcohol.

That so many students find themselves in cars without sober drivers is frightening. Involving student teams in the design of better transportation systems for teenagers may offer potential solutions to this problem.

Learning Circles provide teachers with direction and support to explore creative ways of integrating communication technology with curriculum and community programs. Knowledge constructed through interaction with community leaders, teachers and classmates is likely to be retained long after information memorized from books is forgotten. However teachers who suggest student involvement in social programs walk a very fine line between encouraging student participation in their community and indoctrinating students with a specific position on controversial issues.

Increased teacher professionalism

Qualitative analysis of the Learning Circles suggests that it also contributes to teacher development (Riel, 1990a, 1992). Teachers collaborate with other educators without leaving their classroom, developing flexible and creative ways to extend learning through telecomputing. This encouraged the diffusion of creative ideas, provided support for difficult challenges, and created a vehicle for cooperative plans to renew schools. In survey results, teachers list their own professional development as one of the most significant reasons for continued participation.

Conclusions

Learning Circles are structured to use teacher creativity and student diversity as resources for educational innovation. Casting students as the local experts on their communities helps them become more involved in learning, and encourages them to seek the help of parents, teachers, and community resources.

Margaret Riel

Students in different social categories (included those that have been labelled as gifted with those labelled as unsuccessful) collaborated in a virtual space; home schooled students work with students from large urban centres; students of native origin work with recent immigrants; private schools students work with those form alternative schools. In these contrasts and many more, students experiment with a sense of voice. They want their ideas heard and understood. Good teachers can use this to help students appreciate reciprocal motivation.

This interpretive process changes education from acquiring known facts to negotiating a sense of self and other in a system of evolving meaning. Our world is socially constructed and dynamic. What is 'truth' or 'fact' for one generation or region is not necessarily so for another. Helping students to be part of a community of interpreters arms them with the intellectual skills needed to face societal change with personal responsibility.

Note

1 Paper presented at the American Educational Research Association Annual Meetings, Alanta Georgia, April 12–16, 1993. For copies write: Dr. Riel, 943 San Dieguito Drive, Encinitas, CA, 92024 (mriel@attmail.com).

Sex and death among the disembodied: VR, cyberspace, and the nature of academic discourse

Allucquére Rosanne Stone

Abstract

As I lift the phone, put my feet up, and settle back in the chair before becoming Leila the Sex Kitten, the past few years of my life as a researcher pass before my hot, mascaraed eyes . . .

Cyberspace. The very name conjured William Gibson's mad, brilliantly dystopic vision of the ultimate collision between society and communication technics. I spent my first few years as an academic convincing other social scientists that such a space existed, that interactions within it were social in character, and that such interactions had meaning. Things have changed now, and I find that I have mixed feelings about the changes. I'm happy not to have to spend part of every colloquium re-digging the disciplinary and methodological ditches, and also heartened and a bit disconcerted with researchers swarming over the virtual landscape, peering around at the virtual natives and writing busily in their virtual field notes. The old neighbourhood just ain't the same no more.

Some of the changes cyberspace has brought to fieldwork are basic and obvious. In a universe in which everything (and everybody) is produced and mediated by text, the floppy disk is the ultimate field recorder. Nothing escapes its panoptic gaze. In other respects, the changes are deeper and far more cryptic. Gibson saw them coming too; his characters' dark realization—'There are things in the Net'—perfectly captures the enigma of emergent phenomena in extremely large information systems. Whether those phenomena are social is part of the core of virtual systems research.

But I was in the process of becoming Leila the Sex Kitten when I was distracted by the need to situate this rant within the context of the discourses of social science, so let's get back to sex. My first encounter with virtual worlds was through studying those social groups who understand better than anyone else the relations between bodies and technologies, virtuality and desire—phone sex workers. I came to the encounter already interested in how information is transformed and compressed in social interaction, and from the point of view of communications technology phone sex is quite simply about practical applications of data compression. Usually sex involves as many of the senses as possible. Taste, touch, smell, sight, hearing—and, for all I know, short-range psychic interactions—all work together to heighten the erotic sense. Consciously or unconsciously phone sex workers translate all the modalities of experience into audible form. They start with a complex, detailed set of behaviours, translate them into a single sense modality, and send them down an ordinary phone line. At the other end of the line the recipient of all this effort reconstitutes the tokens into a fully detailed set of images and interactions in multiple sensory modes.

It also seems clear that what's being sent back and forth over the wires isn't merely information, it's bodies—not physical objects, but the information necessary to reconstruct the meaning of body to almost any desired depth and complexity. In general, the idea of body is part of the idea of erotic interaction and its concomitants, and the erotic sensibilities are mobilized and organized around the idea of a physical body which is the seat of sensual interaction. The sex workers' descriptions were invariably and quite directly about physical bodies and what they were doing or what was being done to them.

The fact that we can and do deal quite effectively with bodies through single-mode narrow-bandwidth communication is a recent development, but one which is merely a continuation of shifts in the way cultural codes work—an evolving change which has been under way for some time. For virtual sex to be possible, other things had to happen—the disappearance of public spaces and the role of the body as spectacle within them, the elaboration of interior space in houses into specialized rooms, the shift from benches to chairs, the development of the diary and the interior monologue, the use of mirrors, portraiture, psychoanalysis, the increasing specialization of work—an evolving wry commentary on the sovereign subject taken to its illogical conclusion. In this scenario the crown of creation is a person alone at a keyboard. But beyond the screen is another social world which—

perhaps problematically—possesses some of the important characteristics of our rapidly vanishing public spaces.

But I'm wandering again. By the usual definitions sex work is work, but it's work which is about play. There is a fine body of research addressed to the topic of play vs. work activities, but from the standpoint of cultural criticism the issue is not one of definitions of work or play, but of how the meanings of those terms are produced and maintained. Both work and play have culture-specific meanings and purposes, and I am conducting a quite culture-specific discussion when I talk about the primacy of play in interactive virtual environments. In order to clarify this, let me mention that there are many definitions of interaction and many opinions about what interaction is for. As I write this, large industry consortiums are finalizing their standards for what they call interactive multimedia platforms. These devices usually consist of a computer, colour monitor, mouse, CD-ROM drive, sound card and a pair of speakers. This electronic instantiation of a particular definition freezes the conceptual framework of interaction in a form most suitable for commercial development—the user moves the cursor to the appropriate place and clicks the mouse, which causes something to happen—or what the interactivist Michael Naimark would call, more pejoratively, poke-and-see technology. On the other hand, the definitions of interactivity used by the early researchers at MIT possessed a certain poignancy that seems to have become lost in the commercial translation. One of the best definitions was set forth by Andy Lippman, who described interaction as mutual and simultaneous activity on the part of both participants, usually working toward some goal—but, he adds, not necessarily. From the beginning of interaction research the primacy of a common goal is in question, and in that fact, among others, inheres interaction's vast ludic dimension—as well as my personal stakes. I'm not interested in computer-supported cooperative work, really, but rather in computer-supported cooperative play. The aleatory, rough-and-tumble quality of CSCP generates an environment in which ideas are continually shaken up, new risks are taken, and new formations emerge.

I find phone sex useful for my work, but it's merely a perspicuous and well-established example of virtual interaction. It is also essentially a point-to-point form of communication, restricted in most instances to two participants. In this sense it is a limited medium by today's standards. That's why for the past sixteen years I have been both writing code for, and researching interaction within, the multiple-user social environments which are most frequently the architectural field within which virtual interactions occur. These are not environments for shared work but rather for shared play. I'll describe a few of them here.

Text-based virtual communities

Bulletin Board Services (BBSs) and text-based virtual communities are instances of emerging electronic environments which are capable of simulating and modeling human societies. The first virtual communities based on communication technology were the on-line bulletin board services of the middle 1970s. These were not dependent upon the widespread ownership of computers, merely of terminals; but even a used terminal cost several hundred dollars, so that access to the first BBSs was mainly limited to electronics experimenters, ham radio operators, and the early computer builders—i.e., white males. BBSs are dialup systems, accessible via telephone lines rather than the Internet. This means that BBS users don't have to be part of the privileged groups in government, industry and academia who are able to log into cyberspace in its larger instantiation. The upside of this is that access is more broadly based; the downside, depending upon who is keeping score, is that with small, individually owned BBSs, dialup communities tend to be geographically local to their hardware platforms. Larger systems, such as Compuserve, used leased wide-area telephone lines for remote connection and therefore have nonlocal constituencies.

BBSs were named after their perceived function. Although they were virtual, they took bulletin boards as their physical metaphor, ie, places where people could post notes for general reading. The first successful BBS programs were primitive, usually allowing the user to search for messages alphabetically, or simply to read messages in the order in which they were posted. These programs were sold by their authors for very little, or given away as ' shareware'—part of the early utopian ethic of electronic virtual communities.

Shortly after the first systems became operational, three San Francisco computer programmers developed a revolutionary kind of BBS which allowed messages to be attached to each other by topics and branching subtopics in a treelike structure. The

CommuniTree Group, as they called themselves, saw their BBS as transformative because of the structure it presupposed and simultaneously created—the mode of tree-structured discourse and the community that would speak it. CommuniTree was not perceived merely as a virtual location, but as an extension of the participant's instrumentality into a social space. By using the word 'tree' the group managed to invoke a kind of organic flavor to their project which fit easily into the 'post-hippie' northern Californian discourse in the 1970s. Each branch of the tree was to be a separate conference that grew naturally out of its root message by virtue of each subsequent message that was attached to it. The continuity between messages grew from whatever thread of thought each reader found interesting.

The Tree's founding group was aware that the networks and hardware within which their utopian project was embedded owed their existence to the military-infotainment complex to whose agendas CommuniTree was opposed. The group wasn't daunted by this knowledge. Rather they believed that their approach, with its emphasis on smallness and multiplicity, decentred command structures, and relatively low-tech components, could exist within or even infect the larger communication structures which they shared with such formidable organizations as the US Defense Department.

CommuniTree #1 started operation in May of 1978 in the San Francisco Bay area, roughly a year after the introduction of the Apple II computer. The opening sentence of the first message was 'We are as gods and might as well get good at it'. This techno-spiritual bumptiousness characterized most of the early conferences. Unlike other BBS users, the CommuniTree conferences saw themselves not as readers of notices, but rather as agents of a new kind of social experiment. They saw the terminal or personal computer as a tool for social transformation by the ways it refigured social interaction in both spatial and temporal terms. Significantly, their online interactions were time-aliased—spoken or written at a different time than the time at which they were heard or read. Thus early BBS conversations were like a kind of public letter writing. Letters were meant to be read and replied to some time later than they were written. Nevertheless their participants saw them as conversations—social acts—and as play, a way of experimenting with new perspectives and identities.

Life wasn't easy for the first virtual community. Grammar-school-aged boys found the Tree's dialup number and jammed the conferences with obscene messages. Other enjoyed the sport of attempting to crash the system by discovering bugs in the command structure and triggering them remotely. The technokids got tremendous excitement and satisfaction from their new power to destroy things at a distance, anonymously and at no risk to themselves—a point which should not be lost on those who study the conduct of war in the age of intelligent machines.

CommuniTree was easy to kill because of the state of technology at the time. First, the amount of disk storage available to the system for message archiving was minuscule by today's standards—less than 300 kilobytes. (CommuniTree's authors had considered the disk space and said 'Three hundred kilobytes? We'll never fill it up!' In 1994 a typical BBS might have 400 megabytes of disk space, or more than thousand times more than the Tree.) Thus it didn't take much garbage to fill the system to capacity. Second, the system had been designed for maximum privacy, so that even the system operator could not tell what messages were being received; consequently garbage went onto the disks along with everything else. Third, the Tree accepted control commands, which not only control but can crash the system, indiscriminately along with text.

After a few months of continual assault the Tree choked to death on 'the consequences of freedom of expression,' as one participant put it. But the Tree's death was accompanied by a proliferation of virtual communities with perhaps less visionary character but with vastly superior message handling capability, and with enhancements that allowed system operators to monitor and disconnect troublemakers. The advent of surveillance and control in cyberspace, with the concomitant issues surveillance inevitably raises, also meant survival and growth for the young virtual communities. As they popped online like mushrooms it was clear that they were incestuous and cannibalistic, enthusiastically stealing each other's code and programming ideas. Most of their system operators knew each other; for the most part the operators were also the system programmers, and the borrowing was for the most part friendly. This situation continued for a few iterations of the most workable code, after which the systems had spread geographically beyond the ability of sysops to know each other directly; a limitation shared by all local dialup systems.

RPGs and MUDs

CommuniTree and its progeny were designed as dialup systems, accessible by modem through phone lines. There are many such dialup conference systems available to the public on a cost-per-minute basis, such as CompuServe, plus the generalized access to the Internet which many academics still enjoy in the golden moment before privatization changes it all irrevocably. Most conference systems offer chat lines, through which many people can interact simultaneously in real time. With the development of high-speed dedicated interconnections between government, military, and academic sites, of which Internet is the perspicuous example, came other kinds of conferencing. In the Internet world there are many such systems with elaborately worked out geographies, designed to be accessible to many users at the same time; these are generally known as Multiple-User thises-and-thats, abbreviated MU*. The first of these were direct descendants of Real Life activities called Role-Playing Games, or RPGs.

Initially RPGs were developed within a small community. Most members of the nascent RPG community were also members of the Society for Creative Anachronism (SCA). The SCA is dedicated to keeping the fine chivalric traditions of the Middle Ages alive—at least as SCA members imagine them to have been—and to this end sponsors periodic tournaments in medieval style. Role-playing games are a way for SCA members to continue their fantasy roles between tournaments, and are also a good deal less expensive and more energy efficient than tournaments. The games strongly engage their participants, are open ended, and improve with the players' imaginations. Some players have kept good games going for years, meeting monthly for several days at a time to eat, sleep, and defecate in role. For some, the game has considerably more appeal then Reality. They express an unalloyed nostalgia for a time when roles were clearly defined, folks lived closer to nature, life was simpler, magic was afoot, and adventure was still possible. They are aware, to a certain extent, that their Arthurian vision of the Middle Ages is thoroughly bogus, but they have no intention of allowing reality to temper their enthusiasm. The gritty side of Middle Age life is invisible in their simulations—just as the gritty aspects of modern life are invisible in most of the coded environments of virtual community.

The first RPG was published in 1972 and called, appropriately enough, Dungeons and Dragons. It was an extension, really, of SCA into a textual world whose parameters could be clearly defined. D&D, as it quickly became known, is still played under a rule set invented by the Austin game designer Steve Jackson called the Generic Universal Role Playing System or GURPS, for constructing characters. Voluminous books contain lists of character attributes, weapons, and powers. A designated Dungeon Master acts as arbiter of disputes and prognosticator of events.

Shortly after Jackson developed GURPS, the first affordable modems became available. For the most part these early devices ran at 300 baud, a measurement of data transfer rate; by comparison, in 1994 average modem speeds are around 14,000 baud or 15 times faster. Once modems were affordable, the programmers in the D&D community began to develop versions of the game that could be played online. The first ones ran on small personal computers (they were developed for Apple IIs). Because of the problems of writing multi-tasking operating systems, which allow several people to log in online at once, the first games were time-aliased, like the first BBSs; that is, only one person could be online at a time, so realtime interaction was impossible. The first of these systems to achieve a kind of success was Mines of Moria. The program contained most of the elements that are still ubiquitous in online RPG systems: Quests, Fearsome Monsters, Treasure, Wizards, Twisty Mazes, Vast Castles, and, because the systems were written by young heterosexual males, the occasional Damsel in Distress.

As the Internet came into being from its earlier and more cloistered incarnation as ARPANET, more people had access to what would later be called connectivity. ARPANET had been built with an eye toward multitasking systems—that is, single computers with the capability to service many users at the same time, such as Bell Laboratories' UNIX. ARPANET was designed as a decentred acephalous network which had no preferred path between nodes; such a system, it was reasoned, would be hard for an enemy to disable because it had no vulnerable central switching facility. Data transfer was fast and efficient, enabling multiple users to interconnect at random from widely separated locations. Among its other uses, the network was host to the first realtime multiple user social environments. These were written in the early 1980s and were named, after their origins, Multiple User Dungeons or MUDs.

When the administrators who oversaw the operation of the

large systems began to notice the MUDs in the mid 1980s, they took offense at such unprofessional use of their equipment. The writers of the MUDs then tried the bald public-relations move of renaming their systems Multiple User Domains in an effort to distance themselves from the offensive odor of play which accompanied the word Dungeon. Later versions came to be called MUSEs (Multiple User Social Environments), MUSHes (Multiple User Social Hosts), and MOOs (Mud Object-Oriented). All of these are somewhat similar, but in a MOO it is possible to create virtual objects and assign attributes to them. A MOO builder might create an object called 'Room' with attributes such as 'wall', 'door', 'table', and so on. Objects can be as complex as the programmers' skill allows. Several MOOs have objects called 'TV sets' that can be tuned to virtual channels and thereby receive virtual television programs generated by other objects called 'TV studios'. Objects and attributes in a MOO are persistent; when the MOO crashes, everything is still in place when it comes back up (usually). This has importance for large commercial systems such as Fujitsu's Habitat and smaller ones that contain many complex objects, such as the MIT Media Lab's MediaMOO and the U.Texas ACTLab's PointMOOt.

The code for the first MOO was written by Pavel Curtis, a researcher at the Xerox Palo Alto Research Center who studies computer mediated group interaction. Curtis' original project, which he named LambdaMOO, has been the source of much of the early data on virtual communities. In terms of social formations LambdaMOO has had an interesting and problematic childhood, hosting, as it did, the first documented case of what has been called virtual rape. Some observers disagree with the term, and a number of hot debates about the meaning of rape in cyberspace have ensued.

The first MOO written specifically to host MOO researchers was created by Amy Bruckman at the MIT Media Lab. Later the site was expanded to include virtual conference rooms and areas for socialization, and a number of ongoing virtual colloquia are conducted there. The first MOO designed specifically for interaction research using a mixed population of researchers and subjects was Point MOOt, written by Alan Allford and his team of programmers under my supervision at the Advanced Communication Technologies Laboratory at the department of Radio, TV and Film of the University of Texas at Austin. Point MOOt is an elaborate environment for virtual interaction research, originally intended to be a virtual model of the city of Austin and later expanded in whimsical ways.

All interactions in PointMOOt are recorded for analysis. The capacity to record all interactions has raised issues of privacy, which are still debated by researchers. A few feel strongly that the privacy of people in a virtual environment is compromised by recording even when fair notice is given (a person logging into PointMOOt is informed that they are entering a research environment and that their conversations may be recorded).

It was possible to identify three types of virtual discourse in the early MOOs. Let's recall Andy Lippman's definition of interactivity: Two or more agents engaged in mutual discussion, sometimes working toward a common goal, but not necessarily. For our purposes here the critical phrase is 'but not necessarily,' and the three types of discourse arise from it. In the first instance, there is a definite common goal. This is the mode of cooperative work in the strictly practical sense, in which there are structured mutual objects of discourse. In the second instance, there is no common goal. This is the phatic virtual mode, the mode of such freeforalls as the irc #hottub channel. In the vast territory between these extremes lie the utterances which at least partially share a common goal. Herein lies the power of the virtual mode. These are the ludic discourses, the zone of the playful, experimental, chance encounter, sometimes mutually instructive interactions. What I observe in them is the power of low bandwidth, and the essence of explorative play and the heightened engagement of imagination and drive for closure which low bandwidth engages.

Some of the more recent MOOs, such as Fujitsu's Habitat in Tokyo, use graphics instead of text to create their environments, and so are higher bandwidth communities. Instead of lines of text describing a room, a graphic MOO displays a drawing or digitized photo of a room. Characters in graphic MOOs are displayed as animated cartoon-like figures. From a technical perspective, graphic-based virtual communities use the so-called head end or client-server method in order to keep down the bandwidth between the mainframe and the user. In this method the user's (client) computer contains all the necessary software to generate the graphics and animation. The mainframe (server) computer keeps track of who is where and only needs to exchange brief bursts of data with the client. For example, to take a walk the client instructs their character to start walking;

this data is sent in only a few bytes to the mainframe, which informs the client which segment of the Habitat geography will come into view and what other characters may be there. The actual animation and displays are performed by the client machine under control of the client software. Client-host animation is a relatively new arena for virtual interaction, but the few extant ones are impressive.

The virtual person who is the user's avatar is represented by a cartoon-like figure which the user may customize from a menu of body parts. When the user wishes their character to speak, s/he types out the words on their keyboard, and these appear in a cartoon-like speech balloon over the head of the user's character; the balloon is visible to any other user nearby in the virtual space. Avatars can change clothes and body parts, and the terms used to describe these changes are worth remarking: An avatar goes to the 'spray shop' to buy body colours or clothes (the Japanese description is ambiguous as to which), to the 'head shop' to buy a new head, but to the 'sex change clinic' to change sex. Changing heads is a commercial transaction, but changing sex is a medical one, a different register of social order, even when what is being changed is a representation created with binary code.

The official Fujitsu descriptor for system administrators is Oracles. Oracles practice management by wandering around, so they are frequently active within the simulation. They are able to observe both the official records of who has signed up for Habitat and also who is inside the simulation. Based upon Fujitsu's figures and the Oracles' and my own observations, the ratio of men to women from the 'real world' who sign up for space in Habitat is four to one. However, among the characters who participate in the simulation, the ratio of men to women is three to one. Habitat Oracles like to interpret this data as indicating that 'the people who are using Fujitsu Habitat are selecting their Habitat gender without much relation to their actual gender'. This is a slight misunderstanding of the data; if everyone in Habitat selected their gender without much relation to their actual gender, the ratios of men to women would run closer to one to one. Some of the avatars are selecting genders that may be at variance with their usual gender presentations, but more likely the data show that more men prefer to use feminine gender presentations than there are women who prefer to use the masculine.

The reasons for this seem the same as those in the text-based virtual communities: On line, women attract more interest and get more attention, whether because of or in spite of their smaller numbers. 'Real world' men quickly figure this out, and appropriate it for their own advantage. Because they understand the role-playing aspects of gender presentation in the ludic space of the simulation, and because their sense of personal gender is warranted in their own bodies, and also importantly because the bandwidth limitations of the Habitat simulation preclude detailed, complex gender presentations, they are able to avail themselves of the advantages of gender switching without incurring the disadvantages. They enjoy the attractive and pleasurable qualities of being othered without having to experience the oppression and disempowerment that are part of its construction as well. Should any unpleasant or even incipiently boring events arise, they can simply log out. It is perhaps this ability more than anything else—the ability to log out—that many feminist analysts of virtual systems find most rankling, and certainly with sufficient reason.

Habitat has its own economy, and as in any economy it is likely that sex will be one of the items for sale; and so it was that I came full circle in my studies of bandwidth and desire. There are sex workers in Habitat, in an environment where sex, insofar as we can call it sex, is free of disease. The most common kind of (quasi)physical erotic stimulation is fellatio. So far this is usually transacted between a male client and a female provider. The client avatar sits in a chair, and the sex worker avatar kneels in front of him to perform fellatio with rapid movements of her head. Habitat does not (yet, perhaps) evince male sex workers, in contrast to such steamy virtual environments as the Minitel Pink service. It is not impossible that alternative sex practices to the heterosexual norm could emerge, but given the character and social conditioning of the majority of the people who have access to Habitat this is not likely to happen very soon. Tokyo's lone lesbian bar is still an island in a sea of what appears to be (perhaps deceptively) stolid sexual conformity.

By the time you read this, there will be several Habitat-like communities online in the US, as Chip Morningstar and Randy Farmer, the authors of the original Lucasfilm Habitat simulation, code away at brave new post-Habitat worlds. The issues they raise, like those of all virtual communities, are complex. How is agency warranted between an offline person and an online persona? What is the nature of presence? How do issues of virtuality, 'bodiless interaction' and multiplicity relate to agendas of social and political control, which depend upon the production of a monistic, localizable political individual through the exercise of physical power? My stakes in these outcomes are high, not least because I am aware that within a few years many children will spend more time playing interactive computer games than they currently spend watching television. I see my daughter at her Mac AV, her enraptured face reflecting the glow of the screen and suggestively taking on its electric aura. The scene encapsulates for me a very personal future—the troubling and productive implosions of neurology and electronics, musculature and hydraulics, thought and computation, biology and technology that signal the close of the mechanical age and the inception of an age which, for want of a better term, let's call the virtual—happening not in some theoretical space but right there in the next room, not to some research subject but to my own flesh and blood.

Finally, in a moment you will notice that this chapter has no closure, no conclusion, no tidiness. Had we world enough and time, I would say something about method, because avoiding closure, even in a brief essay at the expense of narrative satisfaction, is itself a specific and deliberate method. Perhaps we can continue that part of the discussion when our personae meet in cyberspace—the problematic and promising space of desire, of play, and—I hope—of possibility.

References

Electronic Sources

ARACHNET. An Association of Electronic Discussion Groups, ARARCH-NET@uottawa.bitnet.'

Burral, W. 'Electronic message sent to the Learning Circle Mentor folder, January, 1994.' 1994.

COMMUNET%UYVMVM.bitnet. 'Communet: Community and Civic network Discussion List.'

Computer Underground Digest, April 21, 1993, 5: 29, ISSN 1004–042X.

'Environmental impacts of the computer age.' *Science News*, October 2, 1993: 219.

'Electronic Gender Salon.' Lewis and Clark College, Oregon, USA: 1992.

Herring, S. 'Gender and democracy in computer-mediated communication.' *Electronic Journal of Communication* 3 (2 1993): (Special issue on computer-mediated communication, edited by T. Benson. Archived on COMSERVE.)

Kunz, S. Electronic mail. skunz@iastate,edu.' February 3, 1993.

Noel, P. Electronic message sent to Shahaf Gal for an NSE sponsored study of the effect of networking on the professional development of teachers, December, 1993.

Reid, B. 'Usenet readership report for July, 1993. news.lists.' August 6, 1993.

Utne Reader Internet Email Salons. utnereader@mr.net.

Bibliography

Abbott, A., (1988), *The System of Professions: An Essay on the Division of Expert Labor*. Chicago: Chicago.

Adler, R., (1988), *Seniornet: Toward a national community of computer-using seniors*. Aspen Institute Project on Enhancing the Social Benefits of New Electronic Technologies, NY: Aspen Institute, Forum Report 5.

Agre, P., (1988), 'The dynamic structure of everyday life.' Ph.D., Artificial Intelligence Laboratory, MIT.

Agre, P., (1993), 'From high tech to human tech: On the sudden market for social studies of technology.' In Bowker, G., Gasser, L., Star, S.L. and Turner, W., (eds), *Beyond the Great Divide: Social Science Research, Technical Systems and Cooperative Work*, Paris: CNRS.

Alpers, S., (1983), *The Art of Describing: Dutch Art in the 17th Century*. Chicago: Chicago.

Amann, K. and Knorr-Cetina, K., (1990), 'The fixation of (visual) evidence.' In Lynch, M. and Woolgar, S. (eds), *Representation in Scientific Practice*, 85–122. Cambridge, MA: MIT.

Ambrose, S., (1985), *Rise to Globalism*. 4th ed., NY: Penguin.

Amerine, R. and Bilmes, J., (1990), Following instructions. In Lynch, M. and Woolgar, S. (eds), *Representation in scientific practice*. 323–336. Cambridge, MA: MIT.

Anderson, J.R., (1990), *Cognitive Psychology and Its Implications*. 3rd ed., NY: Freeman.

Ang, I., (1985), *Watching Dallas: Soap Opera and the Melodramatic Imagination*. NY: Routledge.

Arnheim, R., (1969), *Visual Thinking*. Berkeley: California.

Arnold, E., (1984), *Computer-Aided Design in Europe*. Sussex: European Research Centre.

Aronowitz, S., (1973), *The Shaping of American Working Class Consciousness*. NY: McGraw-Hill.

Austin, J.L., (1975), *How to Do Things with Words*. 2nd ed., Cambridge, MA: Harvard.

Babrow, A.S., (1989), 'An expectancy-value analysis of the student soap opera audience.' *Communication-Research* 16: 155–178.

Bakhtin, M.M., (1981), *The Dialogic Imagination*. Austin: Texas.

Bakhtin, M.M., (1986), *Speech Genres and Other Late Essays*. Austin: Texas.

Balsamo, A., (1993), 'The virtual body in cyberspace.' *Journal of Research in Technology and Philosophy* 13: 119–139.

Barnes, B., (1982), 'The science-technology relationship: A model and a query.' *Social Studies of Science* 12: 166–172.

Barnes, B. and Edge, D. (eds), (1982), *Science in Context*. Cambridge, MA: MIT.

Barnes, B. and Shapin, S. (eds), (1979), *Natural Order: Historical Studies of Scientific Culture*. London: Sage.

Barthes, R., (1970), *S/Z*. New York: Hill & Wang.

Bateson, G., (1972), *Steps to an Ecology of Mind*. Sand Francisco: Chandler.

Bateson, G. and Mead, M., (1942), *Balinese Character: A Photographic Analysis*. New York: New York Academy of Sciences.

Bateson, G. and Mead, M., (1976), 'For God's sake, Margaret'. *The Coevolution Quarterly* (Summer, 1976): 32–44.

Bauman, R., (1992a), 'Contextualization, tradition, and the dialogue of genres: Icelandic legends of the *kraftaskald*.' In Duranti, A. and Goodwin, C. (eds), *Rethinking Context: Language as an Interactive Phenomenon*, 125–146. New York: Cambridge.

Bauman, R., (1992b), 'Verbal art as performance.' *American Anthropologist* 77: 290–311.

Baxandall, M., (1972), *Painting and Experience in Fifteenth Century Italy*. London: Oxford.

Baym, N., (1992), 'Computer-mediated soap talk: communication, community and entertainment on the net.' Paper delivered to the Speech Communication Association, Chicago.

Baym, N. (1994) 'Communication, interpretation, and relationships: a study of a computer-mediated fan community.' Ph.D., Illinois.

References

Beck, E.E. and Bellotti, V.M.E., (1993), 'Informed opportunism as strategy: Supporting coordination in distributed collaborative writing.' In de Micheli, G., Simone, C. and Schmidt, K. (eds), *ECSCW '93, The Third European Conference on Computer Supported Cooperative Work*. Dordrecht: Kluwer.

Becker, H.S., (1986), 'A school is a lousy place to learn anything in.' In *Doing Things Together*, 173–190. Evanston, IL: Northwestern.

Becker, H.S., (1982), *Art Worlds*. Berkeley: California.

Benedikt, M., (ed.) (1991), *Cyberspace: First Steps*. Cambridge, MA: MIT.

Beniger, J.R., (1986), *The Control Revolution: Technological and Economical Origins of the Information Society*. Cambridge, MA: Harvard.

Berger, J., (1972), *Ways of Seeing*. London: Penguin.

Berkowitz, L. and Squitier, K.A., (1986), *Thesaurus Linguae Graecae Canon of Greek Authors and Works*. New York: Oxford.

Bernstein, B., (1971), *Class, Codes and Control*. London: Routledge.

Bijker, W.E., Hughes, T.P. and Pinch, T. (eds), (1987), *The Social Construction of Technological Systems: New Directions in the Sociology and History of Technology*. Cambridge, MA: MIT.

Block, N., (1981), *Imagery*. Cambridge, MA: MIT.

Bloor, D., (1976), *Knowledge and Social Imagery*. London: Routledge.

Bloor, D., (1991), *Knowledge and Social Imagery*. 2nd ed., Chicago: Chicago.

Blye, S., (1988), 'A use of drawing surfaces in different collaborative settings.' In *Second conference on Computer-Supported Cooperative Work*, Portland, Oregon.

Bødker, S., (1991), *Through the Interface*. Hillside, NJ: Erlbaum.

Bødker, S., Christiansen, E., Ehn, P., Markusen, R., Morgensen, P. and Trigg, R., (1991), *Computers in context: Report from the AT project in progress*. Report of the 1991 NES-SAM Conference, Ebeltoft, Denmark.

Boland, R. and Day, W., (1989), 'The experience of system design: A hermeneutic of organizational action.' *Scandinavian Journal of Management* 5: 87–104.

Bolgar, R.R., (1981), 'The Greek Legacy.' In Finley, M.I. (eds), *The Legacy of Greece: A New Appraisal*. Oxford: Clarendon.

Bolter, Jay David, (1991), *Writing Space: The Computer, Hypertext, and the History of Writing*. Hillsdale, New Jersey: Lawrence Erlbaum.

Booker, P., (1963), *A History of Engineering Drawing*. London: Chatto and Windus.

Borning, A., (1987), 'Computer System Reliability and Nuclear War.' *Communications of the ACM* 30: 112–131.

Bourdieu, P., (1977), *Outline of a Theory of Practice*. Cambridge: Cambridge.

Bourdieu, P., (1990), *The Logic of Practice*. Stanford, CA: Stanford.

Bourdieu, P.(1991), *Language and Symbolic Power*. Cambridge: Polity.

Bowker, G., (1994), 'Information Mythology and Infrastructure.' In Bud., L. (ed.), *Information Acumen: The Understanding and Use of Knowledge in Modern Business*, 231–247. London: Routledge.

Bowker, G., Gasser, L., Star, S.L., and Turner, W. (eds), (1993), *Beyond the Great Divide: Social Science Research, Technical Systems and Cooperative Work*. Paris: CNRS.

Bowker, G. and Star, S.L., (1994), 'Knowledge and infrastructure in international information management: Problems of classification and coding.' In Bud, L., (ed.), *Information Acumen: the Understanding and Use of Knowledge in Modern Business*, 187–213. London: Routledge.

Bowker, G. and Star, S.L., (1991), 'Situations vs. standards in long-term, wide-scale decision-making: The case of the International Classification of Diseases.'

In *Hawaiian International Conference on Systems Sciences*, IEEE Computer Society.

Braidotti, R., (1991), *Patterns of Dissonance: A Study of Women in Contemporary Philosophy*. Cornwall: Polity.

Brook, P., (1990), *The empty space*. Harmondsworth: Penguin.

Brown, E., 'On line in the big sky.' *Missoula Independent*, November 14, 1991: 10.

Brown, M.E., (1990), 'Motley moments: Soap opera, carnival, gossip and the power of the utterance.' In Brown, M.E. (ed.), *Television and Women's Culture*, 183–200. Newbury Park, CA: Sage.

Bruer, J.T., (1993), *Schools for thought: a science of learning in the classroom*. Cambridge, MA: MIT.

Brunner, T.F., (1987), 'Data banks for the humanities: Learning from the Thesaurus Linguae Graecae.' *Scholarly Communication*.

Brunner, T.F., (1988), 'Overcoming "Verzettelung".' *Humanities* 9.

Brunner, T.F., 'The Thesaurus Linguae Graecae: Classics and the computer.' *Library Hi Tech* 33 (September 1991): 61–64.

Bucciarelli, L.L., (1988), 'An ethnographic perspective on engineering design.' *Design Studies* 9: 159–168.

Buckingham. D., (1987), *Public Secrets: Eastenders and its Audience*. London: British Film Institute.

Bush, Vannevar, (1945), 'As We May Think.' Atlantic Monthly 176: 101–8.

Callon, M., Law, J. and Rip, A. (eds), (1986), *Mapping the Dynamics of Science and Technology*. London: Macmillan.

Calvert, M., 91967), *The American Engineer in America, 1830–1910*. Baltimore: Johns Hopkins.

Cambrosio, A. and Keating, P., (1988), ' "Going monoclonal": Art, science, and magic in day-to-day use of hybridoma technology.' *Social Problems* 35: 244–260.

Chan, C., (1990), 'Cognitive processes in architectural design problem solving.' *Design Studies* 11: 60–80.

Chi, M., Feltovich, P. and Glaser, R., (1981), 'Categoriation and representation of physics problems by experts and novices.' *Cognitive Science* 5: 121–152.

Cicourel, A., (1981), 'Notes on the integration of micro- and macro-levels of analysis.' In Knorr-Cetina, K. and Cicourel, A.V. (eds), *Advances in Social Theory and Methodology: Toward an Integration of Micro- and Macro-Sociologies*, 51–80. Boston: Routledge.

Clanchy, M.T., (1979), *From Memory to Written Record*. London: Edward Arnold.

Clark, W.J., 'Spreadsheets versus data base management systems.' *Financial and Accounting Systems* (Spring 1991): 10–14.

Clarke, A.E., 'Modernity, postmodernity and reproductive Processes, c1890–1990: or, "Mommy, where do cyborgs come from anyway?".' Paper presented at the Gender, Science and Technology Conference, Melbourne, Australia, 1993.

Clarke, A.E. and Gerson, E., (1990), 'Symbolic interactionism in social studies of science.' In Becker, H.S. and McCall, M.M. (eds), *Symbolic Interaction and Cultural Studies*, 179–214. Chicago: Chicago.

Cockburn, C., (1983), *Brothers: Male Dominance and Technological Change*. Suffolk: Pluto.

Cockburn, C., (1992), 'The circuit of technology: gender, identity and power.' In Silverstone, R. and Hirsch, E. (eds), *Consuming Technologies: Media and Information in Domestic Spaces*. Cornwall: Routledge.

References

Cockburn, C. and Ormrod, S., (1993), *Gender and Technology in the Making.* Newbury Park, CA: Sage.

Cohen, M. and Riel, M., (1989), 'The effect of distant audiences on students' writing.' *American Educational Research Journal* 26: 143–159.

Collins, H.M., (1974), 'The TEA Set: Tacit knowledge and scientific networks.' *Science Studies* 4: 165–186.

Collins, H.M., (1985), *Changing Order: Replication and Induction in Scientific Practice.* London: Sage.

Collins, H.M., (1990), *Artificial Experts: Social Knowledge and Intelligent Machines.* Cambridge, MA: MIT.

Condon, M.C. and Schweingruber, D., (1994), 'The Morality of Time and the Organization of a Men's Emergency Shelter.' Unpublished manuscript, Dept. of Sociology, University of Illinois, Urbana-Champaign.

Cooper, M.M. and Self, C.L., (1990), 'Computer conferences and learning: Authority, resistance, and internally persuasive discourse.' *College English* 52: 847–869.

Coulter, J., (1991), 'Logic: Ethnomethodology and the logic of language.' In Button, G. (ed.), *Ethnomethodology and the Human Sciences*, 20–50. Cambridge: Cambridge.

Cowan, R.S., (1983), *More Work for Mother: The Ironies of Household Technology from the Open Hearth to the Microwave.* New York: Basic Books.

Cronberg, T., (1987), *Det Teknologiske Spillerum I Hverdagen.* Frederiksberg: Byt fra samfundsvidenskaberne.

Cuff, D., (1991), *Architecture: The Story of Practice.* Cambridge, MA: MIT.

Czarniawska-Joerges, B., (1992), *Exploring Complex Organizations: A Cultural Perspective.* London: Sage.

Darnton, R., (1980), 'Intellectual and Cultural History.' In Kammen, M. (ed.), *The Past Before Us: Contemporary Historical Writing in the United States*, 327–354. Ithaca: Cornell.

de Lauretis, T., (1987), *Technologies of Gender: Essays on Theory, Film, and Fiction.* Bloomington, IN: Indiana.

Dertouzos, M.L., Cerf, V.G., Tesler, L.G., Weiser, M., Negroponte, N.P., Sproull, L., Kiesler, S., Malone, T.W., Rockart, J.F., Kay, A.C., Gore, A., Branscomb, A.W. and Kapor, M., (1991), 'Communications, computers, and networks: How to work, play and thrive in cyberspace.' *Scientific American* 265.

Deutsche, R., (1991), 'Uneven development: Public art in New York City.' Pp. 107–132 in Ferguson, R., Gever, M., Minh-ha, T.T. and West, C. (eds), *Marginalization and Contemporary Cultures.* Cambridge, MA: MIT Press.

Diamond, I., (1994), *Fertile Ground: Women, the Earth, and the Limit of Control.* Boston: Beacon.

Dibbell, J., (1993), 'A rape in cyberspace, or How an evil clown, a Haitian trickster spirit, two wizards, and a cast of dozens turned a database into a society.' *The Village Voice*, December 21, 36–42.

Dickson, P., (1976), *The Electronic Battlefield.* Bloomington: Indiana.

Douglas, M., (1970), *Natural Symbols.* London: Barrie and Rockliff.

Downey, G., Donovan, A. and Elliott, T., (1988), 'The invisible engineer: How engineering ceased to be a problem in science and technology studies.' *Knowledge and Society: Studies in the Sociology of Science Past and Present* 8: 189–216.

Dunlop, C. and Kling, R. (eds), (1991), *Computerization and Controversy: Value Conflicts and Social Choices*. NY: Academic.

Eagleton, T., (1983), *Literary Theory—An Introduction*. Oxford: Blackwell.

Eagleton, T., (1991), *Ideology—An Introduction*. London: Verso.

Ebben, M. and Kramarae, C., (1993), 'Women and information technologies: Creating a cyberspace of our own.' In Taylor, H.J., Kramarae, C. and Ebben, M. (eds), *Women, Information Technology and Scholarship*, 15–28. Urbana, IL: Center for Advanced Study.

Eckert, P., (1989), *Jocks and Burnouts*. NY: Teachers' College.

Edgerton, S., (1980), 'The Renaissance artist as quantifier.' In Hagen (ed.), *The Perception of Pictures*. NY: Academic.

Edwards, P.N., *The Closed World: Computers and the Politics of Discourse*. Cambridge, MA: MIT, forthcoming.

Eisenstein, E.L., (1979), *Printing as The Agent of Change*. Cambridge: Cambridge.

Eisenstein, E.L., (1983), *The Printing Revolution in Early Modern Europe*. Cambridge: Cambridge.

Ekman, K., (1978), *Hekseringene*. Rødovre: Samlerens Forlag.

Engeström, Y., (1989), *Developing thinking at the changing workplace: Toward a redefinition of expertise*. Center for Human Information Processing, U. California, San Diego, Report 130.

Engeström, Y., (1990), *Learning, Working and Imagining*. Helsinki: Orienta-Konsultit Oy.

Feltovich, P.J., Spiro, R.J., and Coulson, R.L., (1989), 'The nature of conceptual understanding in biomedicine: The deep structure of complex ideas and the development of misconceptions'. In Evans, D. and Patel, V. (eds), *The Cognitive Sciences in Medicine* 113–172. Cambridge, MA: MIT.

Feigenbaum, E. and McCorduck, P., (1983), *The Fifth Generation: Japan's Computer Challenge to the World*. Reading, MA: Addison-Wesley.

Feigenbaum, E., McCorduck, P. and Nii, H.P., (1988), *The Rise of the Expert Company: How Visionary Companies Are Using Artificial Intelligence to Achieve Higher Productivity and Profits*. NY: Times Books.

Ferguson, E., (1977), 'The mind's eye: Nonverbal thought in technology.' *Science* 197: 827.

Ferguson, E., (1985), 'La fondation des machines modernes: Des dessins.' In *Les 'vues' de l'ésprit (Special Issue of Culture Technique.)* 207–213.

Ferguson, E., (1992), *Engineering and the Mind's Eye*. Cambridge, MA: MIT.

Fink, A., (1991), *Kvinder, Vindenskab og Autoritet*. Sorring, Denmark: Privately printed.

Flamm, K., (1987), *Targeting the Computer: Government Support and International Competition*. Washington, D.C.: Brookings Institution.

Flamm, K., (1988), *Creating the Computer: Government, Industry, and High Technology*. Washington, D.C.: Brookings Institution.

Forman, J., (ed.), (1992), *New Visions of Collaborative Writing*. Portsmouth, NH: Boynton/Cook Heinemann.

Frauenfelder, M., 'Moebius.' *Wired*, January 1994, 96–99.

Fujimura, J., (1987), 'The social construction of doable problems in cancer research: Articulating alignment.' *Social Studies of Science* 17: 257–293.

Fyfe, G. and Law, J. (eds), (1988), *Picturing Power: Visual Depictions and Social Relations*. London: Routledge.

Gal, S., (1992), 'Between speech and silence: The problematics of research on

References

language and gender.' In di Leonardo, M., (ed.) *Gender at the Crossroads of Knowledge: Feminist Anthropology in the Postmodern Era*, 175–203. Berkeley: California.

Gallini, J. and Helman, N., (1993), 'Collaborative learning in vitually extended classrooms.' In *American Educational Research Association*, Atlanta.

Gantt, M. and Nardi, B., (1992), 'Gardeners and gurus: Patterns of cooperation among CAD users.' In *Computer-Human Interaction* 107–118. New York: ACM.

Gardner, H., (1984), *Frames of Mind: The Theory of Multiple Intelligences*. New York: Basic Books.

Gardner, H., (1985), *The Mind's New Science*. New York: Basic Books.

Gaskins, S., Miller, P.J. and Corsaro, W.A., (1992), 'Theoretical and methodological perspectives in the interpretive study of children.' In Corsaro, W.A. and Miller, P.J. (eds), *Interpretive Approaches to Children's Socialization*, 5–24. 58. San Francisco: Jossey-Bass.

Gasser, L., (1986), 'The integration of computing and routine work.' *ACM Transactions on Office Information Systems* 4: 205–225.

Geertz, C., (1973), *The Interpretation of Cultures*. New York: Basic Books.

Geraghty, C., (1991), *Women and Soap Opera*. Cambridge: Polity.

Gibson, J., (1986), *The Perfect War: The War We Couldn't Lose and How We Did*. New York: Vintage Books.

Gibson, W., (1984), *Neuromancer*. New York: Ace Books.

Giddens, A., (1990), *The Consequences of Modernity*. Cornwall: Polity.

Goel, V. and Pirolli, P., (1992), 'The structure of design problem spaces.' *Cognitive Science* 16: 395–429.

Goffman, E., (1981), *Forms of Talk*. Philadelphia: Pennsylvania.

Goodwin, C. and Duranti, A., (1992), 'Rethinking Context: An Introduction.' In Duranti, A. and Goodwin, C. (eds), *Rethinking Context: Language as an Interactive Phenomenon*, 1–42. Cambridge: Cambridge.

Gray, C.H., (1991), 'Computers as Weapons and Metaphors: The U.S. Military 1940–1990 and Postmodern War.' Ph.D., California, Santa Cruz.

Greenfield, P., (1984), *Mind and Media*. Cambridge, MA: Harvard.

Gregory, K.L., (1983), 'Native-view paradigms: Multiple cultures and culture conflicts in organizations.' *Administrative Sciences Quarterly* 28: 359–376.

Griffin, S., (1978), *Woman and Nature: The Roaring Inside Her*. New York: Harper and Row.

Gumperz, J., (1992), 'Contextualization and understanding.' In Duranti, A. and Goodwin, C. (eds), *Rethinking Context: Language as an Interactive Phenomenon*, 229–252. Cambridge: Cambridge.

Gumperz, J.J. and Hymes, D., (1972), *Directions in Sociolinguistics: The Ethnography of Communication*. New York: Holt, Rinehart and Winston.

Gunn, A., 'Computer bulletin boards not just boy toy.' *New Directions for Women*, November/December 1991, 7.

Hacker, Sally, (1990), *Doing It the Hard Way: Investigations of Gender and Technology*. Boston: Unwin Hyman.

Hagaman, D., 'The joy of victory, the agony of defeat: Stereotypes in newspaper sports feature photographs.' *Visual Sociology* 8 (2 1993): 48–66.

Hales, M., (1980), *Living Thinkwork—Where Do Labour Processes Come From?* London: Free Association.

Hales, Mike, (1993), 'Human-centred systems, gender and computer supported cooperative work.' In Probert, B. and Wilson, B. (eds), *Pink Collar Blues: Work, Gender and Technology*, 101–125. Melbourne: Melbourne.

Hales, Mike, (1994a), 'Durable changes and systems that don't get in the way of the work.' In Bradley, G. and Hendrick, H.W. (eds), *Human Factors in Organization Design and Management*, IV. 399–404. Amsterdam: Elsevier/North Holland.

Hales, Mike, (1994b), 'Where are designers? Styles of design practice, objects of design and views of users in computer supported cooperative work.' In Rosenburg, D. and Hutchinson, C. (eds), *Design Issues in CSCW*, 151–177. London: Springer Verlag.

Hales, M., Marsh, S. and Sang, B., (1994), 'The theory and practice of getting humans into global organisations—Performing rather than preforming.' In R. Baskerville, O. Ngwenyama, S. Smithson and J.I. DeGross (eds), *Transforming organisations with information technology* (IFIP Transactions in Computer Science and Technology A-49), 175–195. Amsterdam: North-Holland.

Hall, R.M. and Sandler, B., (1982), *The classroom climate: A chilly one for women*. Washington, D.C., Association of American Colleges Project on the Status and Education of Women.

Halliday, F., (1986), *The Making of the Second Cold War*. London: Verso.

Harasim, L., (1990), *Online Education*. NY: Praeger.

Haraway, D., (1991a), A cyborg manifesto: Science, technology and socialist-feminism in the late twentieth century.' In Haraway, D. (ed.), *Simians, Cyborgs and Women: The Reinvention of Nature*, 149–181. London: Free Association.

Haraway, D., (1991b), *Simians, Cyborgs, and Women: The Reinvention of Nature*. New York: Routledge.

Haraway, D.J., (1985), 'A manifesto for cyborgs: Science, technology, and socialist feminism in the 1980s.' *Socialist Review* 15: 65–107.

Haraway, D.J., (1992), 'The Promises of Monsters.' In Grossberg, L., Nelson, C. and Treichler, P.A. (eds), *Cultural Studies*, New York: Routledge.

Harding, S., (1986), *The Science Question in Feminism*. New York: Open University.

Harper, D., (1987), *Working Knowledge: Skill and Community in a Small Shop*. Chicago: Chicago.

Hartley, L.P., (1966), *The Go-Between*. London:

Hartsock, N.C.M., (1985), *Money, Sex and Power. Towards a Feminist Historical Materialism*. Michigan: Northeastern.

Hawkins, S., (1968), 'The two worlds of Shakespearean comedy.' In Leeds Barroll, J. (ed.), *Shakespeare Studies*, 62–80. III. Cincinnati, OH: The Center for Shakespeare Studies.

Heath, C. and Luff, P., (1991), 'Collaborative activity and technological design: Task coordination in London Underground control rooms.' In Bannon, L., Robinson, M. and Schmidt, K. (eds), *ECSCW '91. Proceedings of the Second European Conference on Computer-Supported Cooperative Work in Amsterdam*, Dordrecht: Kluwer.

Heim, M., (1991), 'The erotic ontology of cyberspace.' In Benedikt, M. (ed.), *Cyberspace: First Steps*, 59–80. Cambridge, MA: MIT.

Henderson, K., (1991), 'Flexible sketches and inflexible data bases: Visual communication, conscription devices, and boundary objects in design engineering.' *Science, Technology and Human Values* 16: 448–473.

Hindle, B., (1991), *Emulation and Invention*. New York: Norton.

References

Hirsch, E.D. Jr., (1976), *The Aims of Interpretation*. Chicago: Chicago.

Hirschhorn, L., (1984), *Beyond Mechanization*. Cambridge, MA: MIT.

Hirschhorn, L., (1985), 'Information technology and the New Services Game.' In Castells, M. (ed.), *High Technology, Space and Society*, 28. Beverly Hills: Sage.

Hirschhorn, L., (1988), *The Workplace Within: Psychodynamics of Organizational Life*. Cambridge, MA: MIT.

Hobson, D., (1982), *Crossroads: The Drama of Soap Opera*. London: Methuen.

Hobson, D., (1989), 'Soap operas at work.' In Seiter, E., Borchers, H., Kreutzner, G. and Warth, E. (eds), *Remote Control: Television, Audiences, and Cultural Power*, 150–167. New York: Routledge.

Howe, L.K., (1977), *Pink Collar Workers*. New York:

Hughes, D., (1991), 'Native American art makes history.' Personal letter to Frank Odasz in *Big Sky Telegraph*.

Hutchins, E., (1990), 'The technology of team navigation.' In Galegher, J., Kraut, R.E. and Egido, C. (eds), *Intellectual Teamwork*, 191–220. Hillsdale, NJ: Lawrence Erlbaum.

Hymes, D., (1975), 'Folklore's nature and the sun's myth.' *Journal of American Folklore* 88: 345–369.

Hymes, D., (1986), 'Models of the interaction of language and social life.' In Gumperz, J. and Hymes, D. (eds), *Directions in Sociolinguistics: The Ethnography of Speaking*, 35–71. New York: Blackwell.

Iacono, S. and Kling, R., (1987), 'Changing office technologies and transformations of clerical work: A historical perspective.' In Kraut, Robert (ed.), *Technology and the Transformation of White Collar Work*. New Jersey: Erlbaum.

Ihde, D., (1979), *Technics and Praxis*. Dordrecht: Reidel.

Ihde, D., (1990), *Technology and the Lifeworld. From Garden to Earth*. Bloomington, IN: Indiana.

Ivins, W.M., (1953), *Prints and Visual Communication*. Cambridge, MA: Harvard.

Ivins, W.M., (1981), *Prints and Visual Communication*. Cambridge, MA: Harvard.

Jacobson, M.J. and Spiro, R.J., (1991) 'Hypertext learning environments and cognitive flexibility: Characteristics promoting the transfer of complex knowledge.' In Birnbaum, L. (ed.), *The International Conference on the Learning Sciences*, 240–248. Charlottesville, Virginia: Association for the Advancement of Computing in Education.

Jacoby, S. and Gonzales, P., (1991), 'The constitution of expert-novice in scientific discourse.' *Issues in Applied Linguistics* 2: 149–181.

Janson, H.W., (1977), *History of Art*. New York: Prentice Hall.

Jenkins, H., (1992), *Textual Poachers: Television Fans and Participatory Cultures*. London: Routledge.

Jones, R.A., (1993), 'La Science positive de la morale en France: les sources allemandes de la De la division du travail social.' In Besnard, P., Borlandi, M. and Vogt, W.P. (eds), *Division du Travail et Lien Social: La These de Durkheim un siecle apres*, 11–41. Paris: Presses Universitaries de France.

Jones, R.A., 'Ambivalent Cartesians: Durkheim, Montesquieu, and method.' *American Journal of Sociology* 100: forthcoming.

Jones, R.A. and Spiro, R.J., (1992), 'Imagined conversations: The relevance of hypertext, pragmatism, and cognitive flexibility theory to the interpretation of "classic texts" in intellectual history.' In Lucarella, D., Nanard, J. and Paolini, R. (eds), 141–149. New York: Association for Computing Machinery.

264

Kanter, R.M., (1977), *Men and Women of the Corporation*. New York: Basic Book.

Keller, E.F., (1985), *Reflections on Gender and Science*. New Haven: Yale.

Kidder, R., (1981), *Soul of a New Machine*. Boston: Little Brown.

Kling, R. and Gerson, E., (1978), 'Patterns of segmentation and intersection in the computing world.' *Symbolic Interaction* 1: 424–438.

Kling, R. and Iacono, S., (1988), 'The mobilization of support for computerization: the role of computerization movements.' *Social Problems* 35: 226–243.

Kling, R. and Iacono, S., (1984), 'The control of information systems development after implementation.' *Communications of the ACM* 27 (12 1984): 1218–1226.

Kling, R. and Scacchi, W., (1979), 'Recurrent dilemmas of computer use in complex organizations.' *AFIPS National Computer Conference*, 107–115.

Kling, R. and Scacchi, W., (1982), 'The web of computing: Computing technology as social organization.' *Advances in Computers* 21: 3–78.

Knorr-Cetina, K. and Amann, K., (1990), 'Image dissection in natural scientific inquiry.' *Science, Technology, and Human Values* 15: 259–283.

Knorr-Cetina, K.D., (1981), *The Manufacture of Knowledge: An Essay on the Constructivist and Contextual Nature of Science*. Oxford: Pergamon.

Kort, B.W., 'Computer networks and informal science education.' *T.I.E. (Telecommunications in Education) News, ISTE (International Society for Technology in Education) Special Interest Group for Telecommunications* 2 (Spring, 1991).

Kraemer, K. and King, J.L., (1977), *Computers and local government*. New York: Praeger.

Kraemer, K. and King, J.L., 'Computer-based models for policy making: uses and impacts in the U.S. federal government.' *Operations Research* 34 (1986): 501–512.

Kramarae, C. and Taylor, H.J., (1993), 'Women and men on electronic networks: A conversation or a monologue?' In Taylor, H.J., Kramarae, C. and Ebben, M. (eds), *Women, Information Technology and Scholarship*, 59–69. Urbana, IL: Center for Advanced Study.

Kramarae, C., Treichler, P.A. and Russo, A., (1992), *Amazons, Bluestockings, and Crones: A Feminist Dictionary*. San Francisco: HarperSanFrancisco.

Kraut, R., Galegher, J., Fish, R. and Chalfonte, B., (1992), 'Task requirements and media choice in collaborative writing.' *Human-Computer Interaction* 7.

Kresik, S. (ed.), (1981), *Contemporary Literary Hermeneutics and Interpretation of Classical Texts*. Ottawa.

Kuhn, T., (1962), *The Structure of Scientific Revolutions*. Chicago: Chicago.

Lakoff, G., (1987), *Women, Fire, and Dangerous Things: What Categories Reveal About the Mind*. Chicago: Chicago.

Lakoff, G. and Johnson, M., (1980), *Metaphors We Live By*. Chicago: Chicago.

Landow, G.P., (1992), *Hypertext: The Convergence of Contemporary Critical Theory and Technology*. Baltimore: Johns Hopkins.

Larkin, J., McDermott, J., Simon, D.P. and Simon, H.A., (1980), 'Expert and novice performance in solving physics problems.' *Science* 208: 1335–1342.

Latour, B., (1986), 'Visualization and cognition: Thinking with eyes and hands.' *Knowledge and Society: Studies in the Sociology of Culture Past and Present* 6: 1–40.

Latour, B., (1987), *Science in Action*. Cambridge, MA: Harvard.

References

Latour, B., (1988a), 'Mixing humans and nonhumans together: The sociology of a door-closer.' *Social Problems* 35: 298–310.

Latour, B., (1998b), *The Pasteurization of France.* Translated by Sheridan, Alan Law, John. Cambridge, MA: Harvard.

Latour, B., (1988c), 'A relativistic account of Einstein's relativity.' *Social Studies of Science* 18: 3–44.

Latour, B., (1990), 'Postmodern? No, simply amodern!: Steps toward an anthropology of science.' *Studies in the History and Philosophy of Science* 21: 145–171.

Latour, B., (1993), *We Have Never Been Modern.* London: Harvester Wheatsheaf.

Latour, B. and Woolgar, S., (1986), *Laboratory Life: The Construction of Scientific Facts.* Princeton, NJ: Princeton.

Laudan, R., (ed.), (1984), *The Nature of Technological Knowledge: Are Models of Scientific Change Relevant?* Dordrecht: Reidel.

Lave, J., (1988), *Cognition in Practice.* New York: Cambridge.

Lave, J. and Wenger, R., (1991), *Situated Learning: Legitimate Peripheral Participation.* Cambridge: Cambridge.

Law, J., (1987), 'On the social explanation of technical change: The case of the Portuguese maritime expansion.' *Technology and Culture* 28: 227–252.

Law, J., (1991), 'Power, discretion and strategy.' In Law, J. (ed.), *A Sociology of Monsters: Essays on Power, Technology and Domination*, 165–191. London: Routledge.

Law, J. and Lynch, M., (1988), 'Lists, field guides, and the descriptive organization of seeing: Birdwatching as an exemplary observational activity.' *Human Studies* 11: 271–.

Law, J. and Whittaker, J., 'Why the PC is not a projectile.'

Law, J. and Williams, R.J., (1982), 'Putting facts together: A study of scientific persuasion.' *Social Studies of Science* 12: 535–558.

Layton, E.T., (1974), 'Technology as knowledge.' *Technology and Culture* 15: 31–41.

Layton, E.T., (1986), *The Revolt of the Engineers: Social Responsibility and the American Engineering Profession.* Baltimore, MD: Johns Hopkins.

Lemke, J.L., (1990), *Talking Science: Language, Learning and Values.* Norwood, NJ: Ablex.

Lerner, G., (1986), *The Creation of Patriarchy.* New York: Oxford.

Leto, V., 1988), ' "Washing, seems it's all we do": Washing technology and women's communication.' In Kamarae, C. (ed.), *Technology and Women's Voices*, 161–179. NY: Routledge.

Levin, J., Riel, M., Miyake, N. and Cohen, M., (1987), 'Education on the electronic frontier: Teleapprentices in globally distributed educational contexts.' *Contemporary Educational Psychology* 12: 254–260.

Lichte, M., (1994), The world enters our classroom—The AT&T Learning Circle Adventure. *Telecommunications in Education News*, 5, 17–21.

Liebes, T. and Katz, E., (1989), 'On the critical abilities of television viewers.' In Seiter, E., Borchers, H., Kreutzner, G. and Warth, W. (eds), *Remote Control: Televisions, Audiences, and Cultural Power*, 204–222. New York: Routledge.

Livingstone, S.M., (1990), 'Interpreting a television narrative: How different viewers see a story.' *Journal of Communication* 40: 72–85.

Loftus, B., (1988), 'Northern Ireland 1968–1988: Enter an art historian in search of a useful theory.' In Fyfe, G. and Law, J. (eds.), *Picturing Power: Visual Depictions and Social Relations*, London: Routledge.

266

Lunsford, A. and Ede, L., (1990), *Singular Texts/Plural Authors: Perspectives on Collaborative Writing*. Carbondale, IL: Southern Illinois.

Lyman, P., (1984), 'Reading, writing and word processing: Towards a phenomenology of the computer age.' *Qualitative Sociology* 7: 75–89.

Lynch, M., (1985a), *Art and Artefact in Laboratory Science: A Study of Shop Work and Shop Talk in a Research Laboratory*. London: Routledge.

Lynch, M., (1985b), 'Discipline and the material form of images: An analysis of scientific visibility.' *Social Studies of Science* 15: 37–66.

Lynch, M., (1988), 'The externalized retina: Selection and mathematization in the visual documentation of objects in the life sciences.' *Human Studies* 11: 201–234.

Lynch, M., (1990), 'The Externalized Retina: Selection and Mathematization in the Visual Documentation of Objects in the Life Sciences.' In Lynch, M. and Woolgar, S. (eds), *Representation in Scientific Practice*, 153–186. Cambridge, MA: MIT.

Lynch, M., 'Demonstrating physic lessons.' In Greeno, J. and Goldman, S.G. (eds), *Thinking Practices*. Hillsdale, NJ: Lawrence Erlbaum, in press.

Lynch, M., Livingston, E. and Garfinkel, H., (1983), 'Temporal order in laboratory work.' In Knorr-Cetina, K. and Mulkay, M. (eds), *Science Observed*, 205–238. Beverly Hills: Sage.

Lynch, M. and Woolgar, S., (1988), 'Introduction: Sociological orientations to representational practice in science.' *Human Studies* 11: 271–304.

Lytje, I. and Markussen, R., (1989), 'Naturvidenskab og køn—Reflektioner over Sandra Harding: *The Science Question in Feminism*.' In Koch, U. (ed.), *Køn og Videnskab*, Aalborg: Aalborg Universitets Forlag.

MacKenzie, D. and Spinardi, G., (1988), 'The shaping of nuclear weapon system technology, Parts I and II.' *Social Studies of Science* 18: 419–463 and 581–624.

MacKenzie, D. and Wajcman, J. (eds), (1985), *The Social Shaping of Technology*. Philadelphia: Open University.

Majchrzak, A. and Salzman, H., (1988), 'Social and organizational dimensions of computer-aided design.' *IEEE Transactions on Engineering Management* 36: 174–180.

Markoff, J., 'Can Machines Think? Humans Match Wits.' *New York Times*, November 9, 1991: 1, 10.

Markussen, R., (1984), 'Butik og kontor—velegnet for kvinder.' In Berg, A.M. (ed.), *Kvindfolk. En Danmarkshistorie fra 1600 til 1980*, 2. Haslev: Nordik Forlag A.S.

Markussen, R., (1994), 'Historical perspectives on work practices and technology.' In Andersen, B., Holmqvist, B. and Jensen, J.F. (eds), *The Computer as Medium*. Cambridge: Cambridge.

Markussen, R. and Foged, B., (1984), *Det Fleksible Køn. Kvinder i Butik og På Kontort*. Viborg: Tiderne Skifter.

Martin, J., (1998a), 'The rise of hermeneutics and the crisis of ocularcentrism.' *Poetics Today* 9:

Martin, J., (1988b), 'Scopic regimes of modernity.' In Roster, H. (ed.), *Visions in Visuality: dia Art Foundation Discussions in Contemporary Culture*, 2. Seattle, WA: Bay Press.

National Council of Teachers of Mathematics, (1989), *Curriculum and evaluation standards for school mathematics*: Reston, VA: National Council of Teachers of Mathematics.

References

McCaffery, L. (ed.), (1991), *Storming the Reality Studio*. Durham, NC: Duke.

McDermott, R.P., Gospodinoff, K. and Aron, Y., (1978), 'Criteria for an ethnographically adequate description of activities and their contexts.' *Semoitica* 24: 245–275.

McIntosh, Peggy, (1992), 'White Privilege and Male Privilege: A Personal Account of Coming to See Correspondences through Work in Women's Studies.' Pp. 70–81 in Anderson, M.L. and Collins, P.H., (eds), *Race, Class and Gender: An Anthology*. Belmont, CA: Wadsworth.

McLuhan, M., (1964), *Understanding Media: The Extensions of Man*. NY: McGraw-Hill.

McNeill, D., (1992), *Hand and Mind: What Gestures Reveal about Thought*. Chicago: Chicago.

Mead, M., (1972), *Blackberry Winter: My Earlier Years*. New York: Morrow.

Mehan, H., (1989), 'Microcomputers in classrooms: Educational technology or social practice?' *Anthropology and Education Quarterly* 20: 4–22.

Mehan, H., (1990), 'The school's work of sorting students.' In Boden, D. and Zimmerman, D.H. (eds), *Talk and Social Structure*. Cambridge: Polity.

Meiksins, P., (1986), 'The "Revolt of the Engineers" reconsidered.' *Technology and Culture* 29:

Meiksins, P., (1989), 'Engineers and managers: An historical perspective on an uneasy relationship.' Paper to the American Sociological Association, San Francisco.

Meyers, G., (1988), 'Every picture tells a story: Illustrations in E.O. Wilson's *Sociobiology*.' *Human Studies* 11: 235.

Miller, P., 'Narrative practices: their role in socialization and self construction.' In Neisser, U. and Fivush, R. (eds), *The Remembering Self: Construction and Accuracy in the Self-Narrative*, Cambridge: Cambridge, in press.

Miller, P. and Hoogstra, L., (1992), 'Language as a tool in the socialization and comprehension of cultural meanings.' In Schwartz, T., White, G. and Lutz, C. (eds), *New Directions in Psychological Anthropology*, New York: Cambridge.

MMAP, (1992), *Designing application projects that optimize student interaction with mathematics*. Institute for Research on Learning, Palo Alto, Report to the NSF.

Morrison, T. (ed.), (1992), *Race-ing justice, En-Gendering Power: Essays On Anita Hill, Clarence Thomas, and the Construction of Social Reality*. New York: Pantheon Books.

Mukerji, C., (1989), *A Fragile Power: Scientists and the State*. Princeton: Princeton.

Mumford, L., (1963), *Technics and Civilization*. New York: Harcourt.

Murphey, M.G., (1973), *Our Knowledge of the Historical Past*. Indianapolis: Bobbs-Merrill.

Mylonas, E. and Bernstein, M., (1992), 'A literacy apprentice.' ALLC/ACH Conference (Oxford University). 181–186. Oxford: Oxford University Press.

Neisser, U. and Kerr, N., (1973), 'Spatial and mnemonic properties of visual images.' *Cognitive Psychology* 5: 138–150.

Newman, R. and Newman, J., (1993), 'Social writing: Premises and practices in computerized contexts.' In Sharples, M. (ed.), *Computer Supported Collaborative Writing*, London: Springer-Verlag.

Nicholson, L., (ed.), (1991), *Feminism/Postmodernism*. London: Routledge.

Nunes, T., Schliemann, A.D. and Carraher, D.W., (1993), _Street Mathematics and School Mathematics_. Cambridge: Cambridge.

O'Keefe, B.J., (1988), 'The logic of message design: Individual differences in reasoning about communication.' _Communication Monographs_ 55: 80–103.

Ochs, R., (1988), _Culture and Language Development_. Cambridge: Cambridge.

Ochs, E., (1991), 'Linguistic resources for socializing humanity.' In _Rethinking Linguistic Relativity in Ocho Rios, Jamaica_.

Ong, W., (1982), _Orality and Literacy_. London: Methuen.

Ortner, S., (1974), 'Is female to male as nature is to culture?' In Rosaldo, M. and Lamphere, L. (eds), _Woman, Culture and Society_. Stanford, CA: Stanford.

Ortner, S.B., (1984), 'Theory in anthropology since the sixties.' _Comparative Studies in Society and History_ 26: 126–166.

Perrow, C., (1984), _Normal Accidents_. New York: Basic Books.

Perrucci, R. and Gerstl, J., (1969), _The Engineer and the Social System_. New York: Wiley.

Philips, S., (1982), _The Invisible Culture_. New York: Longmans.

Pickering, A., (1982), 'Interests and analogies.' In Barnes, B. and Edge, D. (eds), _Science in Context_. Cambridge, MA: MIT.

Piercy, Marge, (1994), _The Longings of Women_. New York: Fawcett Columbine.

Pinch, T., (1985), 'Towards an analysis of scientific observation: The externality and evidential significance of observational reports in physics.' _Social Studies of Science_ 15: 3–36.

Plowman, L., (1993), 'Tracing the evolution of a co-authored text.' _Language and Communication_ 13: 149–161.

Polanyi, M. (1958), _Personal Knowledge_. Chicago: Chicago.

Polanyi, M., (1966), _The Tacit Dimension_. New York: Doubleday.

Posner, I., (1991), 'A Study of collaborative writing.' M.Sc., Toronto.

Pye, D., (1964), _The Nature of Design_. New York: Reinhold.

Ragin, C.C., (1992), 'Introduction: Cases of "What is a case?" ' In Ragin, C.C. and Becker, H.S. (eds), _What Is a Case?: Exploring the Foundations of Social Inquiry_, 1–17. Cambridge: Cambridge.

Reedy, J., (1988), 'Cultural literacy and the classics.' _The Classical Journal_ 84: 41–46.

Reid, E.M. (1991), _Electropolis: Communication and community on internet relay chat_. Melbourne: Australia.

Rengstorf, K.H., (1983), _A Complete Concordance to Flavius Josephus, in cooperation with B. Justis, G. Kontoulis, Jr. Royse, H. Schreckenberg, J. Schwark_. Vol. IV. Leiden: E.J. Brill.

Resnick, L.N. and Resnick, D.P., (1991), 'Assessing the thinking curriculum: New tools for educational reform.' In Gifford. B.R. and O'Connor, M.C. (eds), _Changing Assessments: Alternative Views of Aptitude, Achievement and Instruction_, 37–75. Boston: Kluwer.

Reynolds, L.D. and Wilson, N.G., (1974), _Scribes and Scholars: A Guide to the Transmission of Greek and Latin Literature_. Oxford: Clarendon.

Rheingold, H., _The Virtual Community: Homesteading on the Electronic Frontier_. New York: Addison-Wesley.

Rich, A., (1977), _Of Woman Born: Motherhood as Experience and Institution_. Bristol: Virago.

Rich, A., (1981), _A Wild Patience Has Taken Me This Far: Poems, 1978–1981_. New York: Norton.

References

Ricoeur, P., (1988), *Time and Narrative*. Vol. 3. Chicago: Chicago.

Riel, M., (1989a), 'The impact of computers in classrooms.' *Journal of Research on Computers in Education* 22: 180–190.

Riel, M., (1989b), Four models of educational telecommunications: Connections to the Future. *Education and Computing* 5, 262–274.

Riel, M., (1990a), 'Cooperative learning across classrooms in electronic learning circles.' *Instructional Science* 19: 445–466.

Riel, M., (1990b), Telecommunications: A tool for reconnecting kids with society. *Interactive Learning Environments* 2, 15–30.

Riel, M., (1992), 'Learning Circles: A functional analysis of educational telecomputing.' *Interactive Learning Environments* 2: 15–30.

Riel, M. and Harasim, L., ' Research perspectives on network learning.' *Journal of Machine-Mediated Communication* (in press).

Riel, M. and Levin, J.A., (1990), 'Building electronic communities: Successes and failure in computer networking.' *Instructional Science* 19: 145–169.

Rimmershaw, R., (1992), 'Collaborative writing practices and writing support technologies.' *Instructional Science* 21: 15–28.

Robinson, M., (1991), 'Double-level languages and cooperative working.' *AI and Society* 5: 34–60.

Rogoff, B., (1990), *Apprenticeship in Thinking: Cognitive Development in Social Context*. New York: Oxford.

Rorty, R., (1979), *Philosophy and the Mirror of Nature*. Princeton: Princeton.

Rorty, R., (1984), 'The historiography of philosophy: Four genres.' In Rorty, R., Schneewind, J. and Skinner, W. (eds), *Philosophy in History*, 49–75. Cambridge: Cambridge.

Rorty, R., (1992), 'The Pragmatist's Progress.' Pp. 89–108 in Collioni, S. (ed.), *Interpretation and Overinterpretation*. 89–108. Cambridge: Cambridge.

Skinner, Q., (1969), 'Meaning and Understanding in the History of Ideas.' *History and Theory* 8: 3–53.

Skinner, W., (1988), 'A Reply to My Critics.' In Tully, J. (ed.), *Meaning and Context: Quentin Skinner and His Critics*, 231–288. Princeton: Princeton.

Rosenberg, R., (1991), 'Debunking computer literacy.' *Technology Review* 94: 58–65.

Rouverol, J., (1984), *Writing for the Soaps*. Cincinnati, OH: Writers Digest.

Rubin, A.M., (1985), 'Uses of daytime television soap operas by college students.' *Journal of Broadcasting and Electronic Media* 29: 241–258.

Rubin, A.M. and Perse, E.M., (1987), 'Audience activity and soap opera involvement: A uses and effects investigation.' *Human Communication Research* 14: 246–268.

Ruby, J., (1991), 'Speaking for, speaking about, speaking with, or speaking alongside: An anthropological and documentary dilemma.' *Visual Anthropology Review* 7: 50–69.

Rudwick, M.J.S., (1976), 'The emergence of a visual language for geological science, 1760–1840.' *History of Science* 14: 149–195.

Ruhleder, K., (1991), 'Information Technology as Instrument of Social Transformation.' PhD. Dissertation, California, Irvine.

Ruhleder, K., 'The Impact of Computerization on Knowledge Production—A Case Study of Classical Scholarship.' In *TDH204 Information Technology and Society CD-ROM*, Milton Keynes, UK: Open University, forthcoming.

Ruhleder, K., (1995), 'Reconstructing artifacts, reconstructing work: From textual edition to on-line databank.' *Science, Technology & Human Values*, 20:39–64.

Ruhleder, K., (1994), 'Knowledge work, new media and the construction of artifacts for information storage and manipulation: The impact of one computer-based research tool on classical scholars.' *Transactions on Office Information Systems, Special Issue on Social Science Methodologies*, 12:208–230.

Ruopp, R., Gal, S., Drayton, B. and Pfister, M., (1993), *LabNet: Toward a Community of Practice*. Hillsdale, New Jersey: Lawrence Erlbaum.

Rutledge-Schelds, V. and Dervin, B., (1993), 'Sense-making in feminist social science research—A call to enlarge the methodological options of feminist studies.' *Womens' Studies International Forum* 16: 65–81.

Sacks, H., (1984), 'On doing "being ordinary".' In Atkinson, J.M. ad Heritage, J. (eds), *Structures of Social Action: Studies in Conversational Analysis*, 413–429. Cambridge: Cambridge.

Salomon, G., (1979), *Interaction of Media, Cognition and Learning*. San Francisco: Jossey-Bass.

Salomon, G. and Cohen, A.A., (1977), 'Television formats, mastery of mental skills and the acquisition of knowledge.' *Journal of Educational Psychology* 69: 612–619.

Salzman, H., (1988), 'Computer-aided design: Limitations in automating design and drafting.' *IEEE Transactions on Engineering Management* 36: 252–262.

Sanderson, D., (1993), *Smileys*. Sebastopol, CA: O'Reilly.

SCANS (Secretary's Commission on Acquiring Necessary Skills), *What work requires of schools: A SCANS report for America 2000*. Washington, DC, US Department of Labor, 1991.

Schegloff, E.A., (1984), 'On some gestures' relation to talk.' In Maxwell, J. and Heritage, J. (eds), *Structures of Social Action*, 266–296. New York: Cambridge.

Scheiffelin, B. and Ochs, E., (1986), 'Language socialization.' *Annual Review of Anthropology* 15: 163–246.

Schmidt, K. and Bannon, L., (1992), 'Taking CSCW seriously: Supporting articulation work.' *Computer Supported Cooperative Work (CSCW): An International Journal* 1: 7–40.

Schmitt, M., (1990), 'Scholars must take the lead in computerization in the humanities.' *The Chronicle of Higher Education*: 44.

Schon, D.A., (1990), 'The design process.' In Howard, V.A., *Varieties of Thinking: Essays from Harvard's Philosophy of Education Research Center*, 110–141. New York: Routledge.

Scribner, S. and Cole, M., (1981), *The Psychology of Literacy*. Cambridge, MA: Harvard.

Seiter, E., Borchers, H., Kreutzner, G. and Warth, E., (1989), 'Don't treat us like we're so stupid and naive': Towards an ethnography of soap opera viewers. In Seiter, E. et al. (eds), *Remote Control: Television, Audiences, and Cultural Power*, 223–247. New York: Routledge.

Sennett, R., (1981), *Authority*. New York: Random House.

Sennett, R. and Cobb, J., (1972), *The Hidden Injuries of Class*. New York: Knopf.

Shaiken, H., (1985), *Work Transformed: Automation and Labor in the computer Age*. New York: Holt, Rinehart and Winston.

Shapin, S., (1984), 'Pump and circumstance: Robert Boyle's literary technology.' *Social Studies of Science* 14: 481–520.

Shepard, R.N. and Cermak, G.W., (1973), 'Perceptual cognitive explorations of a toroidal set of free form stimuli.' *Cognitive Psychology* 4: 351–357.

References

Sinclair, M.A., Siemieniuch, C.E. and John, P.A., (1988), 'A user-centered approach to define high-level requirements for next generation CAD systems for mechanical engineering.' *IEEE Transactions on Engineering Management* 36: 262–271.

Sizer, T., (1992), *Horace's School: Redesigning the American High School.* New York: Houghton Mifflin.

Smith, J. and Balka, E., (1988), 'Chatting on a feminist computer network.' In Kramarae, C. (ed.), *Technology and Women's Voices*, 82–97. New York: Routledge, 1988.

Smith, M.I., (1964), *Spatial Ability.* London: U. London.

Spaulding, C. and Lake, D., (1991), 'Interactive effects of computer network and student characteristics on students' writing and collaborating.' In *American Educational Research Association*, Chicago.

Spiro, R.J., Coulson, R.L., Feltovich, P.J. and Anderson, D., (1988), 'Cognitive flexibility theory: Advanced knowledge acquisition in ill-structured domains. *Tenth Annual Conference of the Cognitive Science Society.* Hillsdale, NJ: Lawrence Erlbaum.

Spiro, R.J., Feltovich, P.J., Coulson, R.L. and Anderson, D., (1989), 'Multiple analogies for complex concepts: Antidotes for analogy-induced misconception in advanced knowledge acquisition'. In Vasniadou, S. and Ortony, A. (eds), *Similarity and Analogical Reasoning*, 498–531. Cambridge, MA: Cambridge.

Spiro, R.J., Feltovich, P.J., Jacobson, M.J. and Coulson, R.L., (1991a), 'Cognitive flexibility, constructivism, and hypertext: Random access instruction for advanced knowledge acquisition in ill-structured domains'. *Educational Technology* 11: 24–33.

Spiro, R.J., Feltovich, P.J., Jacobson, M.J. and Coulson, R.L. (1991b), 'Knowledge representation, content specification, and the development of skill in situation-specific knowledge assembly: Some constructivist issues as they relate to cognitive flexibility theory and hypertext'. *Educational Technology* 31: 22–26.

Spiro, R.J., and Jehng, J.C., (1990), 'Cognitive flexibility and hypertext: Theory and technology for the nonlinear and multidimensional traversal of complex subject matter'. In Nix, D. and Spiro, R.J. (eds), *Cognition, Education, and Multimedia: Explorations in High Technology*, 163–105. Hillsdale, NJ: Lawrence Erlbaum.

Spiro, R.J., Vispoel, W.L., Schmitz, J., Samarapungavan, A. and Boerger, A., (1987), 'Knowledge acquisition for application: Cognitive flexibility and transfer in complex content domains'. In Britton, B.C. and Glynn, S. (eds), Hillsdale, NJ: Lawrence Erlbaum Associates.

Sproull, L. and Kiesler, S., (1986), 'Reducing social cues: Electronic mail in organizational communication.' *Management Science* 32: 1492–1512.

Sproull, L. and Kiesler, S., (1991), *Connections: New Ways of Working in the Networked Organization.* Cambridge, MA: MIT.

Star, S.L., (1983), 'Simplification in scientific work: An example from neuroscience research.' *Social Studies of Science* 13: 208–226.

Star, S.L., (1985), 'Scientific work and uncertainty.' *Social Studies of Science* 15: 391–427.

Star, S.L., (1988), 'Introduction: The sociology of science and technology.' *Social Problems* 35.

Star, S.L., (1989a), 'Layered space, formal representations and long-distance control: The politics of information.' *Fundamenta Scientiae* 10: 125–55.

Star, S.L., (1989b), 'The structure of ill-structured solutions: Heterogeneous problem-solving, boundary objects and distributed artificial intelligence.' In Hahns, M. and Gasser, L. (eds), *Distributed Artificial Intelligence 2*, 37–54. Menlo Park: Morgan Kauffman.

Star, S.L., (1991a), 'Invisible work and silenced dialogues in representing knowledge.' In Eriksson, I.V., Kitchenham, B.A. and Tijdens, K.G. (eds), *Women, Work and Computerization: Understanding and Overcoming Bias in Work and Education*, 81–92. Amsterdam: North Holland.

Star, S.L., (1991b), 'Power, technology and the phenomenology of conventions: On being allergic to onions.' In Law, . (ed.), *A Sociology of Monsters: Essays on Power, Technology and Domination*, 25–56. London: Routledge.

Star, S.L., (1992), 'The Trojan door—Organisations, work and the "open black box".' *Systems/Practice* 5: 395–410.

Star, S.L., (1993), 'Cooperation without consensus in scientific problem solving: Dynamics of closure in open systems.' In Easterbrook, S. (ed.), *CSCW: Cooperation or Conflict?*, 93–105. London: Springer-Verlag.

Star, S.L., 'Working together: Symbolic interactionism, activity theory and distributed artificial intelligence.' In Middleton, D and Engström, Y. (eds), *Distributed Cognition and the Workplace*. Cambridge: Cambridge, in press.

Star, S.L. and Griesemer, J.R., (1989), 'Institutional ecology, "translations" and boundary objects—Amateurs and professionals in Berkeley's Museum of Vertebrate Zoology, 1907–39.' *Social Studies of Science* 19: 387–420.

Stengers, I. (1994), *Metamorphoses of Science. Feminism and Shifts of Paradigms*. Working Paper from the Feminist Research Network on Gender-Nature-Culture, Odense, Denmark.

Sterling, B., (ed.), (1986), *Mirrorshades: The Cyberpunk Anthology*. New York: Ace.

Stone, A.R. (1991), 'Will the real body please stand up? Boundary stories about virtual cultures.' In Benedikt, M. (ed.), *Cyberspace: First Steps*, 82–118. Cambridge, MA: MIT.

Stone, A.R., (1995) *The War of Desire and Technology at the Close of the Mechanical Age*. Cambridge: MIT Press.

Stone, A.R., (1994), 'Split Subjects, Not Atoms, or How I Fell In Love With My Prosthesis.' In R. Reid (ed.), *Configurations (Special Issue): Located Knowledges*. New York: Johns Hopkins.

Stout, J., (1982), 'What is the meaning of a text?' *New Literary History* 14: 1–12.

Strauss, A., (1985), 'Work and the division of labor.' *The Sociological Quarterly* 26: 1–19.

Strauss, A., (1988), 'The articulation of project work: An organizational process.' *Sociological Quarterly* 29: 163–178.

Suchman, L., (1987), *Plans and Situated Actions: The Problem of Machine-Human Communication*. Cambridge: Cambridge.

Suchman, L., (1988), 'Representing practice in cognitive science.' *Human Studies* 11: 305–326.

Suchman, L., (1993), 'Do categories have politics? The language/action perspective reconsidered.' In *European Conference on Computer Supported Cooperative Work (ECSCW '93)*, 1–14. Amsterdam: Kluwer.

References

Suchman, L.A. and Trigg, R.H., (1993), 'Artificial intelligence as craftwork.' In Chaiklin, S. and Lave, J. (eds), *Understanding practice: perspectives on activity and context*, 144–178. New York: Cambridge.

Sudnow, D., (1981), *Ways of the Hand*. New York: Harper.

Tang, J. and Leifer, L., (1988), 'A framework for understanding the workspace activity of design teams.' In *Computer-Supported Cooperative Work*.

Taylor, H.J., Kramarae, C. and Ebben, M., (1993), *Women, Information Technology and Scholarship*. Urbana, IL: Center for Advanced Study.

Thorne, B., Kramarae, C. and Henley, N. (eds) (1985), *Language, Gender and Society*. Cambridge, MA: Newbury House.

Tibbets, P., (1988), 'Representation and the realist-constructivist controversy.' *Human Studies* 11: 117–.

Timmermans, S., Bowker, G. and Star, S.L., 'The Architecture of Difference: Visibility, Control and Comparability in Building a Nursing Interventions Classification.' In Berg, M. and Mol, A. (eds), *Differences in Medicine*, in press.

Traweek, S., (1988), *Beamtimes and Lifetimes: The World of High Energy Physicists*. Cambridge: Harvard.

Tully, J., (1988), *Meaning and Context: Quentin Skinner and His Critics*. Princeton: Princeton.

Turing, A., (1950), 'Computing machinery and intelligence.' *Mind* 59: 433–460.

Turkle, S., (1984), *The Second Self: Computers and the Human Spirit*. New York: Simon and Schuster.

Turkle, S. 'Constructions and reconstructions of self in virtual reality: Playing in the MUDs.' *Mind, Culture and Activity* 1: 158–167.

Turnbull, D., (1993), 'The ad hoc collective work of building Gothic cathedrals with templates, string, and geometry.' *Science, Technology and Human Values* 18: 315–340.

Ullman, D., Stauffer, L. and Dietterich, T., (1987), 'Toward expert CAD.' *Computers in Mechanical Engineering*.

Van Creveld, M., (1985), *Command in War*. Cambridge, MA: Harvard.

Verdier, Y., (1981), *Tvätterskan, sömmerskan, kokerskan. Livet i en fransk by genom tre kvinnoyrken*. Värnamo, Sweden: Atlantis.

von Wilamowitz-Moellendorff, U., (1982), *History of Classical Scholarship*. London: Duckworth.

Wagner, I., 'Technology and women's voice: The case of nursing information systems.' *AI & Society* (in press).

Wajcman, J., (1991), *Feminism Confronts Technology*. Cambridge: Polity.

Weisman, Leslie Kanes, (1974–6), 'Birkby/Weisman Collection of Women's Environmental Fantasy Drawings (1974–1976).'

Weisman, L.K., (1992), *Discrimination by Design: A Feminist Critique of the Man-Made Environment*. Urbana, IL: Illinois.

Whalley, P., (1986), *The Social Production of Technical Work*. Albany, NY: SUNY.

Wiener, N., (1948), *Cybernetics: Control and Communication in the Animal and the Machine*. New York; Wiley.

Wilkes, M., (1988), *The Concept of Disciple in Matthew's Gospel as Reflected in the Use of the Term [Mathetes]*. leiden: E.J. Brill.

Will, R., (1991), 'True and false dependence on technology: Evaluation with an expert system.' *Computers in Human Behavior* 7: 171–183.

William, R., (1976), *Keywords: A Vocabulary of Culture and Society*. Glasgow: Fontana.

Williams, R., (1961), *Culture and Society—1780–1950*. Harmondsworth: Penguin.

Williams, R., (1981), *Culture*. London: Fontana.

Winner, L., (1980), 'Do artifacts have politics?' *Daedelus* 109: 121–136.

Wittgenstein, L., (1958), *Philosophical Investigations*. Translated by G.E.M. Anscombe. New York: Macmillan.

Wolf, D., Bixby, J., Glenn, J. and Gardner, H., (1991), 'To use their minds well: investigating new forms of student assessment.' *Review of Research in Education* 17: 31–74.

Woolgar, S., (1985), 'Why not a sociology of machines? The case of sociology and artificial intelligence.' *Sociology* 19: 557–572.

Woolgar, S., (1988), 'Time and documents in researcher interaction: Some ways of making out what is happening in experimental science.' *Human Studies* 11: 171–200.

Youtie, H.C., (1974), *The Textual Criticism of Documentary Papyrii*. 2nd edn., London: Institute of Classical Studies.

Yoxen, E., (1987), 'Seeing with sound: A Study of the development of medical images.' In Bijker, W., Hughes, T. and Pinch, T. (eds), *The Social Construction of Technological Systems: New Directions in the Sociology and History of Technology*, Cambridge, MA: MIT.

Zackheim, M., (1992), 'The cafe series.' *Frontiers: A Journal of Women's Studies* 13: Editorial page.

Zilsel, E., 'The sociological roots of science.' In Kearney, (ed.), *Origins of Scientific Revolution*, London: Longman, Green.

Zuboff, S., (1954), *In the Age of the Smart Machine*. New York: Basic Books.

Zusman, R., (1985), *Mechanics of the Middle Class*. Berkeley: California.

Notes on contributors

Nancy Baym (PhD University of Illinois, 1994) is an assistant professor of communication at Wayne State University. Her work focuses on the creation of computer-mediated culture.

Eevi Beck received her doctorate at the School of Cognitive and Computing Sciences at the University of Sussex, UK. She wrote her thesis on 'Supporting Collaboration in Writing' and now works at the Institute for Informatics, University of Oslo.

Paul N. Edwards teaches in the Program in Science, Technology, and Society and the Dept. of Computer Science at Stanford University. His first book, *The Closed World: Computers and the Politics of Discourse in Cold War America*, will be published by MIT Press in 1995. He hopes to travel the Information Superhighway in a Ferrari, but fears he will have to take the Greyhound bus instead.

Dianne Di Paola Hagaman is a photographer who works in digital imagery. She is completing a photographic book on religion and developing several large-scale visual hypertexts.

Mile Hales is a Senior Research Fellow in the University of Brighton's Centre for Research in Innovation Management (CENTRIM). Under the various auspices of systems thinking, Marxism and cultural materialism he has pursued theory-of-practice in chemical engineering and operational research, the Radical Science Journal editorial collective, labour movement activism in design and manufacturing (Hales, 1982) and the London Industrial Strategy of the Greater London Council. He now does action research in a business school and participates in the neo-modernist debate which calls itself 'computer supported cooperative work'.

Rogers Hall is an Assistant Professor in the Division for Education in Mathematics, Science, and Technology (EMST) at the University of California, Berkeley, and a Research Scientist at the Institute for Research on Learning (IRL) in Palo Alto, California. His research includes studies of representational practices for mathematical work in and out of school and the participatory design of learning environments for mathematics and science.

Kathryn Henderson is an Assistant Professor in Sociology at Texas A&M University. Her MFA in Art Criticism and Ph.D. in Sociology are from University of California, San Diego. She is interested in the connections between technology, art, science, feminism and sustainable development. Her forthcoming book, *On Line and On Paper* (MIT Press) is an ethnographic study of the impact of computer graphics on the visual practices of design engineers.

Robert Alun Jones is professor of sociology, history, and religious studies at the University of Illinois. His primary research interests are in the history of social thought (particularly French and British from 1850 to 1914); the methodology of the history of ideas; and electronic documents and networked information systems.

Randi Markussen is associate professor in the Department of Information and Media Science, Faculty of Arts, Århus University, Denmark. Her background is in History, Communication and Women's Studies.

Margaret Riel is an educational researcher who has developed and assessed educational programs through telecommunications for more than a decade. She has worked with AT&T to design the educational structure and write the curriculum guides for electronic 'Learning Circles' on the AT&T Learning Network.

Karen Ruhleder joined the Management Department at Worcester Polytechnic Institute in 1992, after teaching for one year at the University of Houston. She earned her PhD. in Computer and Information Sciences from the University of California, Irvine, in 1991, a graduate of a special program in the social and organizational analysis of computing. Her interests include the impact of computerization on knowledge work, the support of cooperative and collaborative work through information technology, and the development of governmental information technology policies.

Rand J. Spiro is Professor of Educational Psychology and Psychology, and an Affiliate of the Beckman Institute for Advanced Science and Technology and the Center for the Study of Reading, at the University of Illinois at Urbana-Champaign. She has also been a Visiting Professor of Psychology and Computer Science at Yale University, where he worked in the Yale Artificial Intelligence Laboratory. His research areas are knowledge acquisition in complex domains, medical cognition, hypermedia computer technologies for learning, and constructive processes in text comprehension and recall. His publications include the books *Schooling and the Acquisition of Knowledge* (with R. Anderson and W. Montague), *Theoretical Issues in Reading Comprehension* (with B. Bruce and W. Brewer), and *Cognition, Education, and Multimedia* (with D. Nix), as well as numerous articles and book chapters.

Susan Leigh Star is Associate Professor of Sociology, Library and Information Science, and Women's Studies at the University of Illinois, Urbana-Champaign, and Associate Research Scientist, Institute for Research on Learning, Palo Alto. She has written on the social and historical aspects of science, medicine and technology, and is interested in how infrastructure, work and knowledge coincide.

Reed Stevens is a graduate student in EMST at Berkeley and a Research Associate at IRL. He is working on a dissertation that traces the development of discipline-specific ways of seeing in mathematics, engineering, and science. Fieldwork for this study presently spans school, work and museum settings.

Allucquére Rosanne Stone is an assistant professor in the department of Radio, TV and Film at the University of Texas at Austin, where she directs the Advanced Communications Technology Laboratory (ACTLab) and teaches in the Interdisciplinary Seminar in Arts and Technology. Her background includes work in neurology, computer programming and film production. Her forthcoming books are *Presence: The war of desire and technology at the close of the mechanical age* and *Transhuman: Tales from the edges of identity.*

Index

Index

Index